A TEXT BOOK OF

OPERATING SYSTEM

For
SEMESTER – VI

THIRD YEAR DEGREE COURSE IN COMPUTER ENGINEERING AND INFORMATION TECHNOLOGY

According to New Revised Syllabus of
North Maharashtra University, Jalgaon.

Pavan R Jaiswal

M. E. (I.T.)
Assistant Professor,
Deptt. of Computer Engineering
Vishwakarma Institute of Information Technology (VIIT)
Kondhwa (BK), Pune.

N3356

OPERATING SYSTEM (TE SEM. VI COMP. & IT – NMU) ISBN : 978-93-5164-409-5
First Edition : **January 2015**
© : **Author**

The text of this publication, or any part thereof, should not be reproduced or transmitted in any form or stored in any computer storage system or device for distribution including photocopy, recording, taping or information retrieval system or reproduced on any disc, tape, perforated media or other information storage device etc., without the written permission of Authors with whom the rights are reserved. Breach of this condition is liable for legal action. Every effort has been made to avoid errors or omissions in this publication. In spite of this, errors may have crept in. Any mistake, error or discrepancy so noted and shall be brought to our notice shall be taken care of in the next edition. It is notified that neither the publisher nor the authors or seller shall be responsible for any damage or loss of action to any one, of any kind, in any manner, therefrom.

Published By :
NIRALI PRAKASHAN
Abhyudaya Pragati, 1312, Shivaji Nagar,
Off J.M. Road, PUNE – 411005
Tel - (020) 25512336/37/39, Fax - (020) 25511379
Email : niralipune@pragationline.com

Printed By :
REPRO INDIA LTD,
Mumbai.

DISTRIBUTION CENTRES
PUNE

Nirali Prakashan
119, Budhwar Peth, Jogeshwari Mandir Lane
Pune 411002, Maharashtra
Tel : (020) 2445 2044, 66022708, Fax : (020) 2445 1538
Email : bookorder@pragationline.com

Nirali Prakashan
S. No. 28/25, Dhyari,
Near Pari Company, Pune 411041
Tel : (022) 24690204 Fax : (020) 24690316
Email : dhyari@pragationline.com
bookorder@pragationline.com

MUMBAI
Nirali Prakashan
385, S.V.P. Road, Rasdhara Co-op. Hsg. Society Ltd.,
Girgaum, Mumbai 400004, Maharashtra
Tel : (022) 2385 6339 / 2386 9976, Fax : (022) 2386 9976
Email : niralimumbai@pragationline.com

DISTRIBUTION BRANCHES

NAGPUR
Pratibha Book Distributors
Above Maratha Mandir, Shop No. 3, First Floor,
Rani Jhanshi Square, Sitabuldi, Nagpur 440012,
Maharashtra, Tel : (0712) 254 7129

BENGALURU
Pragati Book House
House No. 1, Sanjeevappa Lane, Avenue Road Cross,
Opp. Rice Church, Bengaluru – 560002.
Tel : (080) 64513344, 64513355,
Mob : 9880582331, 9845021552
Email:bharatsavla@yahoo.com

JALGAON
Nirali Prakashan
34, V. V. Golani Market, Navi Peth, Jalgaon 425001,
Maharashtra, Tel : (0257) 222 0395
Mob : 94234 91860

KOLHAPUR
Nirali Prakashan
New Mahadvar Road,
Kedar Plaza, 1st Floor Opp. IDBI Bank
Kolhapur 416 012, Maharashtra. Mob : 9855046155

CHENNAI
Pragati Books
9/1, Montieth Road, Behind Taas Mahal, Egmore,
Chennai 600008 Tamil Nadu, Tel : (044) 6518 3535,
Mob : 94440 01782 / 98450 21552 / 98805 82331, Email : bharatsavla@yahoo.com

RETAIL OUTLETS
PUNE

Pragati Book Centre
157, Budhwar Peth, Opp. Ratan Talkies,
Pune 411002, Maharashtra
Tel : (020) 2445 8887 / 6602 2707, Fax : (020) 2445 8887

Pragati Book Centre
Amber Chamber, 28/A, Budhwar Peth,
Appa Balwant Chowk, Pune : 411002, Maharashtra,
Tel : (020) 20240335 / 66281669
Email : pbcpune@pragationline.com

Pragati Book Centre
676/B, Budhwar Peth, Opp. Jogeshwari Mandir,
Pune 411002, Maharashtra
Tel : (020) 6601 7784 / 6602 0855

PBC Book Sellers & Stationers
152, Budhwar Peth, Pune 411002, Maharashtra
Tel : (020) 2445 2254 / 6609 2463

MUMBAI
Pragati Book Corner
Indira Niwas, 111 - A, Bhavani Shankar Road, Dadar (W), Mumbai 400028, Maharashtra
Tel : (022) 2422 3526 / 6662 5254, Email : pbcmumbai@pragationline.com

Dedicated to…

My Beloved Parent

Shri Ramlal, Smt. Mamta

My Beloved Wife

Dr. Khushbu

… Pavan R. Jaiswal

PREFACE

It gives me pleasure to present the book of **"Operating System"** for the students of Third Year Degree Course in Computer Engineering and Information Technology, of North Maharashtra University, Jalgaon.

The book is written strictly as per New Revised Syllabus which has been implemented from Academic Year (2015).

Although the book is written for student community, it will be also useful for the teaching faculty.

The objectives of this textbook are :

- **Unit I** : It covers operating system architecture, it's evolution, it's services and components.
- **Unit II** : It covers process scheduling, various scheduling algorithms, inter process communication and problems in concurrent programming.
- **Unit III** : It covers deadlock and its characterization, memory management, memory partitioning and virtual memory management.
- **Unit IV** : It covers file concepts, disk allocation techniques and disk scheduling algorithms.
- **Unit V** : It covers secondary storage structure, protection, security and introduction to UNIX.

I would like to extend my sincere thanks to Management of V.I.I.T. (B.R.A.C.T.), Dr. Mrs. B. S. Karkare (Principal, V.I.I.T.), Dr. Mr. S. R. Sakhare (Head, Comp. Dept., V.I.I.T.) for their kind support.

My special thanks to publisher Mr. Dineshbhai K. Furia, Mr. Jignesh C. Furia, Mr. M.P. Munde and Mrs. Depali Lachake (Co-ordinator), all the team members namely Mrs. Ulka Chavan, Mrs. Pratibha Bele and Miss Mandakini Jadhvar of Nirali Prakashan, for their efforts in bringing out this book.

I am also thankful to **Shri P. M. More**, Branch Manager, Jalgaon Offfice for their valuable help and efforts for promotion of my book.

Thanks to all those who directly and indirectly helped me for completion of this book.

Any suggestions for the improvement of this book are always welcome.

January, 2015   **Author**
Pune.

SYLLABUS

UNIT I : Operating System Overview   8 Hours

a. **Introduction :** Computer system organization, Architecture, Evolution of OS, Need of OS, User view and System view of OS.

b. **Types of Operating System :** Batch, Timesharing, Multiprogramming, Multitasking, RTOS, Distributed.

c. **Operating System Services and Components :** Different OS services and OS components, System calls and its types.

d. **Operating System Structures :** Monolithic, Layered, Kernel, Microkernel, Virtual Machine.

e. **Threads :** Overview, Benefits, Models (Introduction Only).

UNIT II : Process and Process Management   8 Hours

a. **Process Concept :** The process, Process states, Process Control Block, Context Switching, SPOOLING, CPU and I/O burst.

b. **Scheduling :** Concept, Objectives, Queuing diagram.

c. **Types of Schedulers :** Long term Scheduler, Middle term Scheduler, Short term Scheduler.

d. **Scheduling Algorithm (For Uniprocessor System) :** FCFS, SJF (preemptive and non preemptive), Priority (preemptive and non preemptive), Round Robin, MLQ with and without feedback.

e. **IPC :** Concept and Types.

f. **Critical Section :** Critical section problem, Solution to critical section problem, Mutual exclusion with busy waiting, TSL, Peterson's solution for two processes, Dijkstra's semaphore.

g. **Problem in Concurrent Programming :** Producer-Consumer problem, Readers–Writers problem, Dinning Philosopher problem, Monitors.

UNIT III : Deadlocks   8 Hours

a. **Deadlock :** System Model, Deadlock Characterization, Deadlock Prevention, Deadlock Avoidance, Deadlock Detection, Recovery from Deadlock.

b. **Memory Management :** Memory Management Requirements.

c. **Memory Partitioning :** Fixed and Dynamic Partitioning.

d. **Memory Allocation :** Allocation strategies (First Fit, Best Fit and Worst Fit), Fragmentation, Swapping, Paging and Segmentation.

e. **Virtual Memory Management :** Background, Demand Paging, Page Replacement (FIFO, LRU, Optimal LRU), Thrashing.

UNIT IV : Storage Management   8 Hours

a. **File concept :** File Organization, Access Methods and Directory Structure.
b. **Allocation of Disk Space :** Contiguous allocation, Non-contiguous allocation (chaining and indexing).
c. **Disk Scheduling :** FCFS, SSTF, SCAN, C-SCAN, LOOK.

UNIT V : Secondary Storage Structure, Protection and Security, Introduction to UNIX.
                                                                             8 Hours

a. **Disk Management :** Disk formatting, Boot block, Bad blocks.
b. **Swap Space Management :** Swap Space Use, Swap Space.
c. **System Protection :** Goals of protection, Domain of protection, Threats, Security attacks.
d. **Introduction to UNIX :** History, System architecture.
e. **Internal Representation of File :** Inode, Structure of regular file, Super block, Pipes (No Algorithms).
f. **Process Control :** Process creation, Process States and Transitions, Process system calls (exec, fork).

CONTENTS

UNIT I	Operating System Overview	1.1 - 1.34
UNIT II	Process and Process Management	2.1 – 2.52
UNIT III	Deadlocks	3.1 – 3.58
UNIT IV	Storage Management	4.1 – 4.30
UNIT V	Secondary Storage Structure, Protection and Security, Introduction to UNIX.	5.1 – 5.44

✠ ✠ ✠

Unit - I

OPERATING SYSTEM OVERVIEW

A. INTRODUCTION

In this unit we study basic computer system organization, operating system architecture, evolution of OS, viewing OS from user and system point of view. Depending on kind of usage, OS has been categorized into batch, time sharing, multiprogramming, multitasking, real time, distributed operating system, etc. In this unit we see core components and services of OS along with few important system calls. We see here that how OS is structured into monolithic, layered and microkernel structures. We see in brief about virtual machine and it is important in today's computer world. Lastly in this unit, we focus on introductory part of threads, its benefits and models.

1.1 COMPUTER SYSTEM ORGANIZATION

Fig. 1.1 shows block diagram of a typical computer system. As mentioned in Fig. 1.1, computer system is divided into two major sections
- Hardware
- Software.

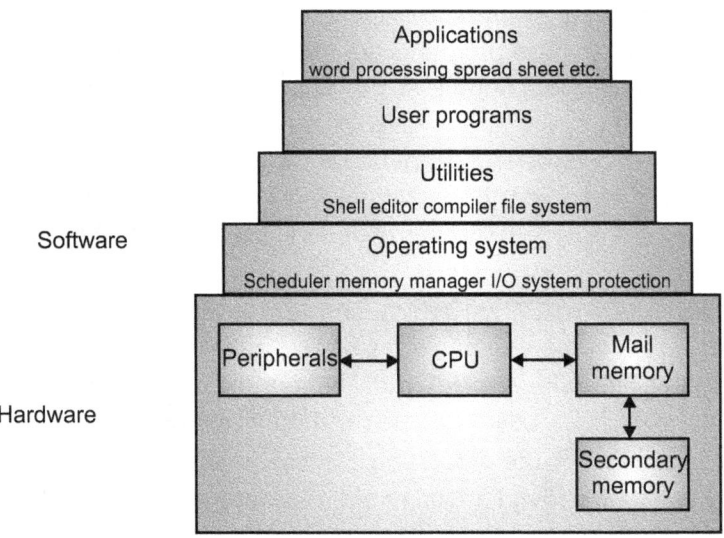

Fig. 1.1 : Computer system block diagram

1.1.1 Computer Hardware an Operating System

The physical machine, consisting of electronic circuits, is called the hardware. It consists of several major units : the Central Processing Unit (CPU), Main Memory, Secondary Memory and Peripherals.

The CPU is the major component of a computer; the "electronic brain" of the machine. It consists of the electronic circuits needed to perform operations on the data. Main memory is where programs that are currently being executed as well as their data are stored. The CPU fetches program instructions in sequence, together with the required data, from main memory and then performs the operation specified by the instruction. Information may be both read from and written to any location in main memory so the devices used to implement this block are called random access memory chips (RAM). The contents of main memory (often simply called memory) are both temporary (the programs and data reside there only when they are needed) and volatile (the contents are lost when power to the machine is turned off).

The secondary memory provides more long term and stable storage for both programs and data. In modern computing systems this secondary memory is most often implemented using rotating magnetic storage devices, more commonly called disks (though magnetic tape may also be used); therefore, secondary memory is often referred to as the disk. The physical devices making up secondary memory, the disk drive, are also known as mass storage devices because relatively large amounts of data and many programs may be stored on them.

1.1.2 Computer Software an Operating System

Hardware is called "hard" because, once it is built, it is relatively difficult to change. However, the hardware of a computer system, by itself, is useless. It must be given directions as to what to do, i.e. a program. These programs are called software; "soft" because it is relatively easy to change both the instructions in a particular program as well as which program is being executed by the hardware at any given time. When a computer system is purchased, the hardware comes with a certain amount of software which facilitates the use of the system. Other software to run on the system may be purchased and/or written by the user. Some major vendors of computer systems include : IBM, DEC, HP, AT&T, Sun, Compaq, and Apple.

The remaining blocks in Fig. 1.1 are typical software layers provided on most computing systems. This software may be thought of as having a hierarchical, layered structure, where each layer uses the facilities of layers below it. The four major blocks shown in the Fig. 1.1 are the Operating System, Utilities, User Programs and Applications.

The primary responsibility of the Operating System (OS) is to "manage" the "resources" provided by the hardware. Such management includes assigning areas of memory to different programs which are to be run, assigning one particular program to run on the CPU at a time, and controlling the peripheral devices. When a program is called upon to be executed (its operations performed), it must be loaded, i.e. moved from disk to an assigned area of memory. The OS may then direct the CPU to begin fetching instructions from this area. Other typical responsibilities of the OS include Secondary Storage management (assignment of space on the disk), a piece of software called the file system, and Security (protecting the programs and data of one user from activities of other users that may be on the same system).

1.1.3 Utility Programs

The layer above the OS is labeled Utilities and consists of several programs which are primarily responsible for the logical interface with the user, i.e. the "view" the user has when interacting with the computer. (Sometimes this layer and the OS layer below are considered together as the operating system). Typical utilities include such programs as shells, text editors, compilers, and (sometimes) the file system.

A program that performs a very specific task, usually related to managing system resources. Operating systems contain a number of utilities for managing disk drives, printers, and other devices.

Utilities differ from applications mostly in terms of size, complexity and function. For example, word processors, spreadsheet programs and database applications are considered applications because they are large programs that perform a variety of functions not directly related to managing computer resources.

The utility program is a type of system software that allows a user to perform maintenance type tasks, usually related to managing computer, its device or it programs.

The utility programs for large computer systems are designed for professional system programmers to either modify or repair the system software. Many utility programs such as programs for finding files, diagnosing and repairing system problems, cleaning up a hard drive, viewing images, playing multimedia files and backing up files. It also helps to secure and safeguard data.

However the utility programs for microcomputers are very often used by end users.

They are user friendly and designed for end users, change the monitor's background pattern, or install computer hardware. It is a software program that performs a specific task, usually related to managing or maintaining a computer system. Most operating system include several built-in utility programs. Some of the principal utility programs are as follows :

1. **File Manager**
   A file manger is a utility that perform functions related to file management.
2. **Data Recovery**
   A data recovery utility is used to "undelete" a file or information that has been accidentally deleted. With this function, users are able to undo the last delete operation that has taken place.
3. **Maintenance Log and Activity Information**
   The operating system can create a log of system users and provide a record of system activity.

4. **Screen Saver**

   A screen saver prevents a monitor's display screen from being etched by an unchanging image.

5. **Backup**

   The backup utility allows users to make a backup (duplicate) copy of the information on the hard disk. During the backup process, the backup utility monitors progress and alert the user of it needs additional media such as CD.

6. **Data Compression**

   Data compression removes redundant elements, gaps, and unnecessary data from a computer's storage space so less space is required to store or transmit data.

1.1.4 User Programs and Applications

Above the utilities in Fig. 1.1 is the block labeled User Programs. It is at this level where a computer becomes specialized to perform a task to solve a user's problem. Given a task that needs to be performed, a programmer can design and code a program to perform that task using the text editors, compilers, debuggers, etc. The program so written may make use of operating system facilities, for example to do I/O (Input/Output) to interact with the program user. It is at this level that the examples, exercises and problems in this text will be written.

However, not everyone who uses a computer is a programmer or desires to be a programmer. As well, if every time a new task was presented to be programmed, one had to start from scratch with a new program, the utility and ease of using the computers would be reduced. These days packages of predefined software, or Applications, are available from many vendors in the industry. Highly functional word processors, desktop publishing packages, spread sheet and data base programs and, yes, games are readily available for computer users as well as programmers. In fact, perhaps most computer users these days access their machines exclusively through these application programs.

1.2 COMPUTER ARCHITECTURE

Computer architecture is a specification detailing how a set of software and hardware technology standards interact to form a computer system or platform. In short, computer architecture refers to how a computer system is designed and what technologies it is compatible with.

A very good example of computer architecture is Von Neumann architecture, which is still used by most types of computers today. This was proposed by the mathematician John Von Neumann in 1945. It describes the design of an electronic computer with its CPU, which includes the arithmetic logic unit, control unit, registers, memory for data and instructions, an input/output interface and external storage functions.

There are three categories of computer architecture :

1.2.1 System Design

This includes all hardware components in the system, including data processors aside from the CPU, such as the graphics processing unit and direct memory access. It also includes memory controllers, data paths and miscellaneous things like multiprocessing and virtualization

1.2.2 Instruction Set Architecture (ISA)

This is the embedded programming language of the central processing unit. It defines the CPU's functions and capabilities based on what programming it can perform or process. This includes the word size, processor register types, memory addressing modes, data formats and the instruction set that programmer use.

1.2.3 Micro Architecture

Otherwise known as computer organization, this type of architecture defines the data paths, data processing and storage elements, as well as how they should be implemented in the ISA.

1.3 EVOLUTION OF OPERATING SYSTEM (OS)

A computer operating system is the software and/or firmware which manages the hardware of the computer and provides those resources, through an API, to application programs. It can also be defined as a program (set of logical instructions) which is responsible for controlling the hardware functionality of a computer or related programmable electronic device.

The first computers did not have operating systems, and could only run one program at a time. The first electronic computing circuits were little more than separate functions and did not really need even a programming language to be tested. In about 1945 computers such as the Eniac were built that took up four square blocks of space and had about the same power as a four function calculator you might get on a key chain today. Programming of these behemoths was done by plug boards that fitted on to something a lot like a telephone switchboard. Since they were experimental engines running on vacuum tubes at that time and maintenance was an issue, little productivity was practical and only a few people knew how to run them. Programming was done in each individual machines own machine language and so operating systems were not required. By the 1950's the invention of the punch card machine made it easier to read in a small program, but all the operating of the system required was the pushing of a few buttons, one to load the cards into memory and another to run the program.

In the mid 1950's, transistors made the computer circuit solid state, which eliminated the need to constantly patrol the innards of the computer to find burned out tubes and clean bugs out of the electrical contacts. The first solid state computers took up large air-conditioned computer rooms with racks of components and were used primarily by Governments to do processing of tables such as ballistic tables needed to aim military weapons. This resulted in a need for more control of the time spent per operation, which saw the separation of the maintenance and operations group from the programmers. At first, programmers wrote out their program on paper and then punched it into cards which the operators would load in sequence into the machine, one stack of cards at a time. Later a Job Control Language was designed that allowed the programmer to declare job information itself as part of their stack of cards and it became possible to run a program called a monitor that read in the stack and stored it on a tape called the input tape. The input tape could then be run on a separate computer, the "Main Frame" and spool its output to a second tape called the output tape, which would be later mounted on the printer to output the response to the program. The batch monitor was the closest thing to an operating system that this early form of computer had. Its job was to read information from the cards and set up the job, automatically freeing up an operator. Also at about this time, FORTRAN was invented and a "compiler" spool could be loaded on the mainframe to allow the programmers to write in a human readable form, while the computer operated still in machine language.

By 1965 the first operating system like programs were beginning to show up, like the FORTRAN Monitoring System, which had to deal with loading three types of programs, the FORTRAN Program, the Compiler and the Machine language program that was the result of complication. This necessitated that the program be able to tell in some manner which type of file it was reading on the tape. A similar system, IBSYS was IBM's operating system for the 7094. Loading the operating system required that a tape containing the operating system be loaded first in order to start the operating system. Early operating systems did not have the bootstrap mechanism which all modern operating systems use to initialize the computer, so start up of a computer was a long and involved process.

By the early 1960's it became obvious that computer companies were having to support two completely different types of computers, 1401 like character based computers and word-oriented 7094 like scientific computers. Maintenance and training on these completely different systems was problematic so IBM invented System/360 and created a range of products that used this common architecture. The IBM 360 was the first computer line to use small scale integrated circuits and thus offered a major cut in price over earlier solid state machines. This radically expanded the market and the power of the machines.

OS360 was written to act as the operating system on all of the System 360 machines from the smallest input processor to the largest number cruncher type processor. It was made up of literally thousands of lines of code written by hundreds of programmers and maintenance was problematic since almost every time a bug was fixed a new one would be generated. Despite the impossibility to maintain such a massive monolithic program it was a distinct improvement on previous second generation operating systems and became quite popular.

One of the concepts that it popularized was the idea of multi-computing, where instead of waiting for a single job, the computer could be running multiple jobs simultaneously. This eliminated waiting periods while the operators mounted the tapes, since the computer could be processing a different program while it waited. One problem with combining business computer operating systems with number crunching system operating systems was that the size of the jobs involved required different strategies. Business jobs were simple and required less time per job and as a result mounting and un-mounting tapes took up 80 to 90 percent of the processing time. While a large number cruncher was still expensive enough that small jobs were not economical so mounting tapes was more like 10 percent of the job and not a significant problem. One way of getting around this was to partition the memory, so that each job could have its own partition. This went along with the Multi-programming concept, because it meant that more than one job could run at the same time on the same computer without interfering with the memory of other jobs.

Along with this concept came the idea of running the card reader from one partition, the number crunching in another and the output to the printer from a third, eliminating the satellite 1401 type computers and reducing the wear and tear on tapes from mounting stress. While third generation units were good for large runs they were essentially still batch systems and as programs began to become more complex, managing the card stacks for a program became unwieldy. This paved the way for timesharing systems where each user had his own terminal and they shared a central mainframe.

Timesharing did not become popular until late in the third generation when the hardware for protection mechanisms became widespread. At that time, the idea of a Computing Utility began to be worked on, the idea being that a single mainframe would supply timesharing opportunities to the whole Boston Area. Out of this concept the first 4th generation operating system MULTICS was born. Of course the idea was based on the small scale integration and the development of LSI and then Later VLSI (Very Large Scale Integration) eventually replaced whole rooms of computers with a small desktop unit. As a result of LSI (Large Scale Integration) it became possible to build a whole computer system on a single rack. These Mini-computers began to compete with IBM for smaller businesses and because their financing terms were not as pecuniary their ability to compete made them replacements for the small and midsized system 360 components. It was not surprising by the 80's to find that a timesharing system used mini-computers as their front ends to handle terminal multiplexing and had a mainframe as the main computing mechanism.

In the 1970's Ken Thompson designed UNIX as a stripped down one user version of MULTICS based on a PDP-7 Minicomputer. Since he published the source code, it became a popular operating system and was used extensively by Universities and small businesses. By the 1990's it was so popular that more software was being written for it by outsiders than was written by ATT. Legal battle started between ATT and Universities as to who owned the rights to the new software involved in Unix V5 resulted in two things, the sale of the operating system to SCO and the development of an alternative kernel by Linus Torvalds that could run the by then public domain software produced by the universities because it met the POSIX standard which had been developed by IEEE.

It was this defiant rewrite of an operating system kernel that created the Open Software Movement that has powered the internet revolution. Most operating systems today have gained by the work of the Open Software Movement because their internet software's sophistication depends on ideas pioneered and spread through free software.

For most purposes today an operating system is best defined as the software that comes on an operating system install CD or DVD. This definition works well for users and operating system vendors. It has even been argued in court.

1.4 NEED OF OPERATING SYSTEM (OS)

In earlier day's user had to design the application according to the internal structure of the hardware. Operating System was needed to enable the user to design the application without concerning the details of the computer's internal structure. In general the boundary between the hardware and software is transparent to the user.

More to this, when we ask question what is the need of OS, is the same question we ask to the persons one of them knows English and the other ones knows Spanish so we need one person who is able to communicate between two same is the answer here for why we need the operating system. It is the communication pathway between the user of the machine and the machine where machine knows only machine language i.e. '1' and '0' on the other hand the man knows the alphabetic language. So operating system gets the alphabetic language from the user and change it to the machine understandable language and vice versa.

Usage of Operating System

- Easy interaction between the human and computer.
- Starting computer operation automatically when power is turned on.
- Loading and scheduling users program.
- Controlling input and output.
- Controlling program execution.
- Managing use of main memory.
- Providing security to users program.

We all have our favorite operating system some of us will only pick from the tree of Apple, while others prefer the Windows seat. It's easy to assume that a computer without an operating system is as useful as a cup of coffee without the cup. But what does an operating system do and can a computer still compute without it?

Let's tackle the first question before we get into the nitty-gritty of a system-less computer. An operating system is basically the general contractor of the computer. While the programs are busy doing their one specialized thing plumbing, electrical, carpentry the operating system is overseeing them all, communicating what they need to the processor and providing a common language that they can all work with to stay on the same page.

There are a few other things your operating system does that you probably do not think about. For instance, it is the operating system (not just the hard drive) that is going to decide how to manage memory. The operating system needs to delegate how much memory each process uses and make sure no memory overlaps. Also keep in mind that your home computer is most likely a single-user, multitasking operating system. That means you only have one processor, but it can run many programs at once.

But here's the kicker it can not actually do that.

When you are downloading files, working on a spreadsheet and listening to music, your computer just appears to be doing these things simultaneously. In reality, the computer is switching between processes at extremely high speeds so high, you do not know it. While you are under the illusion that your CPU and operating system have a hand in every pot, your programs are under the impression that they have complete control of the operating system at any given moment.

So really, your operating system is designed to let the CPU deal with one thing at a time. But because it is a computer and not a harried secretary, it can multitask so fast that the user would not even know.

1.5 USER VIEW AND SYSTEM VIEW OF OS

1.5.1 User View

The user view of the computer varies by the interface being used. Most computer users sit in front of a PC consisting of a monitor, keyboard, mouse and system unit. Such a system is designed for one user to monopolize its resources to maximize the work that the user is performing. In this case, the operating system is designed mostly for ease of use, with some attention paid to performance and none paid to resource utilization.

Some users sit at a terminal connected to a mainframe or minicomputer. Other users are accessing the same computer through other terminals. These users share resources and may exchange information. The operating system is designed to maximize resource utilization.

Other users sit at workstations, connected to networks of other workstations and servers. These users have dedicated resources at their disposal, but they also share resources such as networking and servers.

Recently, many varieties of handheld computers have come into fashion. These devices are mostly standalone, used singly by individual users. Some are connected to networks, either directly by wire or through wireless modems. Due to power and interface limitations they perform relatively few remote operations. These operating systems are designed mostly for individual usability, but performance per amount of battery life is important as well.

Some computers have little or no user view. For example, embedded computers in home devices and automobiles may have numeric keypad and may turn indicator lights on or off to show status, but mostly they and their operating systems are designed to run without user intervention.

1.5.2 System View

We can view an operating system as a resource allocator. A computer system has many resources hardware and software that may be required to solve a problem. The operating system acts as the manager of these resources.

An operating system can also be viewed as a control program that manages the execution of user programs to prevent errors and improper use of the computer. It is especially concerned with the operation and control of I/O (Input/Output) devices.

We have no universally accepted definition of what is part of the operating system. A simple view point is that it includes everything a vendor ships when you order "an operating system".

A more common definition is that the operating system is the one program running at all times on the computer (usually called the kernel), with all else being application programs. This is the one that we generally follow.

B. TYPES OF OPERATING SYSTEM

1.6 BATCH OPERATING SYSTEM

The users of batch operating system do not interact with the computer directly. Each user prepares his job on an off-line device like punch cards and submits it to the computer operator. To speed up processing, jobs with similar needs are batched together and run as a group. Thus, the programmers left their programs with the operator. The operator then sorts programs into batches with similar requirements. Fig. 1.2 below illustrates batch operating system.

The problems with batch systems are :
- Lack of interaction between the user and job.
- CPU is often idle, because the speed of the mechanical I/O devices is slower than CPU.
- Difficult to provide the desired priority.

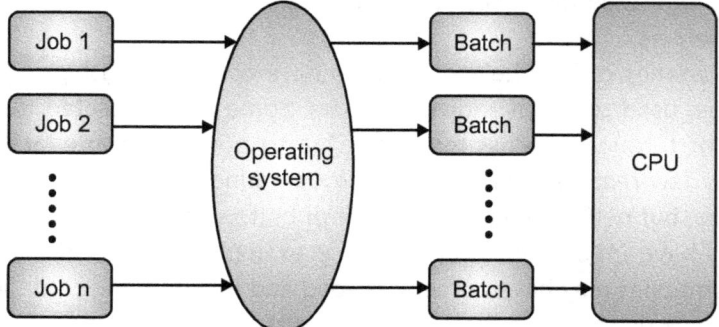

Fig. 1.2 : Batch operating system

1.7 TIME SHARING OR MULTI TASKING OPERATING SYSTEM

Time sharing is a technique which enables many people located at various terminals, to use a particular computer system at the same time. Time sharing or multitasking is a logical extension of multiprogramming. Processor's time which is shared among multiple users simultaneously is termed as time sharing. The main difference between Multiprogrammed Batch Systems and Time Sharing Systems is that in case of Multiprogrammed batch systems, objective is to maximize processor use, where as in Time Sharing Systems objective is to minimize response time.

Multiple jobs are executed by the CPU by switching between them, but the switches occur so frequently. Thus, the user can receive an immediate response. For example, in a transaction processing, processor execute each user program in a short burst or quantum of computation. That is if n users are present, each user can get time quantum. When the user submits the command, the response time is in few seconds at most.

Operating system uses CPU scheduling and multiprogramming to provide each user with a small portion of a time. Computer systems that were designed primarily as batch systems have been modified to time sharing systems.

Fig. 1.3 below illustrates time sharing system.

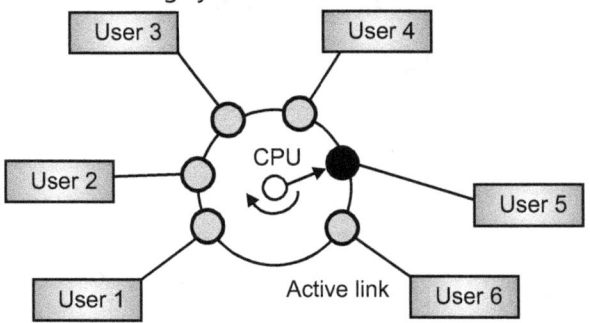

Fig. 1.3 : Time sharing system

In above Fig. 1.3 the user 5 is active but user 1, user 2, user 3 and user 4 are in waiting state where as user 6 is in ready status.

As soon as the time slice of user 5 is completed, the control moves on to the next ready user i.e. user 6. In this state user 2, user 3, user 4 and user 5 are in waiting state and user 1 is in ready state. The process continues in the same way and so on.

The time shared systems are more complex than the multi-programming systems. In time shared systems multiple processes are managed simultaneously which requires an adequate management of main memory so that the processes can be swapped in or swapped out within a short time.

Note : The term "Time Sharing" is no longer commonly used. It has been replaced by 'Multitasking System'.

Advantages of Time Sharing Operating Systems
- Quick response.
- Avoids duplication of software.
- Reduces CPU idle time.

Disadvantages of Time Sharing Operating Systems
- Problem of reliability.
- Question of security and integrity of user programs and data.
- Problem of data communication.

1.8 MULTIPROGRAMMING OPERATING SYSTEM

When two or more programs are residing in memory at the same time, then sharing the processor is referred to the multiprogramming. Multiprogramming assumes a single shared processor. Multiprogramming increases CPU utilization by organizing jobs so that the CPU always has one to execute.

Following Fig. 1.4 shows the memory layout of a multiprogramming system.

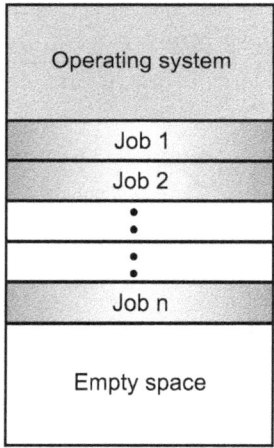

Fig. 1.4 : Memory layout of multiprogramming system

Operating system does the following activities related to multiprogramming :
- The operating system keeps several jobs in memory at a time.
- This set of jobs is a subset of the jobs kept in the job pool.
- The operating system picks and begins to execute one of the jobs in the memory.
- Multiprogramming operating system monitors the state of all active programs and system resources using memory management programs to ensures that the CPU is never idle unless there are no jobs.

Advantages of Multiprogramming System
- High and efficient CPU utilization.
- User feels that many programs are allotted CPU almost simultaneously.

Disadvantages of Multiprogramming System
- CPU scheduling is required.
- To accommodate many jobs in memory, memory management is required.

1.9 REAL TIME OPERATING SYSTEM (RTOS)

Real time system is defined as a data processing system in which the time interval required to process and respond to inputs is so small that it controls the environment. Real time processing is always on line whereas on line system need not be real time. The time taken by the system to respond to an input and display of required updated information is termed as response time. So in this method response time is very less as compared to the online processing.

Real time systems are used when there are rigid time requirements on the operation of a processor or the flow of data and real time systems can be used as a control device in a dedicated application. Real time operating system has well defined, fixed time constraints otherwise system will fail. For example Scientific experiments, medical imaging systems, industrial control systems, weapon systems, robots and home appliance controllers, Air traffic control system etc.

A Real Time Operating System (RTOS) is an operating system that guarantees a certain capability within a specified time constraint. For example, an operating system might be designed to ensure that a certain object was available for a robot on an assembly line. In what is usually called a "hard" real time operating system, if the calculation could not be performed for making the object available at the designated time, the operating system would terminate with a failure. In a "soft" real time operating system, the assembly line would continue to function but the production output might be lower as objects failed to appear at their designated time, causing the robot to be temporarily unproductive. Some real time operating systems are created for a special application and others are more general purpose. Some existing general purpose operating systems claim to be a real time operating systems. To some extent, almost any general purpose operating system such as Microsoft's Windows 2000 or IBM's OS/390 can be evaluated for its real time operating system qualities. That is even if an operating system does not qualify, it may have characteristics that enable it to be considered as a solution to a particular real time application problem.

In general, real time operating systems are said to require :
- Multitasking
- Process threads that can be prioritized
- A sufficient number of interrupt levels

Real time operating systems are often required in small embedded operating systems that are packaged as part of micro-devices. Some kernels can be considered to meet the requirements of a real time operating system. However, since other components, such as device drivers, are also usually needed for a particular solution, a real time operating system is usually larger than just the kernel.

There are two types of real time operating systems.
1. Hard Real Time System
2. Soft Real Time System

1.9.1 Hard Real Time Systems

Hard real time systems guarantee that critical tasks complete on time. In hard real time systems secondary storage is limited or missing with data stored in ROM. In these systems virtual memory is almost never found.

Hard real time system is purely deterministic and time constraint system for example users expected the output for the given input in 10sec, then system should process the input data and give the output exactly by 10th second. Here in the above example 10 sec. is the deadline to complete process for given data. Hard real systems should complete the process and give the output by 10th second. It should not give the output by 11th second or by 9th second, exactly by 10th second it should give the output. In the hard real time system meeting the deadline is very important if deadline is not met the system performance will fail. Another example is defense system if a country launched a missile to another country the missile system should reach the destiny at 4:00 to touch the ground what if missile is launched at correct time but it reached the destination ground by 4:05 because of performance of the system, with 5 minutes of difference destination is changed from one place to another place or even to another country. Here system should meet the deadline.

1.9.2 Soft Real Time Systems

Soft real time systems are less restrictive. Critical real time task gets priority over other tasks and retains the priority until it completes. Soft real time systems have limited utility than hard real time systems. For example; multimedia, virtual reality, advanced scientific projects like undersea exploration and planetary rovers etc.

In soft real time system, the meeting of deadline is not compulsory for every time for every task but process should get processed and give the result. Even the soft real time systems cannot miss the deadline for every task or process according to the priority it should meet the deadline or can miss the deadline. If system is missing the deadline for every time the performance of the system will be worse and cannot be used by the users. Best example for soft real time system is personal computer, audio and video systems, etc.

Memory Management : In simple words how to allocate memory for every program which is to be run and get processed in the memory (RAM or ROM). The schemes like demand paging, virtual memory, segmentation will under this management only.

Segmentation : It is a memory management scheme where the physical memory is dividing into logical segments according to the length of the program. In the segmentation it will avoid unused memory, sharing will be done easily, protection for the program. Sometime Main memory cannot allocate memory to the segments Because of it variable length and large segments.

Paging : in this scheme the physical memory is divided in to fixed size pages. It has all functions of segmentation and also solves its disadvantages. Virtual memory is a memory management scheme where some part of secondary storage device will be used a physical memory when program lacks the physical memory to run the program.

Process Management : thread contains set of instructions which can execute independently of other programs. Collection of thread is called the process or we can say process contains the sequential execution of program and state control of the operating system. Every operating system works by executing series of processes by the processor and give result back to the main memory. Operating systems contains two types of process

System Process : these processes are main responsible for working of operating system.

Application Process : These processes are invoked when particular application is stared and start executing with the help of other system process.

1.10 DISTRIBUTED OPERATING SYSTEM

Distributed systems use multiple central processors to serve multiple real time application and multiple users. Data processing jobs are distributed among the processors accordingly to which one can perform each job most efficiently.

The processors communicate with one another through various communication lines (such as high-speed buses or telephone lines). These are referred as loosely coupled systems or distributed systems. Processors in a distributed system may vary in size and function. These processors are referred as sites, nodes and computers and so on.

Fig. 1.5 below illustrates distributed system. In Fig. 1.5 we see that distributed operating system runs on multiple independent computers, connected through communication network, but appears to its users as single virtual machine and runs its own OS. Each computer node has its own computer memory. Examples of distributed systems are Internet, Intranet, Mobile and ubiquitous computing.

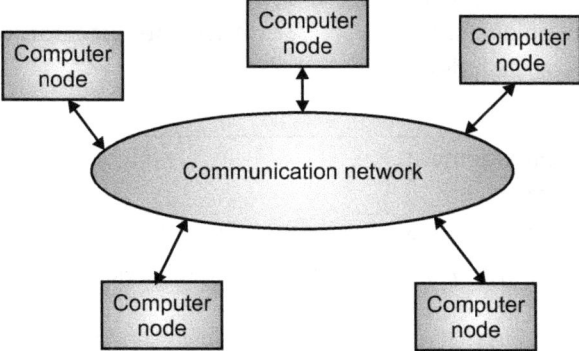

Fig. 1.5 : Architecture of distributed system

The Advantages of Distributed Systems
- With resource sharing facility user at one site may be able to use the resources available at another.
- Speedup the exchange of data with one another via electronic mail.

- If one site fails in a distributed system, the remaining sites can potentially continue operating.
- Better service to the customers.
- Reduction of the load on the host computer.
- Reduction of delays in data processing.

C. OPERATING SYSTEM SERVICES AND COMPONENTS

1.11 OPERATING SYSTEM SERVICES AND COMPONENTS

Following components reflects services made available by OS.

1.11.1 Process Management

- Process is a program in execution.
- Process creation/deletion (bookkeeping).
- Process suspension/resumption (scheduling, system vs. user).
- Process synchronization.
- Process communication.
- Deadlock handling.

1.11.2 Memory Management

- Maintain bookkeeping information.
- Map processes to memory locations.
- Allocate/de-allocate memory space as requested/required.

1.11.3 I/O Device Management

- Disk management functions such as free space management, storage allocation, fragmentation removal, head scheduling.
- Consistent, convenient software to I/O device interface through buffering/caching, custom drivers for each device.

1.11.4 File System

It is built on top of disk management.
- File creation/deletion.
- Support for hierarchical file systems.
- Update/retrieval operations : read, write, append, seek.
- Mapping of files to secondary storage.

1.11.5 Protection

Protection means here controlling access to the system :
- Resources CPU cycles, memory, files, devices.
- Users authentication, communication.
- Mechanisms, not policies.

1.11.6 Network Management

It is often built on top of file system :
- TCP/IP, IPX, IPng.
- Connection/Routing strategies.
- "Circuit" management circuit, message, packet switching.
- Communication mechanism.
- Data/Process migration.

1.11.7 Network Services (Distributed Computing)

It is built on top of networking.
- Email, messaging (GroupWise).
- FTP.
- Gopher, WWW.
- Distributed file systems : NFS, AFS, LAN Manager.
- Name service : DNS, YP, NIS.
- Replication : gossip, ISIS.
- Security : Kerberos.

1.11.8 User Interface

- Character-Oriented shell : sh, csh, command.com (User replaceable).
- GUI : X, Windows 7, Ubuntu.

1.12 SYSTEM CALLS PROVIDING THESE SERVICES

Some of the generic system calls are :
1. Process Management
Scheduling, deadlock detection is transparent :
- Fork, vfork, exit, exec.
- wait.
- Signals, pipes, streams, sockets.

2. Memory Management
For the most part it is transparent to the user :
- Malloc, free.

3. I/O Device Management
Devices are treated as files in UNIX, so I/O devices are supported by the file system.

4. File System
- Create, open, close.
- Lseek, read, write.
- Stat, chmod, chown.
- Link, unlink.
- Mkdir, rmdir.
- Sync.

D. OPERATING SYSTEM STRUCTURES

1.13 INTRODUCTION TO OPERATING SYSTEM STRUCTURES

Computer operating systems have been around for more than half a century so there is not much to add to the definition. Whether you are in the software industry or the academia, I assume you know what an operating system means but in few words an OS is the piece of software that sits between computing hardware and user applications. In this section, we summarize and contrast some of the most popular operating systems architectures from a high level perspective. Generally speaking, an operating system consists of two parts : a privileged mode called kernel space and unprivileged mode called user space. The separation is a need rather than an option otherwise process protection cannot be achieved. Depending on which processes run in what space, we can classify operating systems into four main architectures : Monolithic kernel, Microkernel, layered and Hybrid or modular kernel operating systems. Let us now explore these architectures and see the good and bad about each one of them.

1.14 MONOLITHIC KERNEL

You can think of a monolithic kernel OS as a single large static binary file process running entirely in a single address space. Basic OS services such as process management, memory management, interrupt handling, I/O communication, file system, device drivers, networking, etc all run in kernel space. Entire services are loaded on boot up and reside in memory and work is done using system calls. Linux is an example on a monolithic kernel based OS. Fig. 1.6 shows monolithic kernel based operating system. Look at the term "monolithic". "Mono" means "one" and "lithic" means "it is like stone". This type of architecture provides high level interface over computer resources and hardware. It provides basic set of system calls via system API.

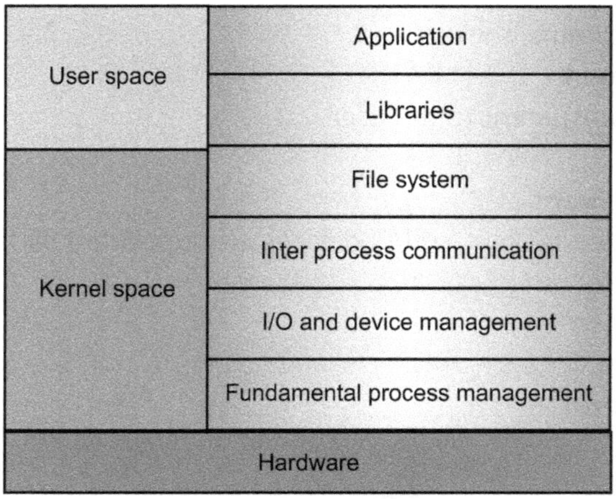

User space	Application
	Libraries
Kernel space	File system
	Inter process communication
	I/O and device management
	Fundamental process management
	Hardware

Fig. 1.6 : Monolithic kernel

Advantages of Monolithic Kernel
- Generally speaking, a monolithic OS kernel is faster due to small source and compiled code size. Less code means also less bugs and security issues.

Disadvantages of Monolithic Kernel
- Monolithic OS being a single big pile of code has disadvantages. For example, making changes is not easy and testing takes more time. It is hard to maintain, patch or extend. Bug fixing or adding new features requires the compilation of the whole source code which is a time and resource consuming process.

Example
- Windows
- UNIX

1.15 MICROKERNEL

The idea behind microkernel OS is to reduce the kernel to only basic process communication and IO control and let other system services run in user space just like any other normal processes. These services are called servers and kept separate and run in different address spaces. Contrary to monolithic OS where services are directly invoked, communication in a microkernel is done via message passing. Mac OS and WinNT are two examples on microkernel OS architecture. Fig. 1.7 shows microkernel based operating system.

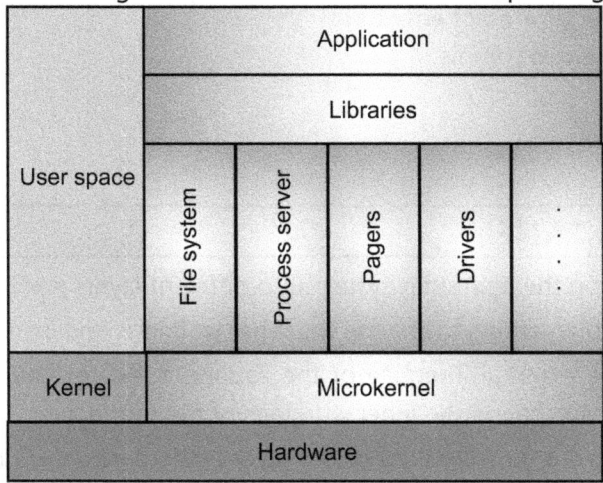

Fig. 1.7 : Micro kernel based operating system

The concept (Fig. 1.7) was to reduce the kernel to basic process communication and I/O control and let the other system services reside in user space in form of normal processes (as so called servers). There is a server for managing memory issues, one server does process management and other one manages drivers and so on. Because the servers do not run in kernel space anymore so called "context switches" are needed to allow user processes to enter privileged mode (and to exit again). That way, the µ-kernel is not a block of system services anymore, but represents just several basic abstractions and primitives to control the communication between the processes and between a process and the underlying hardware. Because communication is not done in a direct way anymore a message system is introduced, which allows independent communication and favors extensibility.

Advantages of Microkernel
- Service separation has the advantage that if one service (called a server) fails others can still work so reliability is the primary feature. For example if a device driver crashes does not cause the entire system to crash. Only that driver need to be restarted rather than having the entire system die. This means more persistence as one server can be substituted with another. It also means maintenance is easier.
- Different services are built into special modules which can be loaded or unloaded when needed. Patches can be tested separately then swapped to take over on a production instance.
- Message passing allows independent communication and allows extensibility.
- The fact that there is no need to reboot the kernel implies rapid test and development.
- Easy and faster integration with 3D party modules.

Disadvantages of Microkernel
- Memory foot print is large.
- Potential performance loss (more software interfaces due to message passing).
- Message passing bugs are not easy to fix.
- Process management is complex.

Example
- Linux

1.16 LAYERED KERNEL

This approach breaks up the operating system into different layers :
1. This allows implementers to change the inner workings and increases modularity.
2. As long as the external interface of the routine does not change, developers have more freedom to change the inner workings of the routines.
3. With the layered approach, the bottom layer is the hardware, while the highest layer is the user interface.
    (i) The main advantage is simplicity of construction and debugging.
    (ii) The main difficulty is defining the various layers.
    (iii) The main disadvantage is that the OS tends to be less efficient than other implementations.

Fig. 1.8 shows Minix layered architecture. As shown in Fig. 1.8., Minix has four layers, each with specific and well defined function.

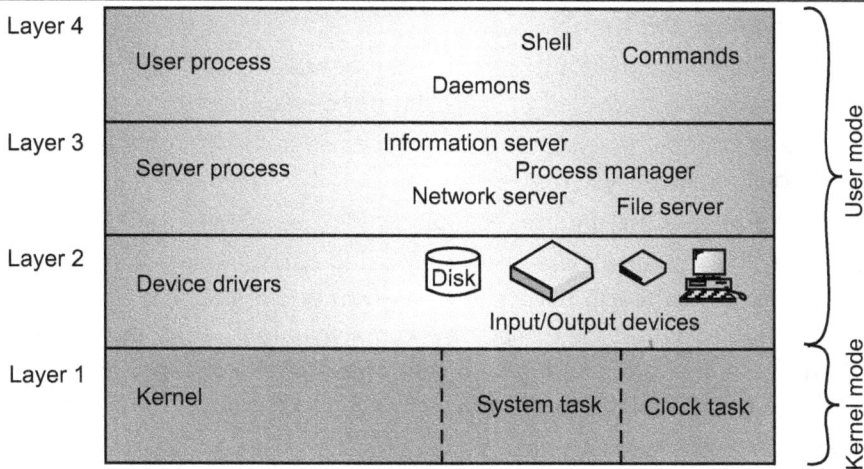

Fig. 1.8 : Minix layered architecture

1.17 HYBRID / MODULAR KERNEL

The hybrid approach is derived from the best of both micro and monolithic kernel architectures. Instead of loading the whole thing into memory, core modules are loaded dynamically to memory on demand. One disadvantage is that a module may destabilize a running kernel.

Many traditionally monolithic kernels are now at least adding (if not actively exploiting) the module capability. The most well known of these kernels is the Linux kernel. The modular kernel essentially can have parts of it that are built into the core kernel binary or binaries that load into memory on demand. It is important to note that a code tainted module has the potential to destabilize a running kernel. Many people become confused on this point when discussing microkernel. It is possible to write a driver for a microkernel in a completely separate memory space and test it before going live. When a kernel module is loaded, it accesses the monolithic portion's memory space by adding to it what it needs, therefore, opening the doorway to possible pollution. Fig. 1.9 shows hybrid kernel based operating system. Hybrid kernels are micro kernels with aspects from monolithic kernel.

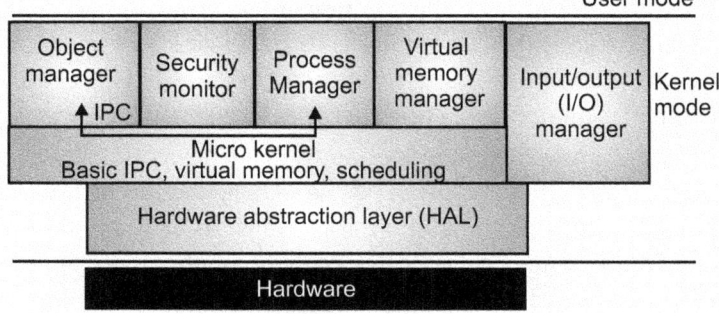

Fig. 1.9 : Hybrid kernel based operating system

Advantages of the Modular Kernel
- Faster development time for drivers that can operate from within modules. No reboot required for testing (provided the kernel is not destabilized).
- On demand capability versus spending time recompiling a whole kernel for things like new drivers or subsystems.
- Faster integration of third party technology

Modules, generally, communicate with the kernel using a module interface of some sort. The interface is generalized (although particular to a given operating system) so it is not always possible to use modules. Often the device drivers may need more flexibility than the module interface affords. Essentially, it is two system calls and often the safety checks that only have to be done once in the monolithic kernel now may be done twice.

Disadvantages of the Modular Kernel
- With more interfaces to pass through, the possibility of increased bugs exists (which implies more security holes).
- Maintaining modules can be confusing for some administrators when dealing with problems like symbol differences.

Examples
- BeOS Kernel
    1. Haiku Kernel
- BSD
    1. DragonFly BSD Kernel
    2. XNU Kernel
- NetWare Kernel
- Plan 9 Kernel
    1. Inferno Kernel
- Windows (NT,2000,2003,XP,Vista) NT Kernel
    1. ReactOS Kernel

Summary of Operating System Structures

A great deal of the advantages and disadvantages of any given design are very much dependent upon the context of the system itself. To generalize and say the monolithic kernel is always faster than its micro or modular counterparts somewhat of a misnomer. There are many ways to illustrate it, one good way however is to look at tuning factors.

A microkernel that is designed for a specific platform or device is only ever going to have what it needs to operate. A monolithic kernel, while initially loaded with subsystems that may not be needed can be tuned to a point where it is as fast as or faster than the one that was specifically designed for the hardware, although more in a general sense.

Another context to keep in mind is the purpose. Not all servers are general, even though they can be. A small web server for example does not necessarily need massive in machine redundancy. If it is small, it should be easy to duplicate on another system or even just restore quickly from backups. A database of medical records, however, is a completely different matter. If the product itself does not have clustering and failover capability or you cannot afford it, using a modular or microkernel servers based system might be a better option.

In summary, there are lots of different kernel types and lots of different situations in which they can be employed.

1.18 VIRTUAL MACHINE

- Virtual Machine, also referred as VM in short, is a software implementation of a computing environment in which an operating system and/or programs can be installed and/or run.
- VM is a program that acts as a virtual computer.
- VM shares physical hardware resources of underlying operating system and supply these resources to other operating system which runs on top of VM.
- In this case, underlying operating system is referred as "**Host Operating System**" and other operating system on top of VM is referred as "**Guest Operating System**".
- Main goal of VM is to provide virtual hardware to guest operating system.
- Virtual hardware includes virtual memory, CPU, network interfaces, hard drive and other devices.
- Such virtual hardware is actually mapped by VM to real hardware on your physical machine. For example virtual machine's virtual hard disk is stored in a file located on your hard drive.
- Virtual machine contains several types of files that are stored on supported storage device.

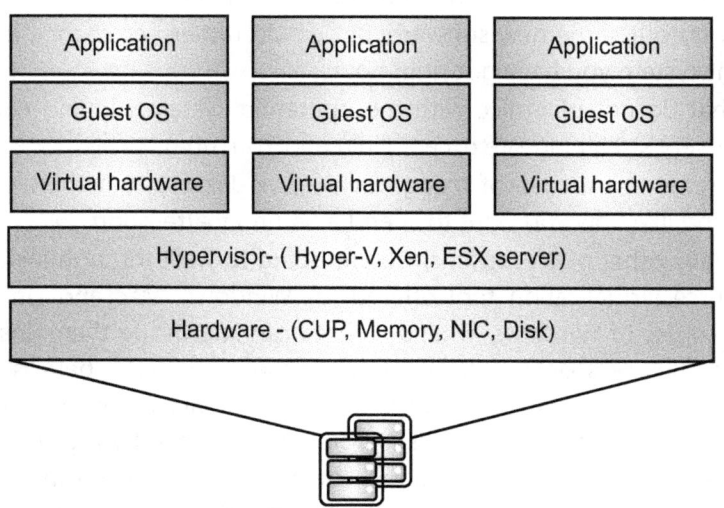

Fig. 1.10 : Virtual machine architecture

- Above Fig. 1.10 illustrates VM architecture. On the top of VM, three guest operating systems are running. In market there are many providers available that allows use of hypervisor to build VM. For example Hyper-V, Xen, ESX Server, etc. Hypervisor (also referred as Virtual machine monitor) is a computer hardware, software or firmware that creates and runs virtual machines. Machine on which hypervisor is running is referred as host machine where as each virtual machine is called as guest machine.

Advantages of Virtual Machine
- Allows running multiple operating systems on single machine.
- Increases energy efficiency by reducing capital cost. It requires less hardware while increasing your server to admin ratio.
- Ensures highest availability and performance.
- Through improved disaster recovery solutions, it builds up business continuity.
- Allows adding new server without buying any additional hardware.

Hardware independence gives freedom to move a virtual machine from one computer to other without making any changes at system level.

1.18.1 Basics of Virtualization

Virtualization is a whole computer concept unto itself, at least on the server/enterprise/big-fancy-corporate level. For home users, talk about "virtual machines" generally refers to x86 virtualization. Basically, it is software that allows an entire operating system (the "guest") to run on another OS (the "Host"), whether in a container window, or full-screen, or in what is sometimes called a "seamless" mode, where just one application is run from the "guest"

Why would you want to run a virtual machine on your computer?
- You like using one OS, but need just an app or two from another running in their natural environments Office or Photoshop in Windows (nine times out of 10), a light-on-resources game, or maybe even some uber-cool Linux app.
- You want to try out some new software, but would rather not chance it mucking up the pretty decent system you have got right now.
- Web sites that do not play nice with the operating system running (we are looking at you, almost every streaming site except Hulu and YouTube).
- You are intrigued at the idea of trying out a Linux desktop, but the word "partitioning" does not sound like how you want to spend a Saturday afternoon.

For those and many other good reasons, we are going to walk through installing VirtualBox, a free, open-source virtualization tool offered for Windows, Mac and Linux desktops and then get virtual copies of Windows XP and Ubuntu running inside them. Installing Windows Vista (Ultimate or Business only, unfortunately) or the Windows 7 beta is about the same process and almost any Linux distribution is friendly as a virtual machine, but this will give you an understanding of the basic process. Before you even ask, by the way, you can not run OS X as a guest system on Windows or Linux, but the VirtualBox can run most anything else including those pre-rolled virtual images you find laying around the internet.

I have to note here that VirtualBox is far from the only competitor in this field in fact, many in the tech community report that VMWare's Workstation offers more features and handles multiple virtual machines better. But VirtualBox is relatively easy to set up, free to install and works on all three major operating systems.

1.18.2 Setup Virtual Machine

Once you have downloaded the .ovf image,

- Start up VirtualBox, then select File>Import Appliance and select the .ovf image that you downloaded.

You may also be able to simply double-click the .ovf file to open it up in your installed virtualization program.

- Next, press the "Import" button.

This step will take a while the unpacked image is about 3 GB.

Finish VM Setup

You will need to complete one more step before you are done with the VM setup.

Select your VM and go to the Settings Tab. Go to Network->Adapter 2. Select the "Enable adapter" box and attach it to "host-only network". (on a new VirtualBox installation you may not have any "host-only network" configured yet. To have one select File menu/Preferences/Network and "Add host-only network" button with default settings. Then you can try the attach.) This will allow you to easily access your VM through your host machine.

At that point you should be ready to start your VM. Press the "Start" arrow icon or double-click your VM within the VirtualBox window.

In the VM console window, log in with the user name and password for your VM. These should both be "mininet"

Note that this user is a sudoer, so you can execute commands with root permissions by typing sudo command, where command is the command you wish to execute with root permission.

1.18.3 Choose Preferred Editor

Nano, Vim, Emacs and Gedit come installed on the OpenFlowTutorial VM. Brief instructions for each :

Nano : You can immediately modify a file. When you are done, hit 'ctrl-x', then say 'Yes' to the prompt, to save and quit.

Vim : to modify a file, type 'i' to enter Insert mode, then use the arrow keys to navigate and edit. When you are done, hit 'esc', type ':wq', then press enter, to save and quit.

Highly recommended for the NOX tutorial : add the following to ~/.vimrc in the VM :

    set tabstop=4

    set expandtab

Emacs : you can immediately modify a file. When you are done, hit 'ctrl-x', 'ctrl-s', then hit 'ctrl-x', 'ctrl-c' to exit.

Gedit : a graphical text editor, no instructions needed.

Eclipse : Eclipse and its dependencies would require about 500MB extra space on the VM image, so it is not shipped by default. If you have Eclipse installed on the host VM, using the Remote Systems Explorer can be a convenient way to access and modify text files on the VM, with many of the advantages of Eclipse, such as syntax highlighting.

If you have another preferred text editor, feel free to install it now :

$ sudo apt-get install <editor>

Command Prompt Notes

In this tutorial, commands are shown along with a command prompt to indicate what subsystem they are intended for . For example,

$ ls

indicates that the ls command should be typed at a Unix (e.g. Linux or OS X) command prompt (which generally ends in $ if you are a regular user or # if you are root.

Other prompts used in this tutorial include

mininet>

for commands entered in the Mininet console and

C:>

for code entered into a Windows command window.

1.18.4 Set Up Network Access

The tutorial VM is shipped without a desktop environment, to reduce its size. All the exercises will be done through X forwarding, where programs display graphics through an X server running on the host OS.

To start up the X forwarding, you will first need to find the guest IP address.

1.18.4.1 VirtualBox

If you are running VirtualBox, you should make sure your VM has two network interfaces. One should be a NAT interface that it can use to access the Internet and the other should be a host-only interface to enable it to communicate with the host machine. For example, your NAT interface could be eth0 and have a 10.x IP address and your host-only interface could be eth1 and have a 192.168.x IP address. You should ssh into the host-only interface at its associated IP address. Both interfaces should be configured using DHCP. If they are not already configured, you may have to run dhclient on each of them, as described below.

1.18.4.2 Access VM via SSH

In this step, you will verify that you can connect from the host PC (your laptop) to the guest VM (OpenFlowTutorial) via SSH.

From the virtual machine console, log in to the VM, then enter :
$ ifconfig -a

You should see three interfaces(eth0, eth1, lo), Both eth0 and eth1 should have IP address assigned. If this is not the case, type
$ sudo dhclient ethX

Replacing ethX with the name of a downed interfaces; sometimes the eth ports appear as eth2 or eth3, you can fix this by editing /etc/udev/rules.d/70-persistent-net.rules and removing the existing configuration lines.

Note the IP address (probably the 192.168 one) for the host-only network; you will need it later. Next, log in, which will depend on your OS.

Mac OS X and Linux

Open a terminal (Terminal.app in Mac, Gnome terminal in Ubuntu, etc). In that terminal, run :
$ ssh -X [user]@[Guest IP Here]

Replace [user] with the correct user name for your VM image.

Replace [Guest] with the IP you just noted. If ssh does not connect, make sure that you can ping the IP address you are connecting to.

Enter the password for your VM image. Next, try starting up an X terminal using
$ xterm

and a new terminal window should appear. If you have succeeded, you are done with the basic setup. Close the xterm. If you get a 'xterm: DISPLAY is not set error', verify your X server installation from above.

1.19 OVERVIEW OF THREADS

A thread is a basic unit of CPU utilization, consisting of a program counter a stack and a set of registers, (and a thread ID).

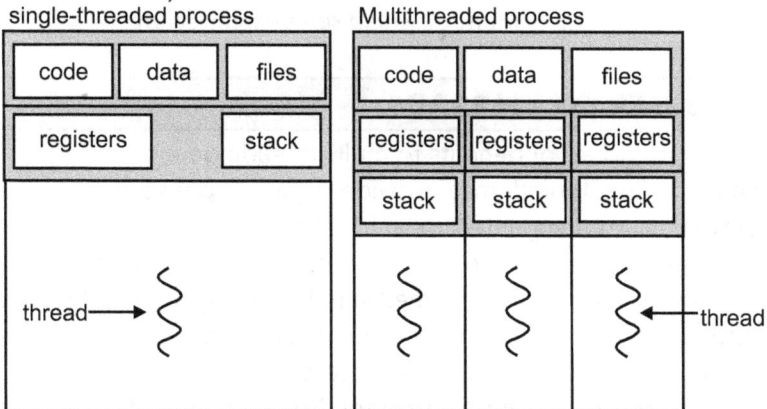

Fig. 1.11 : Single-threaded and multi-threaded processes

Traditional (heavyweight) processes have a single thread of control There is one program counter and one sequence of instructions that can be carried out at any given time.

As shown in Fig. 1.11, multi-threaded applications have multiple threads within a single process, each having their own program counter, stack and set of registers, but sharing common code, data and certain structures such as open files.

1.20 MOTIVATION OF THREADS

- Threads are very useful in modern programming whenever a process has multiple tasks to perform independently of the others. This is particularly true when one of the tasks may block and it is desired to allow the other tasks to proceed without blocking.
- For example in a word processor, a background thread may check spelling and grammar while a foreground thread processes user input (keystrokes), while yet a third thread loads images from the hard drive and a fourth does periodic automatic backups of the file being edited.
- Another example is a web server Multiple threads allow for multiple requests to be satisfied simultaneously, without having to service requests sequentially or to fork off separate processes for every incoming request. (The latter is how this sort of thing was done before the concept of threads was developed. A daemon would listen at a port, fork off a child for every incoming request to be processed and then go back to listening to the port.)

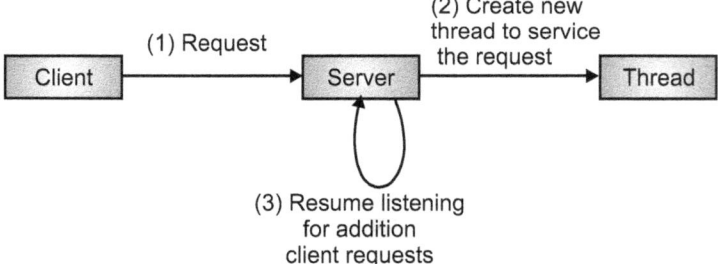

Fig. 1.12 : Multi threaded server architecture

1.21 ADVANTAGES OF THREADS

There are four major categories of benefits to multi-threading :
1. **Responsiveness :** One thread may provide rapid response while other threads are blocked or slowed down doing intensive calculations.
2. **Resource Sharing :** By default threads share common code, data and other resources, which allow multiple tasks to be performed simultaneously in a single address space.
3. **Economy :** Creating and managing threads (and context switches between them) is much faster than performing the same tasks for processes.
4. **Scalability, i.e. Utilization of Multiprocessor Architectures :** A single threaded process can only run on one CPU, no matter how many may be available, whereas the execution

of a multi-threaded application may be split amongst available processors. (Note that single threaded processes can still benefit from multi-processor architectures when there are multiple processes contending for the CPU, i.e. when the load average is above some certain threshold.)

1.22 MULTITHREADING MODELS

There are two types of threads to be managed in a modern system :
- User threads
- kernel threads.

User threads are supported above the kernel, without kernel support. These are the threads that application programmers would put into their programs.

Kernel threads are supported within the kernel of the OS itself. All modern OS support kernel level threads, allowing the kernel to perform multiple simultaneous tasks and/or to service multiple kernel system calls simultaneously.

In a specific implementation, the user threads must be mapped to kernel threads, using one of the following strategies.

1.22.1 Many-to-One Model

- In the many-to-one model, many user level threads are all mapped onto a single kernel thread.
- Thread management is handled by the thread library in user space, which is very efficient.
- However, if a blocking system call is made, then the entire process blocks, even if the other user threads would otherwise be able to continue.
- Because a single kernel thread can operate only on a single CPU, the many-to-one model does not allow individual processes to be split across multiple CPUs.
- Green threads for Solaris and GNU Portable Threads implement the many-to-one model in the past, but few systems continue to do so today.

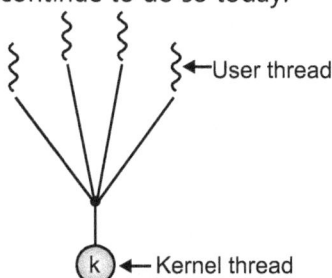

Fig. 1.13 : Many-to-one model

1.22.2 One-to-One Model

- The one-to-one model creates a separate kernel thread to handle each user thread.
- One-to-one model overcomes the problems listed above involving blocking system calls and the splitting of processes across multiple CPUs.

- However the overhead of managing the one-to-one model is more significant, involving more overhead and slowing down the system.
- Most implementations of this model place a limit on how many threads can be created.
- Linux and Windows from 95 to XP implement the one-to-one model for threads.

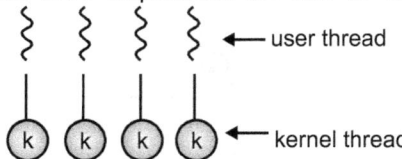

Fig. 1.14 : One-to-one model

1.22.3 Many-to-Many Model

- The many-to-many model multiplexes any number of user threads onto an equal or smaller number of kernel threads, combining the best features of the one-to-one and many-to-one models.
- Users have no restrictions on the number of threads created.
- Blocking kernel system calls do not block the entire process.
- Processes can be split across multiple processors.
- Individual processes may be allocated variable numbers of kernel threads, depending on the number of CPUs present and other factors.

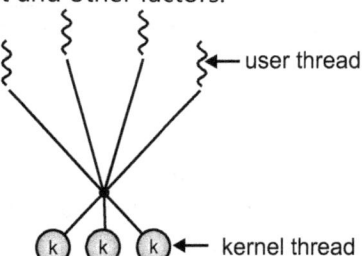

Fig. 1.15 : Many-to-many model

1.23 THREAD LIBRARIES

Pthread libraries provide programmers with an API for creating and managing threads.

Thread libraries may be implemented either in user space or in kernel space. The former involves API functions implemented solely within user space, with no kernel support. The latter involves system calls and requires a kernel with thread library support.

There are three main thread libraries in use today :

1. **POSIX Pthreads :** may be provided as either a user or kernel library, as an extension to the POSIX standard.
2. **Win32 Threads :** provided as a kernel-level library on Windows systems.
3. **Java Threads :** Since Java generally runs on a Java Virtual Machine, the implementation of threads is based upon whatever OS and hardware the JVM is running on, i.e. either Pthreads or Win32 threads depending on the system.

The interface to multithreading support is through a subroutine library, libpthread for POSIX threads and libthread for Solaris threads. They both contain code for :
- creating and destroying threads
- passing messages and data between threads
- scheduling thread execution
- saving and restoring thread contexts

The POSIX Threads Library : libpthread, <pthread.h>

Creating a (Default) Thread

Use the function pthread_create() to add a new thread of control to the current process. It is prototyped by :

> int pthread_create(pthread_t *tid, const pthread_attr_t *tattr,
> void*(*start_routine)(void *), void *arg);

When an attribute object is not specified, it is NULL and the *default* thread is created with the following attributes :
- It is unbounded
- It is nondetached
- It has a a default stack and stack size
- It inherits the parent's priority

You can also create a default attribute object with pthread_attr_init() function and then use this attribute object to create a default thread.

An example call of default thread creation is :

```
#include <pthread.h>
pthread_attr_t tattr;
pthread_t tid;
extern void *start_routine(void *arg);
void *arg;
int ret;
/* default behavior*/
ret = pthread_create(&tid, NULL, start_routine, arg);
/* initialized with default attributes */
ret = pthread_attr_init(&tattr);
/* default behavior specified*/
ret = pthread_create(&tid, &tattr, start_routine, arg);
```

The pthread_create() function is called with attr having the necessary state behavior. start_routine is the function with which the new thread begins execution. When start_routine returns, the thread exits with the exit status set to the value returned by start_routine.

When pthread_create is successful, the ID of the thread created is stored in the location referred to as tid.

Creating a thread using a NULL attribute argument has the same effect as using a default attribute; both create a default thread. When tattr is initialized, it acquires the default behavior.

pthread_create() returns a zero and exits when it completes successfully. Any other returned value indicates that an error occurred.

1.23.1 Wait for Thread Termination

Use the pthread_join function to wait for a thread to terminate. It is prototyped by :

```
int pthread_join(thread_t tid, void **status);
An example use of this function is :
#include <pthread.h>
pthread_t tid;
int ret;
int status;
/* waiting to join thread "tid" with status */
ret = pthread_join(tid, &status);
/* waiting to join thread "tid" without status */
ret = pthread_join(tid, NULL);
```

The pthread_join() function blocks the calling thread until the specified thread terminates. The specified thread must be in the current process and must not be detached. When status is not NULL, it points to a location that is set to the exit status of the terminated thread when pthread_join() returns successfully. Multiple threads cannot wait for the same thread to terminate. If they try to, one thread returns successfully and the others fail with an error of ESRCH. After pthread_join() returns, any stack storage associated with the thread can be reclaimed by the application.

The pthread_join() routine takes two arguments, giving you some flexibility in its use. When you want the caller to wait until a specific thread terminates, supply that thread's ID as the first argument. If you are interested in the exit code of the defunct thread, supply the address of an area to receive it. Remember that pthread_join() works only for target threads that are nondetached. When there is no reason to synchronize with the termination of a particular thread, then that thread should be detached. Think of a detached thread as being the thread you use in most instances and reserve nondetached threads for only those situations that require them.

1.23.2 Threads Example

In this Simple Threads fragment below, one thread executes the procedure at the top, creating a helper thread that executes the procedure fetch, which involves a complicated database lookup and might take some time.

The main thread wants the results of the lookup but has other work to do in the meantime. So it does those other things and then waits for its helper to complete its job by executing pthread_join(). An argument, pbe, to the new thread is passed as a stack parameter. This can be done here because the main thread waits for the spun-off thread to terminate. In general, though, it is better to malloc() storage from the heap instead of passing an address to thread stack storage, which can disappear or be reassigned if the thread terminated.

The source for thread.c is as follows :

```c
    void mainline (...)
{
    struct phonebookentry *pbe;
    pthread_attr_t tattr;
    pthread_t helper;
    int status;
    pthread_create(&helper, NULL, fetch, &pbe);
    /* do something else for a while */
    pthread_join(helper, &status);
    /* it is now safe to use result */
}
    void fetch(struct phonebookentry *arg)
{
    struct phonebookentry *npbe;
    /* fetch value from a database */
    npbe = search (prog_name)
    if (npbe != NULL)
    *arg = *npbe;
    pthread_exit(0);
}
    struct phonebookentry
{
    char name[64];
    char phonenumber[32];
    char flags[16];
}
```

1.23.3 Detaching a Thread

The function pthread_detach() is an alternative to pthread_join() to reclaim storage for a thread that is created with a detachstate attribute set to PTHREAD_CREATE_JOINABLE. It is prototyped by :

```
int pthread\_detach(thread\_t tid);
A simple example of calling this fucntion to detatch a thread is given by :
#include <pthread.h>
pthread_t tid;
int ret;
/* detach thread tid */
ret = pthread_detach(tid);
```

The pthread_detach() function is used to indicate to the implementation that storage for the thread tid can be reclaimed when the thread terminates. If tid has not terminated, pthread_detach() does not cause it to terminate. The effect of multiple pthread_detach() calls on the same target thread is unspecified.

pthread_detach() returns a zero when it completes successfully. Any other returned value indicates that an error occurred. When any of the following conditions are detected, pthread_detach() fails and returns the an error value.

QUESTIONS

1. Explain with neat block diagram computer system organization.
2. Explain with examples utility programs in operating system.
3. What is operating system? Explain operating system architecture.
4. Write in short evolution of operating system.
5. Why operating system is needed? Elaborate with the help of examples.
6. Explain in short user view and system view of operating system.
7. Explain batch operating system in detail.
8. Explain time sharing operating system in detail.
9. Explain multiprogramming operating system in detail.
10. Explain real time operating system in detail.
11. Define terms - hard real time systems and soft real time systems.
12. Explain distributed operating system in detail.
13. What are the operating system services and components?
14. Explain with example, system calls used to perform operating systems core functions.
15. Compare and contrast monolithic and micro kernel architectures.
16. Explain with neat diagram layered kernel architecture.

✠ ✠ ✠

Unit - II

PROCESS AND PROCESS MANAGEMENT

2.0 INTRODUCTION

This unit majorly focus on process and its management. Process is referred as program in execution. During its lifetime, process is always in one of the states like ready, running, blocked, completed, etc. Process related all the important information is stored in Process Control Block (PCB). In this unit, we discuss process scheduling, its objective. We see how schedulers are categorized in long term, short term and medium term scheduler. We see most popularly used scheduling algorithms like First Come First Serve (FCFS), priority, Round Robin (RR), MLQ with and without feedback. Then in detail we explain basics of Inter Process Communication (IPC), its applications and types or mechanisms. Later on we put light on critical section, critical section problem and solution to critical section problems. Lastly in this unit we see concurrent programming and classical concurrent programming problems like producers-consumers problem, readers-writers problem, dinning philosopher problem.

A. PROCESS CONCEPT

2.1 THE PROCESS

Process is a program in execution. The execution of a process must progress in a sequential fashion. Definition of process is as following :

A process is defined as an entity which represents the basic unit of work to be implemented in the system.

Components of process are following :

- **Object Program :** Code to be executed.
- **Data :** Data to be used for executing the program.
- **Resources :** While executing the program, it may require some resources.
- **Status :** Verifies the status of the process execution. A process can run to completion only when all requested resources have been allocated to the process. Two or more processes could be executing the same program, each using their own data and resources.

2.2 PROCESS STATES

As a process executes, it changes state. The state of a process is defined as the current activity of the process.

Process can have one of the following five states at a time as shown in Fig. 2.1.

- **New :** The process is being created.
- **Ready :** The process is waiting to be assigned to a processor. Ready processes are waiting to have the processor allocated to them by the operating system so that they can run.
- **Running :** Process instructions are being executed (i.e. the process that is currently being executed).
- **Waiting :** The process is waiting for some event to occur (such as the completion of an I/O operation).
- **Terminated :** The process has finished execution.

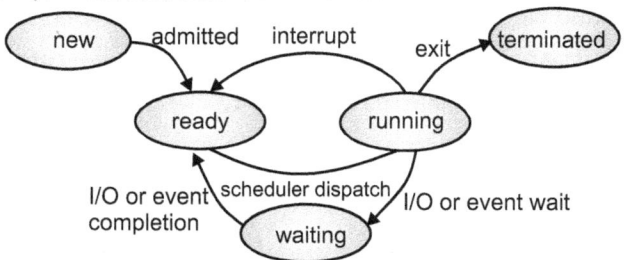

Fig. 2.1 : Five state process model

2.3 PROCESS CONTROL BLOCK (PCB)

Each process is represented in the operating system by a Process Control Block (PCB) also called a task control block. PCB is the data structure used by the operating system. Operating system groups all information that needs about particular process.

PCB contains many pieces of information associated with a specific process which is described below. Fig. 2.2 shows process control block.

1. **Pointer :** Pointer points to another process control block. Pointer is used for maintaining the scheduling list.
2. **Process State :** Process state may be new, ready, running, waiting and so on.
3. **Process Counter :** Program Counter indicates the address of the next instruction to be executed for this process.
4. **CPU Registers :** CPU registers include general purpose register, stack pointers, index register and accumulator etc. number of register and type of register totally depends upon the computer architecture.

5. **Memory Management Information :** This information may include the value of base and limit registers, the page tables, or the segment tables depending on the memory system used by the operating system. This information is useful for deallocating the memory when the process terminates.
6. **Accounting Information :** This information includes the amount of CPU used, time limits, job or process numbers, account numbers etc.

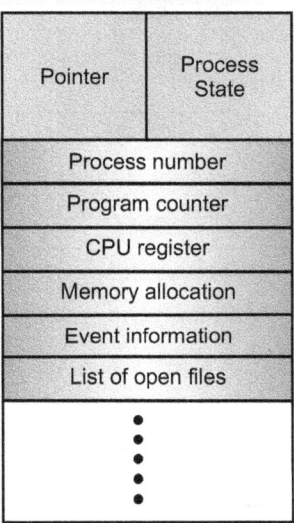

Fig. 2.2 : Process control block

Process control block includes CPU scheduling, I/O resource management, file management information etc.. The PCB serves as the repository for any information which can vary from process to process. Loader/linker sets flags and registers when a process is created. If that process gets suspended, the contents of the registers are saved on a stack and the pointer to the particular stack frame is stored in the PCB. By this technique, the hardware state can be restored so that the process can be scheduled to run again.

2.4 CONTEXT SWITCHING

A context switch is the mechanism to store and restore the state or context of a CPU in Process Control Block (PCB) so that a process execution can be resumed from the same point at a later time. Using this technique a context switcher enables multiple processes to share a single CPU. Context switching is an essential part of a multitasking operating system features.

When the scheduler switches the CPU from executing one process to execute another, the context switcher saves the content of all processor registers for the process being removed from the CPU, in its process descriptor. The context of a process is represented in the process control block of a process.

Context switch time is pure overhead. Context switching can significantly affect performance as modern computers have a lot of general and status registers to be saved. Content switching times are highly dependent on hardware support. Context switch requires (n + m) (bxK) time units to save the state of the processor with n general registers, assuming b are the store operations are required to save n and m registers of two process control blocks and each store instruction requires K time units.

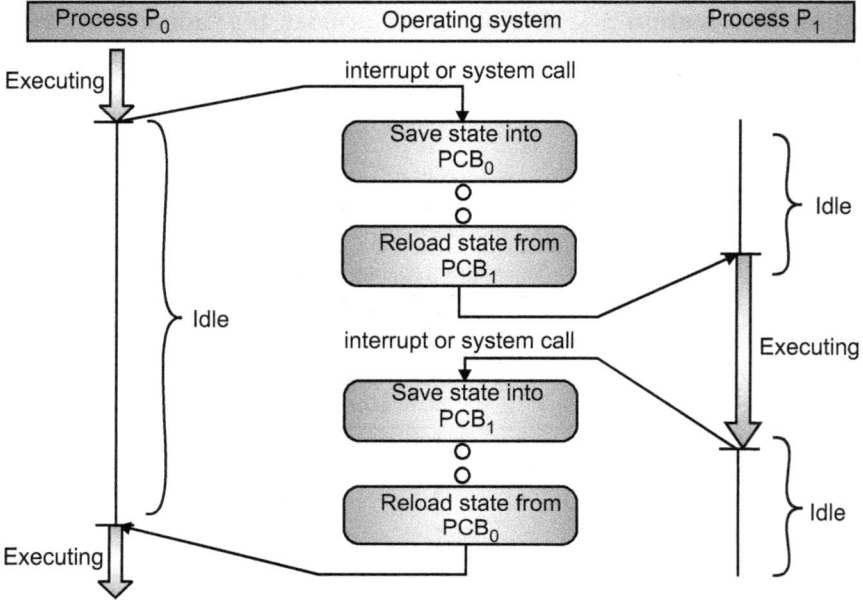

Fig. 2.3 : Context switching

Some hardware systems employ two or more sets of processor registers to reduce the amount of context switching time. When the process is switched, the following information is stored.

- Program Counter.
- Scheduling Information.
- Base and limit register value.
- Currently used register.
- Changed State.
- I/O State.
- Accounting.

2.5 SPOOLING

The term "spool" is an acronym of "Simultaneous Peripheral Off-line Output Listing". Spooling is a process of transferring data by placing in a temporary working area and using it when necessary. Spooling is the process of a sending data to a spool, or temporary storage area in the computer's memory. This data may contain files or processes. Like a spool of thread, the data can build up within the spool as multiple files or jobs are sent to it. However, unlike a spool of thread, the first jobs sent to the spool are the first ones to be processed (FIFO, not LIFO).

The most common type of spooling is print spooling, where print jobs are sent to a print spool before being transmitted to the printer. For example, when you print a document from within an application, the document data is spooled to a temporary storage area while the printer warms up. As soon as the printer is ready to print the document, the data is sent from the spool to the printer and the document is printed.

Print spooling gets its name from technology used in the 1960s, when print jobs were stored on large reels of magnetic tape. The data from these reels was physically spooled to electrostatic printers, which printed the output saved to the tape.

2.6 CPU AND I/O (INPUT/OUTPUT) BURST

CPU Burst : CPU burst is that when CPU waits for input process and after completion input burst CPU do process on that job. CPU burst is like a car and input output burst is like a pedestrian. Because CPU speed is much faster than input output burst. We cannot reduce the speed of CPU burst but we can increase the input output speed.

CPU Burst is "The amount of time the process uses the processor before it is no longer ready".

Types of CPU burst :

1. **Long Burst :** Process is CPU bound.
2. **Short Burst :** Process is I/O bound.

I/O Burst : "Input / Output burst is that after completion the input burst CPU do process on that job".

Concept
- Almost all programs have some alternating cycle of CPU number crunching and waiting for I/O of some kind. (Even a simple fetch from memory takes a long time relative to CPU speeds.)
- In a simple system running a single process, the time spent waiting for I/O is wasted and those CPU cycles are lost forever.
- A scheduling system allows one process to use the CPU while another is waiting for I/O, thereby making full use of otherwise lost CPU cycles.
- The challenge is to make the overall system as "efficient" and "fair" as possible, subject to varying and often dynamic conditions and where "efficient" and "fair" are some what subjective terms, often subject to shifting priority policies.

CPU-I/O Burst Cycle
- Almost all processes alternate between two states in a continuing cycle, as shown in Fig. 2.4 below :

1. A CPU burst of performing calculations and
2. An I/O burst, waiting for data transfer in or out of the system.

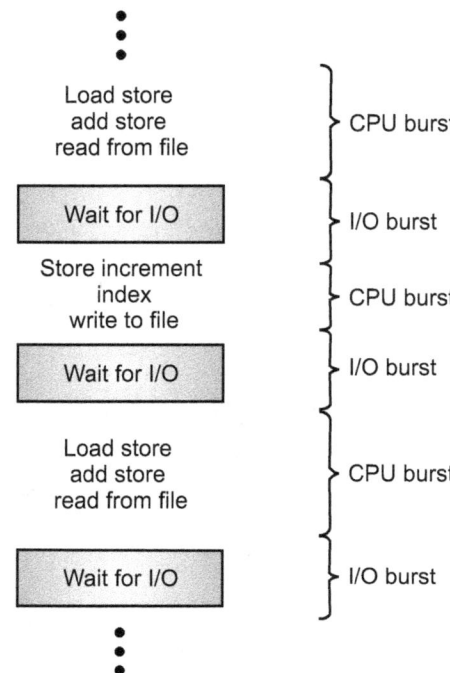

Fig. 2.4 : Alternating sequence of CPU and I/O burst

CPU bursts vary from process to process and from program to program, but an extensive study shows frequency patterns similar to that shown in Fig. 2.5 below

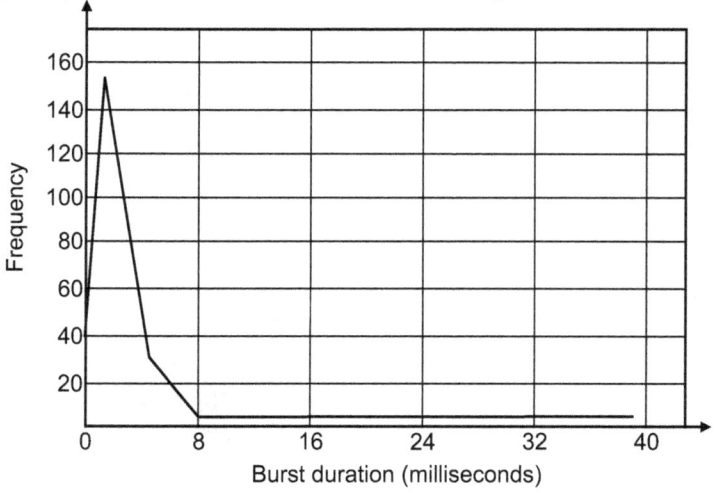

Fig. 2.5 : Histogram of CPU-burst durations

B. SCHEDULING

2.7 CONCEPT OF SCHEDULING

The process scheduling is the activity of the process manager that handles the removal of the running process from the CPU and the selection of another process on the basis of a particular strategy.

Process scheduling is an essential part of a Multiprogramming operating system. Such operating systems allow more than one process to be loaded into the executable memory at a time and loaded process shares the CPU using time multiplexing.

2.8 OBJECTIVES OF SHCEDULING

The primary objective of scheduling is to improve system performance. Various objectives of the scheduling are as follows :

- **Maximize Throughput :** Scheduling should attempt to service the largest possible number of processes per unit time. Maximize the number of interactive user receiving acceptable response times.
- **Be Predictable :** A given job should utilise the same amount of time and should cost the same regardless of the load on the system.
- **Minimize Overhead :** Scheduling should minimize the wasted resources overhead.
- **Balance Resource Use :** The scheduling mechanisms should keep the resources of the system busy. Processes that will use underutilized resources should be favoured.
- **Achieve a Balance Between Response and Utilization :** The best way to guarantee good response times is to have sufficient resources available whenever they are needed. In real time system fast responses are essential and resource utilization is less important.
- **Avoid Indefinite Postponement :** It would be fair if all processes are treated the same and no process can suffer indefinite postponement.
- **Enforce Priorities :** In environments in which processes are given priorities, the scheduling mechanism should favour the higher-priority processes.
- **Give Preference to Processes Holding Key Resources :** Even though a low priority process may be holding a key resource, the process may be in demand by high priority processes. If the resource is not perceptible, then the scheduling mechanism should give the process better treatment that it would ordinarily receive so that the process will release the key resource sooner.
- **Degrade Gracefully Under Heavy Loads :** A scheduling mechanism should not collapse under heavy system load. Either it should prevent excessive loading by not allowing new processes to be created when the load in heavy or it should provide service to the heavier load by providing a moderately reduced level of service to all processes.

2.9 SCHEDULING QUEUES

Scheduling queues refers to queues of processes or devices. When the process enters into the system, then this process is put into a job queue. This queue consists of all processes in the system. The operating system also maintains other queues such as device queue. Device queue is a queue for which multiple processes are waiting for a particular I/O (Input/Output) device. Each device has its own device queue. This Fig. 2.6 shows the queuing diagram of process scheduling.

- Queue is represented by rectangular box.
- The circles represent the resources that serve the queues.
- The arrows indicate the process flow in the system.

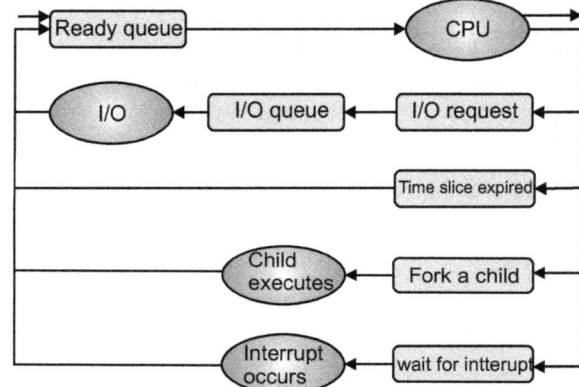

Fig. 2.6 : Queuing diagram

Queues are of two types :
1. Ready queue
2. Device queue

A newly arrived process is put in the ready queue. Processes waits in ready queue for allocating the CPU. Once the CPU is assigned to a process, then that process will execute. While executing the process, any one of the following events can occur :

1. The process could issue an I/O request and then it would be placed in an I/O queue.
2. The process could create new sub process and will wait for its termination.
3. The process could be removed forcibly from the CPU, as a result of interrupt and put back in the ready queue.

2.10 TWO STATES PROCESS MODEL

Two state process model refers to running and non-running states which are described below :

1. Running

When new process is created by Operating System that process enters into the system as in the running state.

2. Not Running

Processes that are not running are kept in queue, waiting for their turn to execute. Each entry in the queue is a pointer to a particular process. Queue is implemented by using linked list. Use of dispatcher is as follows. When process is interrupted, that process is transferred in the waiting queue. If the process has completed or aborted, the process is discarded. In either case, the dispatcher then selects a process from the queue to execute.

C. TYPES OF SCHEDULARS

2.11 SCHEDULER

Scheduler is special system software which handles process scheduling in various ways. Their main task is to select the jobs to be submitted into the system and to decide which process to run. Schedulers are of three types :

1. Long term scheduler
2. Short term scheduler
3. Medium term scheduler

2.12 LONG TERM SCHEDULER

It is also called job scheduler. Long term scheduler determines which programs are admitted to the system for processing. Job scheduler selects processes from the queue and loads them into memory for execution. Process loads into the memory for CPU scheduling. The primary objective of the job scheduler is to provide a balanced mix of jobs, such as I/O (Input/Output) bound and processor bound. It also controls the degree of multiprogramming. If the degree of multiprogramming is stable, then the average rate of process creation must be equal to the average departure rate of processes leaving the system.

On some systems, the long term scheduler may not be available or minimal. Time-sharing operating systems have no long term scheduler. When process changes the state from new to ready, then there is use of long term scheduler.

Long term scheduling obviously controls the degree of multiprogramming in multitasking systems, following certain policies to decide whether the system can honour a new job submission or, if more than one job is submitted, which of them should be selected. The need for some form of compromise between degree of multiprogramming and throughput seems evident, especially when one considers interactive systems. The higher the number of processes, in fact, the smaller the time each of them may control CPU for, if a fair share of responsiveness is to be given to all processes. Moreover we have already seen that a too high number of processes causes waste of CPU time for system housekeeping chores (trashing in virtual memory systems is a particularly nasty example of this). However, the number of active processes should be high enough to keep the CPU busy servicing the payload (i.e. the user processes) as much as possible, by ensuring that on average there always be a sufficient number of processes not waiting for I/O.

Simple policies for long term scheduling are :

- Simple First Come First Served (FCFS) : It is essentially a FIFO scheme. All job requests (e.g. a submission of a batch program or an user trying to log in in a time shared system) are honoured up to a fixed system load limit, further requests being refused tout court, or enqueued for later processing.
- Priority schemes. Note that in the context of long term scheduling ``priority'' has a different meaning than in dispatching here it affects the choice of a program to be entered the system as a process, there the choice of which ready process process should be executed.

2.13 SHORT TERM SCHEDULER

It is also called CPU scheduler. Main objective is increasing system performance in accordance with the chosen set of criteria. It is the change of ready state to running state of the process. CPU scheduler selects process among the processes that are ready to execute and allocates CPU to one of them.

Short term scheduler also known as dispatcher, which executes most frequently and makes the fine grained decision of which process to execute next. Short term scheduler is faster than long term scheduler.

Short term scheduling concerns with the allocation of CPU time to processes in order to meet some pre-defined system performance objectives. The definition of these objectives (scheduling policy) is an overall system design issue and determines the ``character'' of the operating system from the user's (i.e. the buyer's) point of view, giving rise to the traditional distinctions among ``multi-purpose, time shared'', ``batch production'', ``real-time'' systems and so on.

From a user's point of view, the performance criteria can be stated as follows :

- **Response Time :** The interval of time from the moment a service is requested until the response begins to be received. In time-shared, interactive systems this is a better measure of responsiveness from a user's point of view than turnaround time, since processes may begin to produce output early in their execution.
- **Turnaround Time :** The interval between the submission of a process and the completion of its execution, including the actual running time, plus the time spent sleeping before being dispatched or while waiting to access various resources. This is the appropriate responsiveness measure for batch production, as well as for time-shared systems that maintain multiple batch queues, sharing CPU time among them.

- **Meeting Deadlines :** The ability of the OS to meet pre-defined deadlines for job completion. It makes sense only when the minimal execution time of an application can be accurately predicted.
- **Predictability :** The ability of the system to ensure that a given task is executed within a certain time interval and/or to ensure that a certain constant response time is granted within a strict tolerance, no matter what the machine load is.

When the overall system performance is considered, additional scheduling criteria must be taken into account :

- **Throughput :** The rate of completion of processes (processes completed per unit time). This is a ``raw'' measure of how much work is performed, since it depends on the execution length of processes, but it's obviously affected by the scheduling policy.
- **User Processor Utilisation :** Time (percentage of unit time) during which the CPU is running user processes. This is a measure of how well the system can serve the payload and keep at minimum time spent in housekeeping chores.
- **Overall Processor Utilisation :** Time percentage during which the CPU is busy. It's a significant criterion for expensive hardware, that must be kept busy as much as possible in order to be justify its cost (e.g. supercomputers for numerical calculus applications).
- **Resource Utilisation Balance :** It extends the idea of processor utilisation to take into account all system resources. A good scheduler should try to keep all the hardware resources in use at any time.

When the interaction between user's needs and overall system performance is considered, additional criteria to be accounted for arise :

- **Fairness :** No process should be left to starve waiting for CPU time; CPU time should be shared fairly : all processes that are equivalent, according to a pre-defined, scheduling policy related definition, should be treated equally by the scheduler.
- **Enforcing Priorities :** Within the limits of a fair scheduling policy, preference should be given to high priority processes, when priorities are defined.

The design of the short term scheduler is one of the critical areas in the overall system design, because of the immediate effects on system performance from the user's point of view. It's usually one of the trickiest as well as since most processor architectures support their own task switching facilities, the implementation of the process switch mechanism is generally machine-dependent. The result is that the actual process switch software is usually written in the assembly language of a particular machine, whether the operating system is meant to be portable across different machines or not.

Independently of the adopted scheduling policy, three basic issues in short term scheduler design can be individuated :

- The process switch must be done efficiently, otherwise the users will suffer from poor system responsiveness. This is a platitude, yet it has an immediate translation in terms of performance specification : The time spent to switch one process out and the next one in must be in the order of a few microseconds (with current technologies). Since most of the time taken to carry out the process switch is sacrificed in saving and restoring the context of processes, it is important that the amount of information to be saved and restored be reduced to the absolute minimum (in other words, it must be a minimal or quasi-minimal representation of the process's state). An effective way to achieve fast process (and context) switches is to remap the (virtual) addresses of the new running processes PCB into an address that the kernel knows about. This requires simply the remapping of one address as opposed to copying the whole PCB data into some storage area.
- Since many data structures are shared among processes (e.g., device tables, timing information, relative priorities, etc.), there must be a consistent method for allowing data access between them. Obviously answer is to store these data structures in memory.
- Since the system manages multiple processes, each of which assumes the only process running on the time shared machine, the system must choose a scheme in which processes have a fair share of time, where the "fairness" is conditioned by the overall system policy.

2.14 MEDIUM TERM SCHEDULER

Medium term scheduling is part of the swapping. It removes the processes from the memory. It reduces the degree of multiprogramming. The medium term scheduler is in charge of handling the swapped out processes.

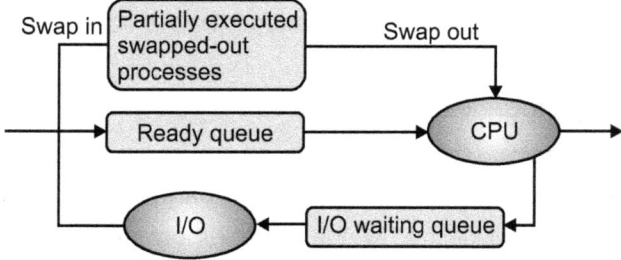

Fig. 2.7 : Illustration of medium term scheduler

Running process may become suspended if it makes an I/O request. Suspended processes cannot make any progress towards completion. In this condition, to remove the process from memory and make space for other process, the suspended process is moved to the secondary storage. This process is called swapping and the process is said to be swapped out or rolled out. Swapping may be necessary to improve the process mix.

2.15 COMPARISON BETWEEN SCHEDULER

Sr. No	Long Term	Short Term	Medium Term
1	It is a job scheduler	It is a CPU scheduler	It is a process swapping scheduler
2	Speed is lesser than short term scheduler	Speed is fastest among other two	Speed is in between both short and long term scheduler
3	It controls the degree of multiprogramming	It provides lesser control over degree of multiprogramming	It reduces the degree of multiprogramming
4	It is almost absent or minimal in time sharing system	It is also minimal in time sharing system	It is a part of Time sharing systems
5	It selects processes from pool and loads them into memory for execution	It selects those processes which are ready to execute	It can re-introduce the process into memory and execution can be continued

D. SCHEDULING ALGORITHM (FOR UNIPROCESSOR SYSTEM)

2.16 PREEMPTIVE SCHEDULING

- CPU scheduling decisions take place under one of four conditions :
    1. When a process switches from the running state to the waiting state, such as for an I/O (Input/Output) request or invocation of the wait( ) system call.
    2. When a process switches from the running state to the ready state, for example in response to an interrupt.
    3. When a process switches from the waiting state to the ready state, say at completion of I/O (Input/Output) or a return from wait( ).
    4. When a process terminates.
- For conditions 1 and 4 there is no choice : A new process must be selected.
- For conditions 2 and 3 there is a choice : To either continue running the current process, or select a different one.
- If scheduling takes place only under conditions 1 and 4, the system is said to be non-preemptive or cooperative. Under these conditions, once a process starts running it keeps running, until it either voluntarily blocks or until it finishes. Otherwise the system is said to be preemptive.

- Windows used non-preemptive scheduling up to Windows 3.x and started using preemptive scheduling with Win95. Macs used non-preemptive prior to OSX and preemptive since then. Note that pre-emptive scheduling is only possible on hardware that supports a timer interrupt.
- Note that preemptive scheduling can cause problems when two processes share data, because one process may get interrupted in the middle of updating shared data structures.
- Preemption can also be a problem if the kernel is busy implementing a system call (e.g. updating critical kernel data structures) when the preemption occurs. Most modern UNIXs deal with this problem by making the process wait until the system call has either completed or blocked before allowing the preemption Unfortunately this solution is problematic for real-time systems, as real time response can no longer be guaranteed.
- Some critical sections of code protect themselves from concurrency problems by disabling interrupts before entering the critical section and re-enabling interrupts on exiting the section. Needless to say, this should only be done in rare situations and only on very short pieces of code that will finish quickly, (usually just a few machine instructions.)

2.17 SCHEDULING CRITERIA

There are several different criteria to consider when trying to select the "best" scheduling algorithm for a particular situation and environment, including :

- **CPU Utilization :** Ideally the CPU would be busy 100% of the time, so as to waste 0 CPU cycles. On a real system, CPU usage should range from 40% (lightly loaded) to 90% (heavily loaded).
- **Throughput :** Number of processes completed per unit time. May range from 10 / second to 1 / hour depending on the specific processes.
- **Turn Around Time :** Time required for a particular process to complete, from submission time to completion. (wall clock time).
- **Waiting Time :** How much time processes spend in the ready queue waiting their turn to get on the CPU.
- **Response Time :** The time taken in an interactive program from the issuance of a command to the commence of a response to that command.

In general one wants to optimize the average value of a criteria (Maximize CPU utilization and throughput and minimize all the others). However sometimes one wants to do something different, such as to minimize the maximum response time.

Sometimes it is most desirable to minimize the variance of criteria than the actual value, i.e. users are more accepting a consistent predictable system than an inconsistent one, even if it is a little bit slower.

2.18 SCHEDULING ALGORITHMS

The following subsections will explain several common scheduling strategies, looking at only a single CPU burst each for a small number of processes. Obviously real systems have to deal with a lot more simultaneous processes executing their CPU-I/O burst cycles.

2.18.1 First Come First Serve (FCFS)

- FCFS is very simple Just a FIFO queue, like customers waiting in line at the bank or the post office or at a copying machine.
- Unfortunately, however, FCFS can yield some very long average wait times, particularly if the first process to get there takes a long time. For example, consider the following three processes :

Table 2.1

Process	Burst Time
P1	24
P2	3
P3	3

- In the first Gantt chart below, process P1 arrives first. The average waiting time for the three processes is (0 + 24 + 27) / 3 = 17.0 ms.
- In the second Gantt chart below, the same three processes have an average wait time of (0 + 3 + 6) / 3 = 3.0 ms. The total run time for the three bursts is the same, but in the second case two of the three finish much quicker and the other process is only delayed by a short amount.

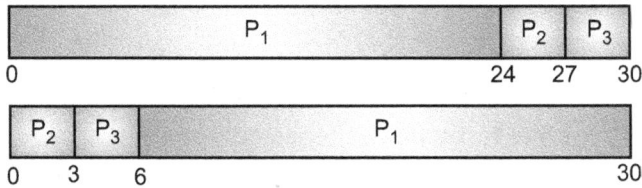

Fig. 2.8

- FCFS can also block the system in a busy dynamic system in another way known as the convoy effect. When one CPU intensive process blocks the CPU a number of I/O intensive processes can get backed up behind it, leaving the I/O devices idle. When the CPU hog finally relinquishes the CPU, then the I/O processes pass through the CPU quickly, leaving the CPU idle while everyone queues up for I/O and then the cycle repeats itself when the CPU intensive process gets back to the ready queue.

2.18.2 Shortest Job First (SJF)

- The idea behind the SJF algorithm is to pick the quickest fastest little job that needs to be done, get it out of the way first and then pick the next smallest fastest job to do next.
- Technically this algorithm picks a process based on the next shortest CPU burst, not the overall process time.

- For example, the Gantt chart below is based upon the following CPU burst times, (and the assumption that all jobs arrive at the same time).

Table 2.2

Process	Burst Time
P1	6
P2	8
P3	7
P4	3

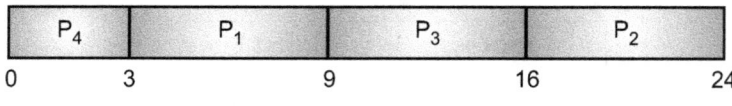

Fig. 2.9

- In the case above the average wait time is (0 + 3 + 9 + 16) / 4 = 7.0 ms, (as opposed to 10.25 ms for FCFS for the same processes.)
- SJF can be proven to be the fastest scheduling algorithm, but it suffers from one important problem, How do you know how long the next CPU burst is going to be?
  - For long-term batch jobs this can be done based upon the limits that users set for their jobs when they submit them, which encourages them to set low limits, but risks their having to re-submit the job if they set the limit too low. However that does not work for short-term CPU scheduling on an interactive system.
  - Another option would be to statistically measure the run time characteristics of jobs, particularly if the same tasks are run repeatedly and predictably. But once again that really is not a viable option for short term CPU scheduling in the real world.
  - A more practical approach is to predict the length of the next burst, based on some historical measurement of recent burst times for this process. One simple, fast and relatively accurate method is the exponential average, which can be defined as follows. (The book uses tau and t for their variables, but those are hard to distinguish from one another and do not work well in HTML.)

    estimate[i + 1] = alpha * burst[i] + (1.0 - alpha) * estimate[i]

- SJF can be either preemptive or non-preemptive. Preemption occurs when a new process arrives in the ready queue that has a predicted burst time shorter than the time remaining in the process whose burst is currently on the CPU. Preemptive SJF is sometimes referred to as shortest remaining time first scheduling.

- For example, the following Gantt chart is based upon the following data :

Table 2.3

Process	Arrival Time	Burst Time
P1	0	8
P2	1	4
P3	2	9
P4	3	5

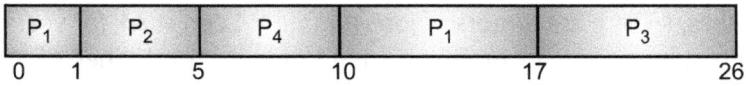

Fig. 2.10

- The average wait time in this case is ((5 - 3) + (10 - 1) + (17 - 2)) / 4 = 26 / 4 = 6.5 ms. (As opposed to 7.75 ms for non-preemptive SJF or 8.75 for FCFS.)

2.18.3 Priority

- Priority scheduling is a more general case of SJF in which each job is assigned a priority and the job with the highest priority gets scheduled first. (SJF uses the inverse of the next expected burst time as its priority. The smaller the expected burst, the higher the priority.)
- Note that in practice, priorities are implemented using integers within a fixed range, but there is no agreed-upon convention as to whether "high" priorities use large numbers or small numbers. This book uses low number for high priorities with 0 being the highest possible priority.
- For example, the following Gantt chart is based upon these process burst times and priorities and yields an average waiting time of 8.2 ms :

Table 2.4

Process	Burst Time	Priority
P1	10	3
P2	1	1
P3	2	4
P4	1	5
P5	5	2

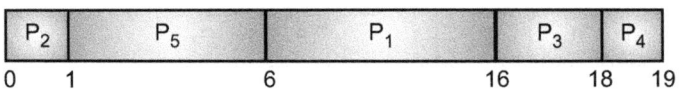

Fig. 2.11

- Priorities can be assigned either internally or externally. Internal priorities are assigned by the OS using criteria such as average burst time, ratio of CPU to I/O activity, system resource use and other factors available to the kernel. External priorities are assigned by users, based on the importance of the job, fees paid, politics etc.
- Priority scheduling can be either preemptive or non-preemptive.
- Priority scheduling can suffer from a major problem known as indefinite blocking or starvation, in which a low-priority task can wait forever because there are always some other jobs around that have higher priority.
- If this problem is allowed to occur, then processes will either run eventually when the system load lightens (at say 2:00 a.m.) or will eventually get lost when the system is shut down or crashes. (There are rumors of jobs that have been stuck for years.)
- One common solution to this problem is aging in which priorities of jobs increase the longer they wait. Under this scheme a low-priority job will eventually get its priority raised high enough that it gets run.

2.18.4 Round Robin (RR)

- Round robin scheduling is similar to FCFS scheduling, except that CPU bursts are assigned with limits called time quantum.
- When a process is given the CPU a timer is set for whatever value has been set for a time quantum :
   1. If the process finishes its burst before the time quantum timer expires, then it is swapped out of the CPU just like the normal FCFS algorithm.
   2. If the timer goes off first, then the process is swapped out of the CPU and moved to the back end of the ready queue.
- The ready queue is maintained as a circular queue, so when all processes have had a turn, then the scheduler gives the first process another turn and so on.
- RR scheduling can give the effect of all processors sharing the CPU equally, although the average wait time can be longer than with other scheduling algorithms. In the following example the average wait time is 5.66 ms.

Table 2.5

Process	Burst Time
P1	24
P2	3
P3	3

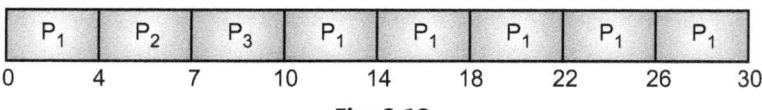

Fig. 2.12

- The performance of RR is sensitive to the time quantum selected. If the quantum is large enough, then RR reduces to the FCFS algorithm; If it is very small, then each process gets 1/nth of the processor time and share the CPU equally.
- BUT, a real system invokes overhead for every context switch and the smaller the time quantum the more context switches there are. shown in Fig. 2.12. Most modern systems use time quantum between 10 and 100 milliseconds and context switch times on the order of 10 microseconds, so the overhead is small relative to the time quantum.

2.18.5 Multilevel Queue Scheduling (MLQ) without Feedback

- When processes can be readily categorized, then multiple separate queues can be established, each implementing whatever scheduling algorithm is most appropriate for that type of job and/or with different parametric adjustments.
- Scheduling must also be done between queues. That is scheduling one queue to get time relative to other queues. Two common options are strict priority (no job in a lower priority queue runs until all higher priority queues are empty) and round robin (each queue gets a time slice in turn, possibly of different sizes).
- Note that under this algorithm jobs cannot switch from queue to queue Once they are assigned a queue, i.e. their queue until they finish.

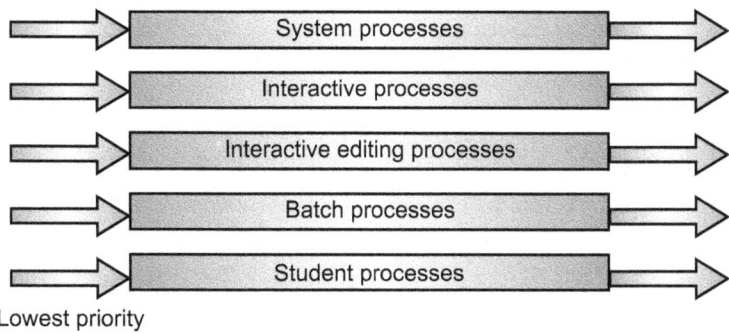

Fig. 2.13 : Multilevel queue scheduling

2.18.6 Multilevel Queue Scheduling (MLQ) with Feedback

- Multilevel feedback queue scheduling is similar to the ordinary multilevel queue scheduling described above, except jobs may be moved from one queue to another for a variety of reasons :
  1. If the characteristics of a job change between CPU intensive and I/O intensive, then it may be appropriate to switch a job from one queue to another.
  2. Aging can also be incorporated, so that a job that has waited for a long time can get bumped up into a higher priority queue for a while.
- Multilevel feedback queue scheduling is the most flexible, because it can be tuned for any situation. But it is also the most complex to implement because of all the adjustable parameters. Some of the parameters which define one of these systems include :

1. The number of queues.
2. The scheduling algorithm for each queue.
3. The methods used to upgrade or demote processes from one queue to another. (Which may be different).
4. The method used to determine which queue a process enters initially.

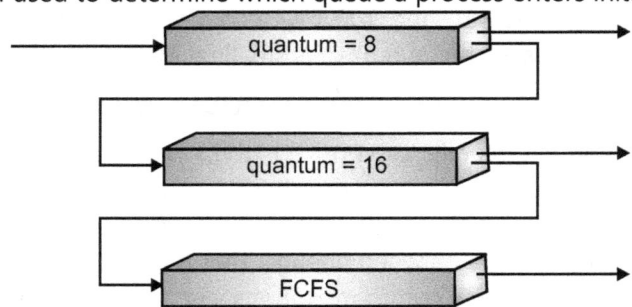

Fig. 2.14 : Multilevel feedback queues

E. (IPC) INTER PROCESS COMMUNICATION

2.19 CONCEPTS OF IPC

In computing, Inter Process Communication (IPC) is a set of methods for the exchange of data among multiple threads in one or more processes. Processes may be running on one or more computers connected by a network. IPC methods are divided into methods for message passing, synchronization, shared memory and Remote Procedure Calls (RPC). The method of IPC used may vary based on the bandwidth and latency of communication between the threads and the type of data being communicated.

There are several reasons for providing an environment that allows process cooperation :

1. Information sharing
2. Computational speedup
3. Modularity
4. Convenience
5. Privilege separation

IPC may also be referred to as inter-thread communication and inter application communication.

The combination of IPC with the address space concept is the foundation for address space independence/isolation.

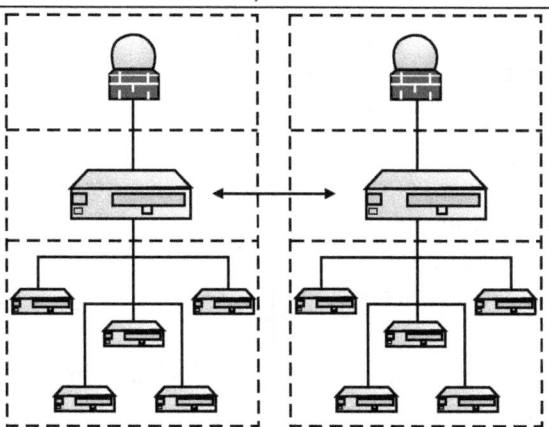

Fig. 2.15 : An example showing a grid computing system connecting many personal computers over the internet using IPC

IPC enables one application to control another application and for several applications to share the same data without interfering with one another. IPC is required in all multiprocessing systems, but it is not generally supported by single process operating systems such as DOS. OS/2 and MS-Windows support an IPC mechanism called DDE.

2.20 MAIN IPC METHOD

Following are the main methods of IPC (Inter Process Communication) :

Method	Short Description	Provided by
File	A record stored on disk that can be accessed by name by any process	Most operating systems
Signal	A system message sent from one process to another, not usually used to store information but instead give commands	Most operating systems some systems, such as Win NT subsystem, implement signals in only the C run-time library and provide no support for their use as an IPC method. But other subsystems like the POSIX subsystem provided by default until windows 2000. Then available with Interix in XP/2003 then with windows services for UNIX (SFU)
Socket	A data stream sent over a network interface, either to a different process on the same computer or to another computer	Most operating systems

Contd...

Message Queue	An anonymous data stream similar to the pipe, but stores and retrieves information in packets	Most operating systems
Pipe	A two way data stream interfaced through standard input and output and is read character by character.	All POSIX systems, Windows
Named Pipe	A pipe implemented through a file on the file system instead of standard input and output.	All POSIX systems, Windows
Semaphore	A simple structure that synchronizes threads or processes acting on shared resources.	All POSIX systems, Windows
Shared Memory	Multiple processes given access to the same memory, allowing all to change it read changes made by other processes	All POSIX systems, Windows
Message Passing (Shared Nothing)	Similar to the message queue	Used in MPI paradigm, Java RMI, CORBA, DDS, MSMQ, MailSlots, QNX, others
Memory-Mapped File	A file mapped to RAM and can be modified by changing memory addresses directly instead of outputting to a stream, shares same benefits as a standard file	All POSIX systems, Windows

2.21 PLATFORM OF IPC

There are several APIs which may be used for IPC. A number of platforms independent of APIs include the following :
- Anonymous pipes and named pipes.
- Common Object Request Broker Architecture (CORBA).

- Freedesktop.org's D-Bus.
- Distributed Computing Environment (DCE).
- Message Bus (Mbus) (specified in RFC 3259).
- MCAPI Multicore Communications API.
- Lightweight Communications and Marshalling (LCM).
- ONC RPC.
- Unix domain sockets.
- XML XML-RPC or SOAP.
- JSON JSON-RPC.

The following are platform or programming language specific APIs :

- Apple Computer's Apple events (previously known as Intra Application Communications (IAC)).
- Enea's LINX for Linux (open source) and various DSP and general purpose processors under OSE.
- IPC implementation from CMU.
- Java's Remote Method Invocation (RMI).
- KDE's Desktop Communications Protocol (DCOP) : Now deprecated. D-Bus is used instead.
- Libt2n for C++ under Linux only, handles complex objects and exceptions.
- The Mach kernel's Mach Ports.
- Microsoft's ActiveX, Component Object Model (COM), Microsoft Transaction Server (COM+), Distributed Component Object Model(DCOM), Dynamic Data Exchange (DDE), Object Linking and Embedding (OLE), anonymous pipes, named pipes, Local Procedure Call, MailSlots, Message loop, MSRPC, .NET Remoting and Windows Communication Foundation (WCF).
- Novell's SPX.
- PHP's sessions.
- POSIX mmap, message queues, semaphores and shared memory.
- RISC OS's messages.
- Solaris Doors.
- System V's message queues, semaphores and shared memory.
- Distributed Ruby.

F. CRITICAL SECTION

2.22 CRITICAL SECTION PROBLEM

- Set of instructions that must be controlled so as to allow exclusive access to one process :
  1. Rarely : Access to the critical section is limited to n processes instead of one process.
- Execution of the critical section by processes is mutually exclusive in time.

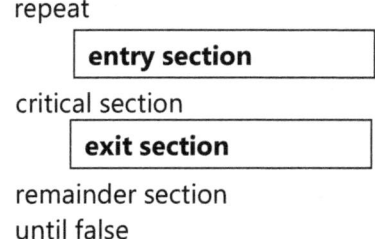

repeat
    entry section
critical section
    exit section
remainder section
until false

"General Structure of a Typical Process P"

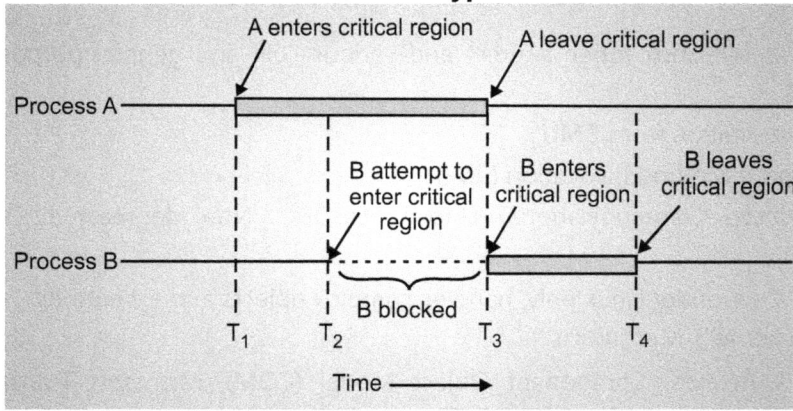

Fig. 2.16 : Mutual exclusion using critical region

- Consider a system consisting of η processes {$P_0, P_1, ..., P_{n-1}$}. Each process has a segment of code called a critical section (CS), in which the process may be changing common variables, updating a table, writing a file and so on.
- The important feature of the system is that, when one process is executing in its CS, no other process is to be allowed to execute in its CS.
- That is not two processes are executing in their CSs at the same time.
- Each process must request permission to enter its CS. The section of code implementing this request is the entry section.
- The CS may be followed by an exit section.
- The remaining code is the remainder section.

2.23 SOLUTION TO CRITICAL SECTION PROBLEM

Solution 1 : The Critical Section Problem must meet three conditions :
1. **Mutual Exclusion :** If process P^i is executing in its critical section, no other process is executing in its critical section.
2. **Progress :** If no process is executing in its critical section and there exists some processes that wish to enter their critical sections, then only those processes that are not executing in their remainder section can participate in the decision of which will enter its critical section next and this decision cannot be postponed indefinitely.
   - If no process is in critical section, can decide quickly who enters.
   - Only one process can enter the critical section so in practice, others are put on the queue.
3. **Bounded Waiting :** There must exist a bound on the number of times that other processes are allowed to enter their critical sections after a process has made a request to enter its critical section and before that request is granted.
   - The wait is the time from when a process makes a request to enter its critical section until that request is granted.
   - In practice, once a process enters its critical section, it does not get another turn until a waiting process gets a turn (managed as a queue).

Solution 2 :

Assumption
- Assume that a variable (memory location) can only have one value; never ``between values''.
- If processes A and B write a value to the same memory location at the ``same time,'' either the value from A or the value from B will be written rather than some scrambling of bits.

Peterson's Algorithm
- A simple algorithm that can be run by two processes to ensure mutual exclusion for one resource (say one variable or data structure).
- Does not require any special hardware.
- It uses busy waiting (a spinlock).

Shared variables are created and initialized before either process starts. The shared variables flag[0] and flag[1] are initialized to FALSE because neither process is yet interested in the critical section. The shared variable turn is set to either 0 or 1 randomly (or it can always be set to say 0),
var flag : **array** [0..1] **of** boolean;

```
turn : 0..1;
%flag[k] means that process[k] is interested in the critical section
flag[0] := FALSE;
flag[1] := FALSE;
turn := random(0..1)
```

After initialization, each process, which is called process i in the code (the other process is process j), runs the following code:

```
repeat
flag[i] := TRUE;
turn := j;
while (flag[j] and turn=j) do no-op;
CRITICAL SECTION
flag[i] := FALSE;
REMAINDER SECTION
until FALSE;
```

Information common to both processes:
```
turn = 0
flag[0] = FALSE
flag[1] = FALSE
```

Example 2.1

Process 0	Process 1
i = 0, j = 1	i = 1, j = 0
flag[0] := TRUE turn := 1 check (flag[1] = TRUE and turn = 1) • Condition is false because flag[1] = FALSE • Since condition is false, no waiting in while loop • Enter the critical section • Process 0 happens to lose the processor	
	flag[1] := TRUE turn := 0 check (flag[0] = TRUE and turn = 0) • Since condition is true, it keeps busy waiting until it loses the processor

Contd...

- Process 0 resumes and continues until it finishes in the critical section
- Leave critical section

flag[0] := FALSE

- Start executing the remainder (anything else a process does besides using the critical section)
- Process 0 happens to lose the processor

	check (flag[0] = TRUE and turn = 0) • This condition fails because flag[0] = FALSE • No more busy waiting • Enter the critical section

Example 2.2

Process 0	Process 1
i=0, j=1	i=1, j=0
flag[0] = TRUE turn = 1 • Lose processor here	
	flag[1] := TRUE turn := 0 check (flag[0] = TRUE and turn = 0) • Condition is true so Process 1 busy waits until it loses the processor
check (flag[1] = TRUE and turn = 1) • This condition is false because turn = 0 • No waiting in loop • Enters critical section	

Example 2.3

Process 0	Process 1
i=0, j=1	i=1, j=0
flag[0] = TRUE • Lose processor here	

Contd...

	flag[1] = TRUE turn = 0 check (flag[0] = TRUE and turn = 0) • Condition is true so, Process 1 busy waits until it loses the processor
turn := 1 check (flag[1] = TRUE and turn = 1) • Condition is true so Process 0 busy waits until it loses the processor	
	check (flag[0] = TRUE and turn = 0) • The condition is false so, Process 1 enters the critical section

2.23.1 Summary of Techniques for Critical Section Problem

Software

1. **Peterson's Algorithm :** Based on busy waiting
2. **Semaphores :** General facility provided by operating system (e.g., OS/2)
    (i) Based on low-level techniques such as busy waiting or hardware assistance
    (ii) Described in more detail below
3. **Monitors :** Programming language technique
    (i) See S&G, pp. 190--197 for more details

Hardware

1. Exclusive access to memory location :
    (i) Always assumed
2. Interrupts that can be turned off :
    (i) Must have only one processor for mutual exclusion
3. **Test-and-Set :** Special machine-level instruction
    (i) Described in more detail below :
4. **Swap :** Atomically swaps contents of two words
    (i) See S&G, pp. 173--174 for more details
    (ii) For example, the Exchange instruction is available in the machine language used on Intel processors.

Test-and-Set

- Hardware assistance for process synchronization.
- A special hardware instruction that does two operations atomically.

- Both operations are executed or neither is :
  (i) Sets the result to current value.
  (ii) Changes current value to true.
  (iii) When describing machine language (CPU) operations, the verb 'set' means 'set to true'.

2.24 MUTUAL EXCLUSION WITH BUSY WAITING, TSL

How do we implement a mutual exclusion policy? No matter what policy we implement a process that is about to enter its critical section must first check to see if any other processes are in their critical sections. As we shall see, there are, potentially, number of ways to enforce mutual exclusion. Ideally, we would like to implement a policy that works in the most efficient way possible.

What about using a lock variable, which must be tested by each process before it enters its critical section? If another process is already in its critical section, the lock is set to 1 and the process currently using the processor is not permitted to enter its critical section. If the value of the lock variable is 0, then the process enters its critical section and it sets the lock to 1. The problem with this potential solution is that the operation that reads the value of the lock variable, the operation that compares that value to 0 and the operation that sets the lock, are three different atomic actions. With this solution, it is possible that one process might test the lock variable, see that it is open, but before it can set the lock, another process is scheduled, runs, sets the lock and enters its critical section. When the original process returns, it too will enter its critical section, violation the policy of mutual exclusion.

The only problem with the lock variable solution is that the action of testing the variable and the action of setting the variable are executed as separate instructions. If these operations could be combined into one indivisible step, this could be a workable solution. These steps can be combined, with a little help from hardware into what is known as a TSL or TEST and SET LOCK instruction. A call to the TSL instruction copies the value of the lock variable and sets it to a nonzero (locked) value, all in one step. While the value of the lock variable is being tested, no other process can enter its critical section, because the lock is set. Let us look at an example of the TSL in use with two operations, enter_region and leave_region :

enter_region : (executed when a process wants to enter its critical section)
```
tsl register, lock    // copy lock to register and set lock to 1
cmp register, 0       // see if lock variable was set
jnz enter_region      // if lock was set, loop
ret                   // enter critical section
```
leave_region : (executed when a process wants to leave its critical section)
```
mov lock, 0           // store a 0 in lock variable
ret                   // done
```

You can see from the example above that if a process is interrupted after executing the TSL, there is no danger that another process might enter its critical section. This is so because the lock variable is set to a non-zero value while the original process is testing it. Another advantage of the TSL instruction is that it works on machines with many processors as well.

Look closely at the code for the "enter_region". For example and you will see that if a process tests a variable which is locked, it will continue to test the variable again and again until it can enter its critical section. In other words, as long as a process is denied access to its critical section, it will stay in a tight loop and wait until it can proceed, all the while wasting processor time. This continuous testing of the lock variable is called busy waiting. Mutual exclusion policies that require busy waiting waste valuable processor time and in some cases can lead to situations where a process will test the lock variable forever a very undesirable occurrence.

2.25 PETERSON'S SOLUTION FOR TWO PROCESSES

Peterson's Algorithm (AKA Peterson's solution) is a concurrent programming algorithm for mutual exclusion that allows two processes to share a single-use resource without conflict, using only shared memory for communication. It was formulated by Gary L. Peterson in 1981. While Peterson's original formulation worked with only two processes, the algorithm can be generalized for more than two processes.

The Algorithm

The algorithm uses two variables, flag and turn. A flag[n] value of true indicates that the process n wants to enter the critical section. Entrance to the critical section is granted for process P0 if P1 does not want to enter its critical section or if P1 has given priority to P0 by setting turn to 0.

```
    bool flag[0] = false;
    bool flag[1] = false;
int turn;
P0:     flag[0] = true;                P1:     flag[1] = true;
P0_gate: turn = 1;                     P1_gate: turn = 0;
    while (flag[1] && turn == 1)           while (flag[0] && turn == 0)
    {                                      {
        // busy wait                           // busy wait
    }                                      }
    // critical section                    // critical section
    ...                                    ...
    // end of critical section             // end of critical section
    flag[0] = false;                       flag[1] = false;
```

The algorithm does satisfy the three essential criteria to solve the critical section problem, provided that changes to the variables turn, flag[0] and flag[1] propagate immediately and atomically. The while condition works even with preemption.

The three criteria are mutual exclusion, progress and bounded waiting.

Mutual Exclusion

P0 and P1 can never be in the critical section at the same time : If P0 is in its critical section, then flag[0] is true. In addition, either flag[1] is false (meaning P1 has left its critical section), or turn is 0 (meaning P1 is just now trying to enter the critical section, but graciously waiting), or P1 is at label P1_gate (trying to enter its critical section, after setting flag[1] to true but before setting turn to 0 and busy waiting). So if both processes are in their critical sections then we conclude that the state must satisfy flag[0] and flag[1] and turn = 0 and turn = 1. No state can satisfy both turn = 0 and turn = 1, so there can be no state where both processes are in their critical sections. (This recounts an argument that is made rigorous in.)

Progress

Progress is defined as the following : If no process is executing in its critical section and some processes wish to enter their critical sections, then only those processes that are not executing in their remainder sections can participate in making the decision as to which process will enter its critical section next. This selection cannot be postponed indefinitely. A process cannot immediately re-enter the critical section if the other process has set its flag to say that it would like to enter its critical section.

Bounded Waiting

Bounded waiting means that "there exists a bound or limit on the number of times that other processes are allowed to enter their critical sections after a process has made a request to enter its critical section and before that request is granted". In Peterson's algorithm, a process will not wait longer than one turn for entrance to the critical section : After giving priority to the other process, this process will run to completion and set its flag to 0, thereby allowing the other process to enter the critical section.

2.26 DIJKSTRA'S SEMAPHORE

Semaphores

Semaphore is a value that indicates the status of common resources. A semaphore, in its most basic form, is a protected integer variable that can facilitate and restrict access to shared resources in a multi-processing environment. The two most common kinds of semaphores are counting semaphores and binary semaphores. Counting semaphores represent multiple resources, while binary semaphores, as the name implies, represents two possible states (generally 0 or 1; locked or unlocked). Semaphores were invented by the late Edsger Dijkstra.

Semaphores can be looked at as a representation of a limited number of resources, like seating capacity at a restaurant. If a restaurant has a capacity of 50 people and nobody is there, the semaphore would be initialized to 50. As each person arrives at the restaurant, they cause the seating capacity to decrease, so the semaphore in turn is decremented. When the maximum capacity is reached, the semaphore will be at zero and nobody else will be able to enter the restaurant. Instead the hopeful restaurant goers must wait until someone is done with the resource, or in this analogy, done eating. When a patron leaves, the semaphore is incremented and the resource becomes available again.

A semaphore can only be accessed using the following operations : wait() and signal(). wait() is called when a process wants access to a resource. This would be equivalent to the arriving customer trying to get an open table. If there is an open table, or the semaphore is greater than zero, then he can take that resource and sit at the table. If there is no open table and the semaphore is zero, that process must wait until it becomes available. signal() is called when a process is done using a resource, or when the patron is finished with his meal. The following is an implementation of this counting semaphore (where the value can be greater than 1) :

```
wait(Semaphore s)
{
    while (s==0);    /* wait until s>0 */
    s=s-1;
}
signal(Semaphore s){
    s=s+1;
}
Init(Semaphore s , Int v){
    s=v;
}
```

Historically, wait() was called P (for Dutch "Proberen" meaning to test) and signal() was called V (for Dutch "Verhogen" meaning to increment). The standard Java library instead uses the name "acquire" for P and "release" for V.

No other process can access the semaphore when P or V are executing. This is implemented with atomic hardware and code. An atomic operation is indivisible, that is, it can be considered to execute as a unit.

If there is only one count of a resource, a binary semaphore is used which can only have the values of 0 or 1. They are often used as mutex locks. Here is an implementation of mutual-exclusion using binary semaphores :

```
do
{
    wait(s);
    // critical section
    signal(s);
    // remainder section
} while(1);
```

In this implementation, a process wanting to enter its critical section it has to acquire the binary semaphore which will then give it mutual exclusion until it signals that it is done.

For example, we have semaphore and two processes, P1 and P2 that want to enter their critical sections at the same time. P1 first calls wait(s). The value of s is decremented to 0 and P1 enters its critical section. While P1 is in its critical section, P2 calls wait(s), but because the value of s is zero, it must wait until P1 finishes its critical section and executes signal(s). When P1 calls signal, the value of s is incremented to P1 and P2 can then proceed to execute in its critical section (after decrementing the semaphore again). Mutual exclusion is achieved because only one process can be in its critical section at any time.

G. PROBLEM IN CONCURRENT PROGRAMMING

2.27 INTRODUCTION TO PROBLEM IN CONCURRENT PROGRAMMING

Usually we have been exclusively concerned with sequential programs that execute a single stream of operations. Concurrent computation makes programming much more complex. In this section, we explore the extra problems posed by concurrency and outline some strategies for managing them.

In a concurrent program, several streams of operations may execute concurrently. Each stream of operations executes as it would in a sequential program except for the fact that streams can communicate and interfere with one another. Each such sequence of instructions is called a thread. For this reason, sequential programs are often called single-threaded programs. When a multi-threaded program executes, the operations in its various threads are interleaved in an unpredictable order subject to the constraints imposed by explicit synchronization operations that may be embedded in the code. The operations for each stream are strictly ordered, but the interleaving of operations from a collection of streams is undetermined and depends on the vagaries of a particular execution of the program. One stream may run very fast while another does not run at all. In the absence of fairness guarantees (discussed below), a given thread can starve unless it is the only "runnable" thread.

A thread is runnable unless it executes a special operation requiring synchronization that waits until a particular condition occurs. If more than one thread is runnable, all but one thread may starve (make no progress because none of its operations are being executed) unless the language makes a fairness guarantee. A fairness guarantee states that the next operation in a runnable thread eventually will execute. The Java language specification currently makes no fairness guarantees but most Java Virtual Machines guarantee fairness.

Threads can communicate with each other in a variety of ways that we will discuss in detail later in this section. The Java programming language relies primarily on shared variables to support communication between processes, but it also supports an explicit signaling mechanism.

In general, writing concurrent programs is extremely difficult because the multiplicity of possible interleaving of operations among threads means that program execution is non-deterministic. For this reason, program bugs may be difficult to reproduce. Furthermore, the complexity introduced by multiple threads and their potential interactions makes programs much more difficult to analyze and reason about. Fortunately, many concurrent programs including most GUI applications follow stylized design patterns that control the underlying complexity.

To demonstrate some of the subtle problems that arise with this sort of programming, consider the following example. We have two threads, A and B, that both have access to a variable ct. Suppose that, initially, ct is 0, but there are places in both A and B where ct is incremented.

A	B
...	...
ct++;	ct++;

To increment a variable x, (i) the value v of x must be fetched from memory, (ii) a new value v' based on v and (iii) v' must be stored in the memory location allocated to variable x. These are three separate actions and there is no guarantee that no other thread will access the variable until all three are done. So it's possible, for instance, that the order of operations from these two threads occurs as follows :

```
fetches ct = 0
B fetches ct = 0
A computes the value ct++ = 1
A stores the value 1 in ct
B computes new value ct++ = 1
B stores the value 1 in ct
```

With this order of the operations, the final value for ct is 1. But in other possible orderings (e.g., if A performs all of its actions first), the final value would be 2.

Below explained are classical concurrent programming problems.

2.28 PRODUCER-CONSUMER PROBLEM

In computing, the producer-consumer problem (also known as the bounded-buffer problem) is a classic example of a multi-process synchronization problem. The problem describes two processes, the producer and the consumer, who share a common, fixed-size buffer used as a queue. The producer's job is to generate a piece of data, put it into the buffer and start again. At the same time, the consumer is consuming the data (i.e., removing it from the buffer) one piece at a time. The problem is to make sure that the producer won't try to add data into the buffer if it's full and that the consumer won't try to remove data from an empty buffer.

The solution for the producer is to either go to sleep or discard data if the buffer is full. The next time the consumer removes an item from the buffer, it notifies the producer who starts to fill the buffer again. In the same way, the consumer can go to sleep if it finds the buffer to be empty. The next time the producer puts data into the buffer, it wakes up the sleeping consumer. The solution can be reached by means of inter-process communication, typically using semaphores. An inadequate solution could result in a deadlock where both processes are waiting to be awakened. The problem can also be generalized to have multiple producers and consumers.

2.28.1 Inadequate Implementation

To solve the problem, a less experienced programmer might come up with a solution shown below. In the solution two library routines are used, sleep and wakeup. When sleep is called the caller is blocked until another process wakes it up by using the wakeup routine. The global variable itemCount holds the number of items in the buffer.

```
int itemCount = 0;
procedure producer() {
   while (true) {
      item = produceItem();

      if (itemCount == BUFFER_SIZE) {
         sleep();
      }
      putItemIntoBuffer(item);
      itemCount = itemCount + 1;
      if (itemCount == 1) {
         wakeup(consumer);
      }
   }
}
procedure consumer() {
   while (true) {
      if (itemCount == 0) {
         sleep();
      }
      item = removeItemFromBuffer();
```

```
    itemCount = itemCount - 1;
    if (itemCount == BUFFER_SIZE - 1) {
       wakeup(producer);
    }
    consumeItem(item);
  }
}
```

The problem with this solution is that it contains a race condition that can lead to a deadlock. Consider the following scenario :

- The consumer has just read the variable itemCount, noticed its zero and is just about to move inside the if block.
- Just before calling sleep, the consumer is interrupted and the producer is resumed.
- The producer creates an item, puts it into the buffer and increases itemCount.
- Because the buffer was empty prior to the last addition, the producer tries to wake up the consumer.
- Unfortunately the consumer wasn't yet sleeping and the wakeup call is lost. When the consumer resumes, it goes to sleep and will never be awakened again. This is because the consumer is only awakened by the producer when itemCount is equal to 1.
- The producer will loop until the buffer is full, after which it will also go to sleep.

Since both processes will sleep forever, we have run into a deadlock. This solution therefore is unsatisfactory.

An alternative analysis is that if the programming language does not define the semantics of concurrent accesses to shared variables (in this case itemCount) without use of synchronization, then the solution is unsatisfactory for that reason, without needing to explicitly demonstrate a race condition.

2.28.2 Using Semaphores

Semaphores solve the problem of lost wakeup calls. In the solution below we use two semaphores, fillCount and emptyCount, to solve the problem. fillCount is the number of items already in the buffer and available to be read, while emptyCount is the number of available spaces in the buffer where items could be written. fillCount is incremented and emptyCount decremented when a new item is put into the buffer. If the producer tries to decrement emptyCount when its value is zero, the producer is put to sleep. The next time an item is consumed, emptyCount is incremented and the producer wakes up. The consumer works analogously.

semaphore fillCount = 0; // items produced
semaphore emptyCount = BUFFER_SIZE; // remaining space :

```
procedure producer() {
   while (true) {
      item = produceItem();
      down(emptyCount);
         putItemIntoBuffer(item);
      up(fillCount);
   }
}
procedure consumer() {
   while (true) {
      down(fillCount);
         item = removeItemFromBuffer();
      up(emptyCount);
      consumeItem(item);
   }
}
```

The solution above works fine when there is only one producer and consumer. With multiple producers sharing the same memory space for the item buffer, or multiple consumers sharing the same memory space, this solution contains a serious race condition that could result in two or more processes reading or writing into the same slot at the same time. To understand how this is possible, imagine how the procedure putItemIntoBuffer() can be implemented. It could contain two actions, one determining the next available slot and the other writing into it. If the procedure can be executed concurrently by multiple producers, then the following scenario is possible :

- Two producers decrement emptyCount
- One of the producers determines the next empty slot in the buffer
- Second producer determines the next empty slot and gets the same result as the first producer.
- Both producers write into the same slot.

To overcome this problem, we need a way to make sure that only one producer is executing putItemIntoBuffer() at a time. In other words we need a way to execute a critical section with mutual exclusion. To accomplish this we use a binary semaphore called mutex. Since the value of a binary semaphore can be only either one or zero, only one process can be executing between down(mutex) and up(mutex). The solution for multiple producers and consumers is shown below.

```
semaphore mutex = 1;
semaphore fillCount = 0;
```

```
semaphore emptyCount = BUFFER_SIZE;
procedure producer() {
  while (true) {
    item = produceItem();
    down(emptyCount);
      down(mutex);
        putItemIntoBuffer(item);
      up(mutex);
    up(fillCount);
  }
}
procedure consumer() {
  while (true) {
    down(fillCount);
      down(mutex);
        item = removeItemFromBuffer();
      up(mutex);
    up(emptyCount);
    consumeItem(item);
  }
}
```

Note : The order in which different semaphores are incremented or decremented is essential: changing the order might result in a deadlock.

2.28.3 Using Monitors

The following pseudo code shows a solution to the producer-consumer problem using monitors. Since mutual exclusion is implicit with monitors, no extra effort is necessary to protect the critical section. In other words, the solution shown below works with any number of producers and consumers without any modifications. It is also noteworthy that using monitors makes race conditions much less likely than when using semaphores.

```
monitor ProducerConsumer {
  int itemCount;
  condition full;
  condition empty;
  procedure add(item) {
    while (itemCount == BUFFER_SIZE) {
```

```
            wait(full);
        }
        putItemIntoBuffer(item);
        itemCount = itemCount + 1;
        if (itemCount == BUFFER_SIZE -1) {
            notify(empty);
        }
    }
    procedure remove() {
        while (itemCount == 0) {
            wait(empty);
        }
        item = removeItemFromBuffer();
        itemCount = itemCount - 1;
        if (itemCount == 1) {
            notify(full);
        }
        return item;
    }
}
procedure producer() {
    while (true) {
        item = produceItem();
        ProducerConsumer.add(item);
    }
}
procedure consumer() {
    while (true) {
        item = ProducerConsumer.remove();
        consumeItem(item);
    }
}
```

Note : The use of while statements in the above code, both when testing if the buffer is full or empty. With multiple consumers, there is a race condition where one consumer gets notified that an item has been put into the buffer but another consumer is already waiting on the monitor so removes it from the buffer instead. If the while was instead an if, too many items might be put into the buffer or a remove might be attempted on an empty buffer.

2.29 READERS-WRITERS PROBLEM

The R-W problem is another classic problem for which design of synchronization and concurrency mechanisms can be tested.

Definition
- There is a data area that is shared among a number of processes.
- Any number of readers may simultaneously write to the data area.
- Only one writer at a time may write to the data area.
- If a writer is writing to the data area, no reader may read it.
- If there is at least one reader reading the data area, no writer may write to it.
- Readers only read and writers only write.
- A process that reads and writes to a data area must be considered a writer (consider producer or consumer).

Semaphore Solution : Readers have Priority

```
int readcount = 0;
semaphore wsem = 1; //
semaphore x = 1; //
void main(){
  int p = fork();
  if(p) reader; // assume multiple instances
  else  writer; // assume multiple instances
}
```

```
void reader(){                        void writer(){
  while(1){                             while(1){
    wait(x);                              wait(wsem)
      readcount++;                        doWriting();
      if (readcount==1)                   signal(wsem)
        wait(wsem);                     }
    signal(x);                        }
    doReading();
    wait(x);
      readcount--;
      if (readcount==0)
        signal(wsem);
    signal(x);
  }
}
```

Once readers have gained control, a flow of reader processes could starve the writer processes.

Rather has the case that when a write needs access, then hold up subsequent reading requests until after the writing is done.

Semaphore Solution : Writers have Priority

```
int readcount, writecount = 0;
semaphore rsem, wsem = 1; //
semaphore x,y,z = 1; //
void main(){
  int p = fork();
  if(p) reader; // assume multiple instances
  else  writer; // assume multiple instances
}
```

```
void reader(){
  while(1){
    wait(z);
    wait(rsem);
    wait(x);
    readcount++;
    if (readcount==1)
        wait(wsem);
    signal(x);
    signal(rsem);
    signal(z);
    doReading();
    wait(x);
    readcount--;
    if (readcount==0)
        signal(wsem);
    signal(x);
  }
}
```

```
void writer(){
  while(1){
    wait(y);
    writecount++;
    if (writecount==1)
        wait(rsem);
    signal(y);
    wait(wsem);
    doWriting();
    signal(wsem);
    wait(y);
    writecount--;
    if (writecount==0)
        signal(rsem);
    signal(y);
  }
}
```

Message Passing Solution

Mailboxes are set up for Read requests, Write requests and each process a mailbox for permission to proceed. The Controller() process performs the necessary coordination among the reader and writers giving writers priority.

Table 2.6

Only Readers	Only Writers	Both w/ Reader First	Both w/ Writer First
• wsem set • no queues	• wsem and rsem set • writers Q on wsem	• wsem set by reader • rsem set by writer • writers Q on wsem • 2nd reader Q on rsem • other readers on z	• wsem set by writer • rsem set by writer • writers Q on wsem • 1st reader Q on rsem • other readers on z

```
void reader(int id){
  message rmsg;
  while(1){
    rmsg = id;
    send("ReadReq",rmsg);
    receive("Reader"+id,rmsg);
    DoReading();
    rmsg = id;
    send("Fini",rmsg);
  }
}
void writer(int id){
  message rmsg;
  while(1){
    rmsg = id;
    send("WriteReq",rmsg);
    receive("Writer"+id,rmsg);
    DoWriting();
    rmsg = id;
    send("Fini",rmsg);
  }
}
```

```
void controller(){
  while(1){
    if(count>0){ //no writer
      if (!empty("Fini")){
        receive("Fini",msg); count++;
      } else if(!empty("WriteReq")){
        receive("WriteReq",msg);
        id = msg.id;
        count -= MAXREADERS;
      } else if(!empty("ReadReq")){
        receive("ReadReq",msg)
        count--;
        send("Reader"+msg.id, "OK");
      }
    }
    if(count==0){//only a writer
      send("Writer"+id, "OK");
      receive("Fini",msg);
      count = MAXREADERS;
    }
    while(count<0){ // 1 wrtr;n rdrs
      receive("Fini",msg);
      count++;
    }
  }
}
```

2.30 DINNING PHILOSOPHER PROBLEM

2.30.1 Problem

The dining philosopher problem is invented by E. W. Dijkstra. Imagine that five philosophers who spend their lives just thinking and eating. In the middle of the dining room is a circular table with five chairs. The table has a big plate of spaghetti. However, there are only five chopsticks available, as shown in the following Fig. 2.17 Each philosopher thinks. When he gets hungry, he sits down and picks up the two chopsticks that are closest to him. If a philosopher can pick up both chopsticks, he eats for a while. After a philosopher finishes eating, he puts down the chopsticks and starts to think.

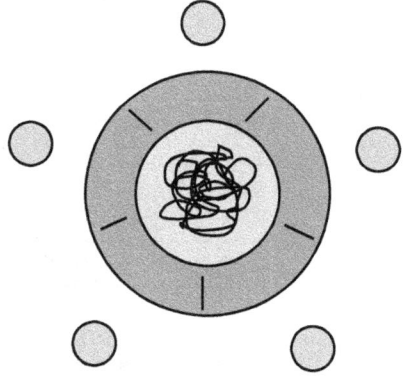

Fig. 2.17

Analysis

How do we write a threaded program to simulate philosophers? First, we notice that these philosophers are in a thinking picking up chopsticks-eating-putting down chopsticks cycle as shown in Fig. 2.18 below.

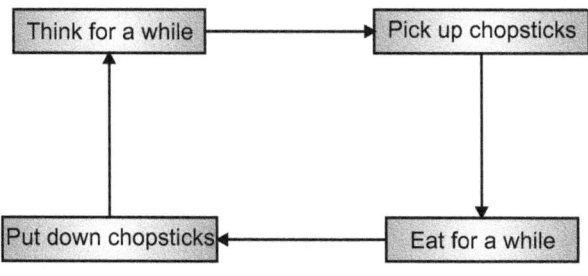

Fig. 2.18

The "pick up chopsticks" part is the key point. How does a philosopher pick up chopsticks? Well, in a program, we simply print out messages such as "Have left chopsticks", which is very easy to do. The problem is each chopstick is shared by two philosophers and hence a shared resource. We certainly do not want a philosopher to pick up a chopstick that has already been picked up by his neighbour. This is a race condition. To address this problem, we may consider each chopstick as a shared item protected by a mutex lock. Each philosopher, before he can eat, locks his left chopstick and locks his right chopstick. If the acquisitions of both locks are successful, this philosopher now owns two locks (hence two chopsticks) and can eat. After finishes easting, this philosopher releases both chopsticks and thinks! This execution flow is as shown in Fig. 2.19 below.

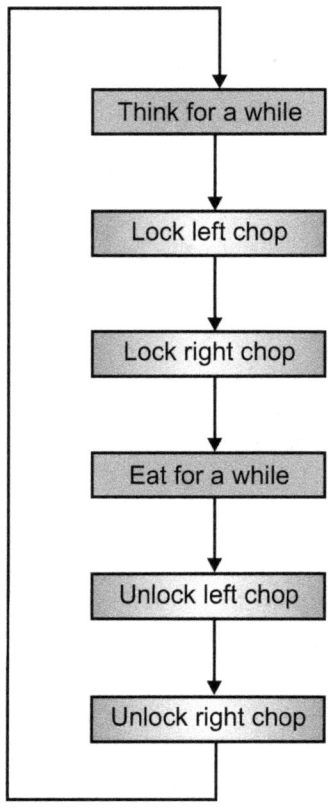

Fig. 2.19

Because we need to lock and unlock a chopstick, each chopstick is associated with a mutex lock. Since we have five philosophers who think and eat simultaneously, we need to create five threads, one for each philosopher. Since each philosopher must have access to the two mutex locks that are associated with its left and right chopsticks, these mutex locks are global variables.

Program 2.1 : Let us see how the above analysis can be converted to a program. Since each philosopher should be run as a thread, we define a Philosopher class as a derived class of class Thread.

```cpp
#include "ThreadClass.h"
#define PHILOSOPHERS   5
class Philosopher: public Thread
{
   public:
      Philosopher(int Number, int iter);
   private:
      int No;
      int Iterations;
      void ThreadFunc();
};
```

The constructor takes two arguments, Number for the number assigned to this philosopher thread and iter for specifying the number of thinking-eating cycles.

The implementation of this class, as shown below, should have all thinking, eating, locking and unlocking mechanisms implemented. Since each chopstick must be protected by a mutex lock, we declare an arrayChopstick[ ] of pointers to Mutex. Since the main program allocates these locks, they are declared as global variables using extern.

Function Filler() generates a char array that contains some spaces. Note that this function is declared to be static so that is can only be used within this file (i.e., Philosopher.cpp).

Let us look at the constructor. It receives two arguments. The first, Number, is assigned by the main program to indicate which philosopher this thread represents. The second, iter, gives the number of thinking-eating cycles for each philosopher. The constructor is very simple. It gives this thread a name. Thus, if the value of Number is 2 (i.e., philosopher 2), this thread will have the name Philosopher2.

```cpp
#include <iostream>
#include "Philosopher.h"
extern Mutex *Chopstick[PHILOSOPHERS];  // locks for chopsticks
static strstream *Filler(int n)
{
```

```
    int i;
    strstream *Space;
    Space = new strstream;
    for (i = 0; i < n; i++)
        (*Space) << ' ';
    (*Space) << '\0';
    return Space;
}
Philosopher::Philosopher(int Number, int iter)
            : No(Number), Iterations(iter)
{
    ThreadName.seekp(0, ios::beg);
    ThreadName << "Philosopher" << Number << '\0';
}
void Philosopher::ThreadFunc()
{
    Thread::ThreadFunc();
    strstream *Space;
    int i;
    Space = Filler(No*2);
    for (i = 0; i < Iterations; i++) {
        Delay();                            // think for a while
        Chopstick[No]->Lock();              // get left chopstick
        Chopstick[(No+1) % PHILOSOPHERS]->Lock();    // gets right chopstick
        cout << Space->str() << ThreadName.str()
             << " begin eating." << endl;
        Delay();                            // eat for a while
        cout << Space->str() << ThreadName.str()
             << " finish eating." << endl;
        Chopstick[No]->Unlock();            // release left chopstick
```

```
        Chopstick[(No+1) % PHILOSOPHERS]->Unlock();  // release right chopstick
    }
    Exit();
}
```

The function ThreadFunc() implements the executable code of a philosopher thread. First of all, it creates a char array of No*2 spaces so that this thread's output would be indented properly. After this, this thread iterates Iteration times. In each cycle, this thread simulates thinking and eating. To this end, we use a method of class Thread : Delay(). The purpose of Delay() is simply delaying the execution of the thread for a random number of times. This simulates "think for a while" and "eat for a while."

Let us look at how locking and unlocking of chopsticks is carried out. Suppose the chopsticks are numbered counter clockwise. For philosopher i, his left chopstick is i and his right chopstick is i+1. Of course, we cannot use i+1 directly, because when i=4, the right chopstick of philosopher is 0 rather than 5. This can easily be done with the remainder operator : (i+1) % PHILOSOPHERS, where PHILOSOPHERS is the number of philosophers. In the above code, philosopher No thinks for a while, locks his left chopstick by calling the method Chopstick[No]->Lock(), locks his right chopstick by calling the methodChopstick[(No+1) % PHILOSOPHERS]->Lock(), eats for a while, unlocks his left chopstick by calling the method Chopstick[No]->Unlock() and unlocks his right chopstick by calling the method Chopstick[(No+1) % PHILOSOPHERS]->Unlock(). This completes one thinking-eating cycle. This cycle repeats for Iteration number of times.

Note : In the above code each philosopher picks up, or locks, his left chopstick first followed by the right one.

The main program, as usual, is easy as shown below. The number of thinking-eating cycles a philosopher must perform is the only command line argument. Since mutex locks must be created before their uses, the main program allocates the mutex locks before the creation of threads. In the following, each mutex lock is created with a name like ChopStick0, ChopStick1, ChopStick4. After all chopstick locks are created, the main thread continues to create philosopher threads and joins with all of its child threads. When all philosopher threads terminate, the main thread returns (i.e., terminates).

```
#include <iostream>
#include <stdlib.h>
#include "Philosopher.h"
Mutex *Chopstick[PHILOSOPHERS];  // locks for chopsticks
```

```
int main(int argc, char *argv[])
{
    Philosopher *Philosophers[PHILOSOPHERS];
    int i, iter;
    strstream name;
    if (argc != 2) {
        cout << "Use " << argv[0] << " #-of-iterations." << endl;
        exit(0);
    }
    else
        iter = abs(atoi(argv[1]));
    for (i=0; i < PHILOSOPHERS; i++) { // initialize chopstick mutex locks
        name.seekp(0, ios::beg);
        name << "ChopStick" << i << '\0';
        Chopstick[i] = new Mutex(name.str());
    }
    for (i=0; i < PHILOSOPHERS; i++) { // initialize and run philosopher threads
        Philosophers[i] = new Philosopher(i, iter);
        Philosophers[i]->Begin();
    }
    for (i=0; i < PHILOSOPHERS; i++)
        Philosophers[i]->Join();
    Exit();
    return 0;
}
```

Discussion

Here are some very important facts about this program :

- If you read the program carefully, we implicitly assign philosopher No to use chopstick ChopStick[No] and chopstick ChopStick[(No+1) % PHILOSOPHERS]. In other word, each philosopher is assigned to a fixed chair. Is it necessary? It is certainly not. For example, when a philosopher is hungry, we can generate a random integer i in the range of 0 and 4. If that chair is occupied, generate another random integer. In this way, we simulate the activity of finding an un-occupied chair. Once an un-occupied chair, say i, is found, this philosopher uses chopstick i and (i + 1) % PHILOSOPHERS. In doing so, our program may be very complex and blur our original focus. After you understand the above program, you can certainly try to make it more realistic.

- The above program forces each philosopher to pick up and put down his left chopstick, followed by his right one. This is also for the purpose of simplicity. In fact, it is easy to see that the order of putting down the chopsticks is irrelevant. Try to reasoning about this yourself.

- The most serious problem of this program is that deadlock could occur! What if every philosopher sits down about the same time and picks up his left chopstick as shown in the following Fig. 2.20. In this case, all chopsticks are locked and none of the philosophers can successfully lock his right chopstick. As a result, we have a circular waiting (i.e., every philosopher waits for his right chopstick that is currently being locked by his right neighbour) and hence a deadlock occurs.

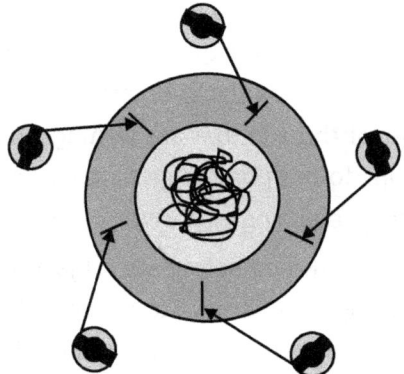

Fig. 2.20

- Starvation is also a problem! Imagine that two philosophers are fast thinkers and fast eaters. They think fast and get hungry fast. Then, they sit down in opposite chairs as shown below. Because they are so fast, it is possible that they can lock their chopsticks and eat. After finish eating and before their neighbors can lock the chopsticks and eat, they come back again and lock the chopsticks and eat. In this case, the other three philosophers, even though they have been sitting for a long time, they have no chance to eat. This is a starvation. Note that it is not a deadlock because there is no circular waiting and everyone has a chance to eat!

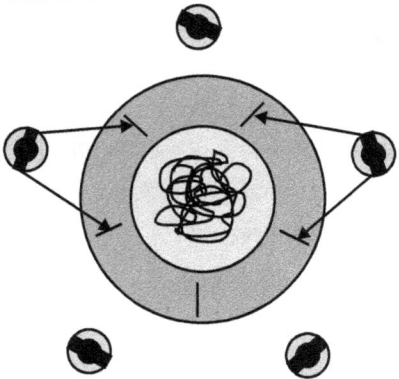

Fig. 2.21

The above Fig. 2.21 shows a simple example of starvation. You can find more complicated thinking-eating sequence that also generates starvation.

2.31 MONITORS

In concurrent programming, a monitor is a synchronization construct that allows threads to have both mutual exclusion and the ability to wait (block) for a certain condition to become true. Monitors also have a mechanism for signalling other threads that their condition has been met. A monitor consists of a mutex (lock) object and condition variables. A condition variable is basically a container of threads that are waiting on a certain condition. Monitors provide a mechanism for threads to temporarily give up exclusive access in order to wait for some condition to be met, before regaining exclusive access and resuming their task.

Another definition of monitor is a thread-safe class, object, or module that uses wrapped mutual exclusion in order to safely allow access to a method or variable by more than one thread. The defining characteristic of a monitor is that its methods are executed with mutual exclusion : At each point in time, at most one thread may be executing any of its methods. Using a condition variable(s), it can also provide the ability for threads to wait on a certain condition (thus using the above definition of a "monitor"). For the rest of this article, this sense of "monitor" will be referred to as a "thread-safe object/class/module".

Monitors were invented by C. A. R. Hoare and Per Brinch Hansen and were first implemented in Brinch Hansen's Concurrent Pascal language.

You might get an experience from studying all semaphore examples that signal and wait calls may scatter everywhere in your program in a not-so-well structured way. If you really get such a feeling, the concept of monitor comes to rescue. The concept of monitor came from C. A. R. Hoare's 1974 paper.

A monitor has four components as shown below: initialization, private data, monitor procedures and monitor entry queue. The initialization component contains the code that is used exactly once when the monitor is created, The private data section contains all private data, including private procedures, that can only be used within the monitor. Thus, these private items are not visible from outside of the monitor. The monitor procedures are procedures that can be called from outside of the monitor. The monitor entry queue contains all threads that called monitor procedures but have not been granted permissions. We shall return to this soon.

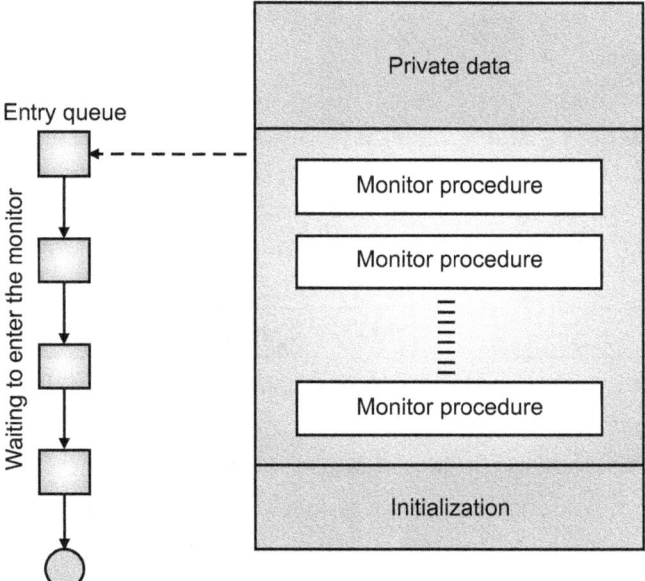

Fig. 2.22

Therefore, a monitor looks like a class with the initialization, private data and monitor procedures corresponding to constructors, private data and methods of that class. The only major difference is that classes do not have entry queues.

Mutual Exclusion of a Monitor

Monitors are supposed to be used in a multithreaded or multi process environment in which multiple threads/processes may call the monitor procedures at the same time asking for service. Thus, a monitor guarantees that at any moment at most one thread can be executing in a monitor! What does this mean? When a thread calls a monitor procedure, we can view the called monitor procedure as an extension to the calling thread. If the called monitor procedure is in execution, we will say the calling thread is in the monitor executing the called monitor procedure. Now, if two threads are in the monitor (i.e., they are executing two, possibly the same, monitor procedures), some private data may be modified by both threads at the same time causing race conditions to occur. Therefore, to guarantee the integrity of the private data, a monitor enforces mutual exclusion implicitly. More precisely, if a thread calls a monitor procedure, this thread will be blocked if there is another thread executing in the monitor. Those threads that were not granted the entering permission will be queued to a monitor entry queue outside of the monitor. When the monitor becomes empty (i.e., no thread is executing in it), one of the threads in the entry queue will be released and granted the permission to execute the called monitor procedure. Although we say "entry queue," you should not view it literally. More precisely, when a thread must be released from the entry queue, you should not assume any policy for which thread will be released.

In summary, monitors ensure mutual exclusion automatically so that there is no more than one thread can be executing in a monitor at any time. This is a very usably and handy capability.

Monitor as a Mini-OS

The concept of a monitor is very similar to an operating system. One can consider the initialization as those data that are initialized when the system is booted up, the private data and code as the internal data structures and functions of an operating system and the monitor procedures as the system calls. User programs are, of course, threads that make service requests. Therefore, a monitor can be considered a mini-OS with limited services.

QUESTIONS

1. What is process? Explain five states process model.
2. Write short note on process control block.
3. What is process scheduling? State and explain objectives of process scheduling.
4. Compare and contrast long term, short term and medium term scheduler.
5. Explain following scheduling algorithms with suitable data
    (a) FCFS
    (b) SJF
    (c) Priority
    (d) RR
6. What is inter process communication? Justify its need in computing environment.
7. What is critical section problem? What are the solutions to it?
8. Explain in short Peterson algorithm.
9. What are the problems in concurrent programming?
10. Explain producer consumer problem with neat diagram.
11. Differentiate producer consumer and reader writer problem.
12. What is monitor? Why and where it is used?

✠ ✠ ✠

Unit - III

DEADLOCKS

3.0 INTRODUCTION

In this unit we see in details and definition of deadlock, necessary conditions for deadlock to occur. Further we see how deadlock is characterized, how to prevent deadlock, how to avoid deadlock, how to detect deadlock and recovering from deadlock. Next to this, we discuss memory management and its requirements. We see how memory partitioning in terms of fixed and dynamic is done. We focus on memory allocation strategies, for e.g. first fit, best fit and worst fit works. We cover address translation using paging and segmentation techniques. At the last we cover virtual memory, its usage in demand paging and concepts of thrashing.

A. DEADLOCK

3.1 DEFINITION OF DEADLOCK

During computation many times it happens that two computer processes shares the same resources and then, these processes are prevented to access the shared resource by each other. Whenever such situation occurs in which none of the processes is progressing further due to non-accessible of shared resource, it is called as Deadlock.

We know that earliest computer operating systems were running single program at a time. So it meant that, whatever resources system was having, it can be given to process as and when required. But these days situations have been changed. Current operating systems are expected to run multiple processes at once. So in order to execute many processes at same time, it is expected that resource requirements of processes must be clear to operating system in advance. So this is why dynamic resource allocation comes into the discussion. It is desirable that dynamic allocation of resources to processes need to be handled effectively by operating system. In case of failure, there are chances of deadlock to exist. Here I present a simple scenario which leads to deadlock.

> Process P1 requests resource R1 and gets it.
> Process P2 requests resource R2 and gets it.
> Process P1 requests resource R2 and is queued up, pending the release of R2.
> Process P2 requests resource R1 and is queued up, pending the release of R1.

As mentioned above, until resource is released, none of the process can proceed further. At this point, it might be difficult for operating system to take action. Best action that can be taken is to stop one of the processes. By this we are clear that handling deadlock plays an important role.

Recall that one definition of an operating system is a resource allocator. There are many resources that can be allocated to only one process at a time and we have seen several operating system features that allow this, such as mutexes, semaphores or file locks.

Sometimes a process has to reserve more than one resource. For example, a process which copies files from one tape to another generally requires two tape drives. A process which deals with databases may need to lock multiple records in a database.

In general, resources allocated to a process are not preemptable; this means that once a resource has been allocated to a process, there is no simple mechanism by which the system can take the resource back from the process unless the process voluntarily gives it up or the system administrator kills the process. This can lead to a situation called deadlock. A set of processes or threads is deadlocked when each process or thread is waiting for a resource to be freed which is controlled by another process. Here is an example of a situation where deadlock can occur.

```
Mutex M1, M2;
/* Thread 1 */
while (1) {
  NonCriticalSection()
  Mutex_lock(&M1);
  Mutex_lock(&M2);
  CriticalSection();
  Mutex_unlock(&M2);
  Mutex_unlock(&M1);
}
/* Thread 2 */
while (1) {
  NonCriticalSection()
  Mutex_lock(&M2);
  Mutex_lock(&M1);
  CriticalSection();
  Mutex_unlock(&M1);
  Mutex_unlock(&M2);
}
```

Suppose thread 1 is running and locks M1, but before it can lock M2, it is interrupted. Thread 2 starts running; it locks M2, when it tries to obtain and lock M1, it is blocked because M1 is already locked (by thread 1). Eventually thread 1 starts running again and it tries to obtain and lock M2, but it is blocked because M2 is already locked by thread 2. Both threads are blocked; each is waiting for an event which will never occur.

Traffic gridlock is as shown in following Fig. 3.1 an everyday example of a deadlock situation.

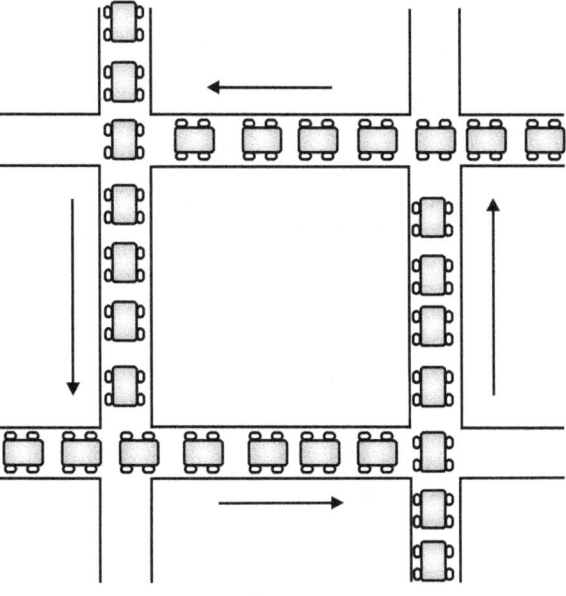

Fig. 3.1

3.2 SYSTEM MODEL

- As far as deadlock is concerned, we model system as a limited resources collection. Such collection can be though as a portioning into different categories as per the need and then there after it can be allocated to processes.
- System resources that we consider here are CD-ROM, tape driver, memory, CPU, printer, files, etc.
- When we put these resources into category, it is expected that, we put them properly so that whenever need comes for a category, one of resources should be able to satisfy that request. It is even better if we divide category deeper for effective resource management.
- For example "storage" resources can be put into "primary" storage and "secondary" storage categories.
- It might be possible that few of the categories may have just a single resource inside it.
- Following sequence can be applied in a regular operation in which a process request a resource before using it and after resource need is satisfied, it releases the resource.
    1. **Request :** If process request a resource and if requested resource is unavailable, then process must wait until resource is made available. Examples of system calls are request(), new(), malloc(), open(), etc.
    2. **Use :** Process receives the resource and uses it.
    3. **Release :** Process is done with resource requirement and releases it to be used by or given to other process. Examples of system calls are release(), free(), close(),etc.

- **Kernel :** A core concern of operating system. It is responsible to keep watch on what resources are freed or allocated. If allocated, to which process they are allocated. Which are the processes in waiting queue?
- As mentioned earlier, set of processes is deadlocked if process holds one resource and needs the other resource which itself is hold by some other process.

3.3 DEADLOCK CHARACTERIZATION

If following four conditions occurs simultaneously in system, then it is said that deadlock exists in a system.

1. **Mutual Exclusion**

   This means that at a time in a system, only one process is allowed to hold shared resource. So in case any other process demands for this resource, then demanding process must have to wait until the resource is released by earlier process that is holding it.

2. **Hold and Wait**

   As name suggest, a process is already holding one resource and demanding another resource which is held by some other process.

3. **No Preemption**

   No preemption means no resource is preempted. At certain point it is required that resource needs to be released. So in this case it has to be released voluntarily by the process that is holding it.

4. **Circular Wait**

   Consider that there exists a set of process say {P0, P1,..Pn} such that P0 is requesting a resource which is currently held by P1, P1 is requesting a resource which is currently held by P2,.., Pn-1 requesting a resource which is currently held by P0.

   For deadlock to exist, all above four conditions must exist simultaneously.

3.3.1 Deadlock with Mutex Locks

Let's see how deadlock can occur in a multithreaded Pthread program using mutex locks. The pthread_mutex_init() function initializes an unlocked mutex. Mutex locks are acquired and released using pthread_mutex_lock 0 and pthread_mutex_unlock 0, respectively. If a thread attempts to acquire a locked mutex, the call to pthread_mutex_lock 0 blocks the thread until the owner of the mutex lock invokes pthread_mutex_unlock Two mutex locks are created in the following code example :

/* Create and initialize the mutex locks */

pthread_mutex_t f irst_mutex ; pthread_mutex_t second_mutex ;

pthread_mutex_init (&f irst_mutex , NULL) ;

pthread_mutex_init (&second_mutex , NULL) ;

Next, two threads thread_one and thread_two are created and both these threads have access to both mutex locks. thread_one and thread_two run in the functions do_work_one () and do_work_two 0, respectively, as shown below :

```
/* thread_one runs in this function */
void *do_work_one (void *param)
{
    pthread_mutex_lock (&f irst _mutex) ; pthread_mutex_lock (&second_mutex) ;
    /** * Do some work */ pthread_mutex_unlock (&second_mutex) ;
    pthread_mutex_unlock (&f irst_mutex) ;
pthread_exit (0) ;
}
/* thread_two runs in this function */
void *do_work_two (void *param)
{
    pthread_mutex_lock (&second_mutex) ;
    pthread_mutex_lock (&f irst_mutex) ;
     /** * Do some work */
    pthread_mutex_unlock(&f irst _mutex) ;
    pthread_mutex_unlock (&second_mutex) ;
    pthread_exit (0) ;
}
```

In this example, thread_one attempts to acquire the mutex locks in the order (1) first_mutex, (2) second_mutex, while thread_two attempts to acquire the mutex locks in the order (1) second_mutex, (2) first _mutex. Deadlock is possible if thread_one acquires first_mutex while thread_two acquires second_mutex. Note that, even though deadlock is possible, it will not occur if thread_one can acquire and release the mutex locks for first_mutex and second_mutex before thread_two attempts to acquire the locks. And, of course, the order in which the threads run depends on how they are scheduled by the CPU scheduler. This example illustrates a problem with handling deadlocks : it is difficult to identify and test for deadlocks that may occur only under certain scheduling circumstances.

3.4 RESOURCE-ALLOCATION GRAPH (RAG)

- Resource-Allocation Graphs helps to understand deadlock much clearly. They have properties as given below :
  1. On graph, set of resource categories, say {R1, R2, .., RN} are referred as "square" nodes. Specific instances of resources are referred as a "dot" inside node. (One dot means one instance, two dots means two instances.)
- Consider set of processes {P1, P2, .., PN}.

- In some cases deadlocks can be understood more clearly through the use of Resource-Allocation Graphs, having the following properties :
    1. Term "request edge" is a set directed arc from process Pi to resource Rj. It means Rj is requested by Pi.
    2. The term "Assignment edge" is a set of directed arc from resource Rj to process Pi. It means Rj is currently hold by Pi.
    3. As soon as request for a particular resource is granted to a process, request edge becomes assignment edge.
    4. As shown in Fig. 3.2, request edge points to square where in assignment edge points to specific instance within square.
    5. For example :

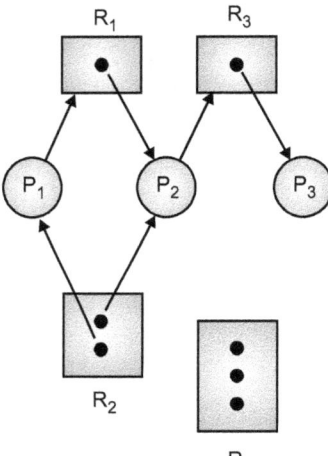

Fig. 3.2 : Resource allocation graph

- We can say that system is not having deadlock if there is no cycle in resource allocation graph. See in Fig. 3.2 above.

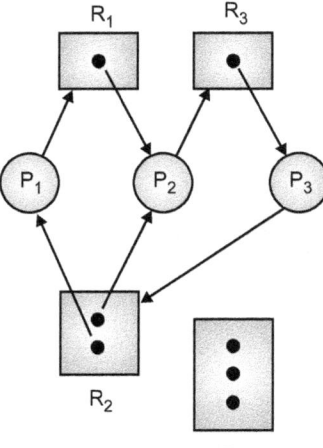

Fig. 3.3 : Resource allocation graph with a deadlock

- We say that deadlock exists in a system if resource allocation graph contains cycle and there is just a single instance in each resource category.
- There might be possibility of deadlock if resource allocation graph contains cycle and resource category contains more than once instance. But this cannot be guaranteed always.
- Consider Figs. 3.3 and 3.4.

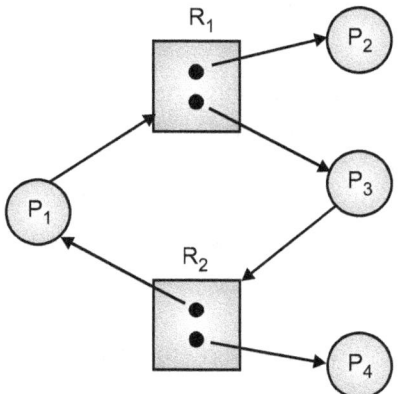

Fig. 3.4 : Resource allocation graph with a cycle but no deadlock

3.5 METHODS FOR HANDLING DEADLOCKS

- Deadlock is handled by the following ways :
    1. **Deadlock Prevention or Avoidance :** It means prevent system from deadlock state.
    2. **Deadlock Detection and Recovery :** It means detect the deadlock state and if found recover the system from it. Recovery can be done by preempting resource(s) from process.
    3. **Ignore the Problem all Together :** If you find that deadlock occurs once a year, then it is better to reboot as required. This is actually better than the overhead (in terms of system performance penalties) that can be caused by deadlock prevention or detection policies. This is an approach that can be seen in UNIX and Windows system.
- If deadlock avoidance is expected then system shall have additional information about all processes. It means future resource requirements of process shall be drawn in advance.
- As far as deadlock detection is considered, it can be treated fairly straightforward. But in case of deadlock recovery, aborting or preempting resources could not be the best option all time.
- System will gradually slow down in case of no deadlock detection or no prevention. In few cases, this slow down cannot be distinguished if real time process itself is doing some heavy computation.

3.6 DEADLOCK PREVENTION

Deadlock prevention is possible when one of the four necessary conditions is prevented :

(a) Mutual Exclusion
- Shared resources such as read-only files do not lead to deadlocks.
- But if resources are tape drives and printers, then such resources actually needs an exclusive access by single process at a time.

(b) Hold and Wait
- If process is prevented from holding one or more resources while it is waiting for other resource simultaneously, then this hold and wait condition can be prevented. This can be achieved by following possibilities.
    1. Processes requests all required resources at one time. But this could not be useful solution when process needs one resource early in its execution and does not need some other resource until much later.
    2. Before requesting new resources, process holding any other resource must release it first and then reacquire the released resource with the new one in single request. This scenario can be harmful when process has partially finished and its resource has been preempted and now difficult to reallocate it again.
    3. Starvation is possible because of either of the methods described above.

(c) No Preemption
- Preemption of process resource allocations can prevent this condition of deadlocks, when it is possible.
- First approach is that if a process is forced to wait when requesting a new resource, then all other resources previously held by this process are implicitly released, (preempted), forcing this process to re-acquire the old resources along with the new resources in a single request, similar to the previous discussion.
- Second approach is that when requested resource is not available, then system looks to see which other processes are holding that resource. If such process is found, then its resources are preempted and such resources are added to the list of resources for which process is waiting.
- Either of these approaches is applicable when resource states can be easily saved and restored. (For example memory, register).

(d) Circular Wait
- If we numbers all resources and if process request the resource strictly in increasing or decreasing order, then circular wait can be avoided.
- In other words, in order to request resource Rj, a process must first release all Ri such that $i >= j$.
- Determining the relative ordering of different resources is a big challenge in this scheme.

- Deadlock prevention is the process of making it logically impossible for one of the 4 deadlock conditions to hold.
- Relaxing mutual exclusion requires making all relevant resources sharable. Some resources can be made sharable. Spooling can make devices like printers or tape drives sharable. Spooling is storing the output on a shared medium, like disk and using a single process to coordinate access to the shared resource. Print spooling is the cannonical example.
- There are generally some resources that cannot be spooled semaphores, for example. Removing mutual exclusion is not always an option.
- Relaxing Hold and Wait requires processes to acquire all their needed resources at once. To acquire new resources in such a system requires a process to relinquish all the processes it holds and try to reacquire all the resources it needs atomically.
- Reasonable systems can be programmed this way, but in practice it's almost never done. Starvation is a real possibility and its probability increases with the number of resources concurrently acquired.
- Relaing non-preemptability for resources other than the CPU is very non intuitive. The idea that a program might lose a lock at any time and have to reacquire it is very counterintuitive. If this is done with physical resources, things can be even more confusing. Other than very specialized cases, relaxing non-preemptability is almost never done.
- The most common method of preventing deadlock is to prevent the circular wait. A simple way to do this, when possible, is to order the resources and always acquire them in order. Because a process can't be waiting on a lower numbered process while holding a higher numbered one, a cycle is impossible.
- One can consider the Dining Philosophers to be a deadlock problem and can apply deadlock prevention to it by numbering the forks and always acquiring the lowest numbered fork first.

```c
#define N 5                          /* Number of philosphers */
#define RIGHT(i) (((i)+1) %N)
#define LEFT(i) (((i)==N) ? 0 : (i)+1)
typedef enum { THINKING, HUNGRY, EATING } phil_state;
phil_state state[N];
semaphore mutex =1;
semaphore f[N];                      /* one per fork, all 1*/
void get_forks(int i)
{
   int max, min;
   if ( RIGHT(i) > LEFT(i) ) {
```

```
        max = RIGHT(i); min = LEFT(i);
    }
    else
{
    min = RIGHT(i); max = LEFT(i);
    }
    P(f[min]);
    P(f[max]);
}
void put_forks(int i)
{
    V(f[LEFT(i)]);
    V(f[RIGHT(i)]);
}
void philosopher(int process)
{
    while(1)
{
    think();
    get_forks(process);
    eat();
    put_forks(process);
    }
}
```

This solution doesn't get maximum parallelism, but it is an otherwise valid solution.

3.7 DEADLOCK AVOIDANCE

- Deadlock prevention is possible when we prevent at least one of the necessary conditions. So general idea behind deadlock avoidance is to prevent deadlock.
- Doing this needs more maximum information about process.
- In some algorithms the scheduler only needs to know the *maximum* number of each resource that a process might potentially use. In more complex algorithms the scheduler can also take advantage of the *schedule* of exactly what resources may be needed in what order.
- When a scheduler sees that starting a process or granting resource requests may lead to future deadlocks, then that process is just not started or the request is not granted.
- A resource allocation state is defined by the number of available and allocated resources and the maximum requirements of all processes in the system.

3.7.1 Safe State

- Safe state is a state in which system allocates all the requested resources to processes without entering into deadlock state.
- For state to be safe, there need to be a safe sequence. Say there exists a safe sequence of processes {P0, P1, P2, ..., PN} such that all of the resource requests for Pi can be granted using the resources currently allocated to Pi and all processes Pj where j < i (i.e. if all the processes prior to Pi finish and free up their resources, then Pi will be able to finish also, using the resources that they have freed up).
- Unsafe state is a sate which is not safe. It means it may lead to deadlock. It is very much feasible to say that all safe states are deadlock free, but not all unsafe states leads to deadlock.

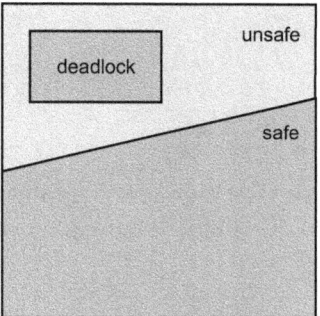

Fig. 3.5 : Safe, unsafe and deadlocked state spaces

For example, consider a system with 12 tape drives, allocated as follows. Is this a safe state? What is the safe sequence?

	Maximum Needs	Current Allocation
P0	10	5
P1	4	2
P2	9	2

What happens to the above table if process P2 requests and is granted one more tape drive? Key to the safe state approach is that when a request is made for resources, the request is granted only if the resulting allocation state is a safe one.

3.7.2 Resource Allocation Graph Algorithm

- As mentioned earlier, deadlock state can be detected by cycles in the resource allocation graphs if there exists single instance in resource categories.
- So if we augment resource allocation graph with claim edges, then unsafe states can be recognized and avoided. Claim edges are denoted by dashed lines, which point from process to resource. Claim edge indicates that resource may be requested by process in the future.
- In order for this technique to work, all claim edges must be added to the graph for any particular process before that process is allowed to request any resources. (Alternatively,

processes may only make requests for resources for which they have already established claim edges and claim edges cannot be added to any process that is currently holding resources)
- After request is made, claim edge Pi → Rj is converted to request edge. Similarly when resource is released, the assignment reverts back to claim edge.
- This approach works by denying requests that would produce cycles in the resource-allocation graph, taking claim edges into effect.
- Consider for example what happens when process P2 requests resource R2 :

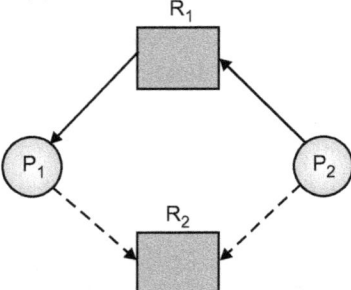

Fig. 3.6 : Resource allocation graph for deadlock avoidance

- The resulting resource-allocation graph would have a cycle in it and so the request cannot be granted.

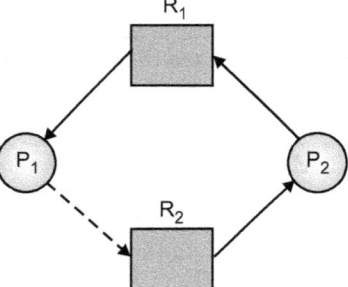

Fig. 3.7 : Unsafe state in a resource allocation graph

3.7.3 Banker's Algorithm

- Resource allocation graph does not work for the resource categories that contain more than one instance. So more complex need to be chosen.
- The Banker's algorithm gets its name because it is a method that bankers could use to assure that when they lend out resources they will still be able to satisfy all their clients.
- A banker won't loan out a little money to start building a house unless they are assured that they will later be able to loan out the rest of the money to finish the house.
- When a process starts up, it must state in advance the maximum allocation of resources it may request, up to the amount available on the system.
- The scheduler determines whether system ensures safe state or not after granting the request that has been made earlier. Process will not be granted unless system safe state is ensured.

- Banker's algorithm uses several data structures. In given explanation, 'n' refers to number of processes and 'm' refers to number of resource categories :
  1. **Available[m] :** This vector indicates currently available resources of each type.
  2. **Max[n][m] :** Refers to maximum demand of each process for each resource.
  3. **Allocation[n][m] :** Indicates the number of each resource category allocated to each process.
  4. **Need[n][m] :** Indicates the remaining resources needed of each type for each process.
  5. **Need[i][j] = Max[i][j] :** Allocation[i][j] for all i, j.
- Consider following notations and observation for simplification :
  1. One row of the Need vector, Need[i], can be treated as a vector corresponding to the needs of process i and similarly for Allocation and Max.
  2. A vector X is considered to be <= a vector Y if X[i] <= Y[i] for all i.

(a) Safety Algorithm

- Before we go ahead with preparing Banker's algorithm, we need an algorithm that determines whether a particular state is safe or not.
- Consider the following algorithm that determines state of system is safe :

  Step 1. Let Work and Finish be vectors of length m and n respectively.

  Step 2. Work is a working copy of the available resources, which will be modified during the analysis.

  Step 3. Finish is a vector of Booleans indicating whether a particular process can finish (or has finished so far in the analysis).

  Step 4. Initialize Work to Available and Finish to false for all elements.

  Step 5. Find i such that both (A) Finish[i] == false and (B) Need[i] < Work. This process has not finished, but could be, with the given available working set. If no such i exists, go to step 4.

  Step 6. Set Work = Work + Allocation[i] and set Finish[i] to true. This corresponds to process i finishing up and releasing its resources back into the work pool. Then loop back to step 2.

  Step 7. If finish[i] == true for all i, then the state is a safe state, because a safe sequence has been found.

- JTB has made few modifications to algorithm. They are as given :
  1. In step 1 instead of making Finish an array of Booleans initialized to false, make it an array of ints initialized to 0. Also initialize an ints = 0 as a step counter.
  2. In step 2, look for Finish[i] == 0.
  3. In step 3, set Finish[i] to ++s. S is counting the number of finished processes.
  4. For step 4, the test can be either Finish[i] > 0 for all i, or s >= n. The benefit of this method is that if a safe state exists, then Finish[] indicates one safe sequence.

(b) Resource-Request Algorithm (The Bankers Algorithm)

- In earlier section, we saw algorithm to determine safe state of system. Now let us understand Banker's algorithm.
- Job of this algorithm to determine whether request is safe or not. Request is granted only if it is safe to do so.
- When a request is made (that does not exceed currently available resources), pretend it has been granted and then see if the resulting state is a safe one. If so grant the request and if not deny the request as follows :
    1. Let Request[n][m] indicate the number of resources of each type currently requested by processes. If Request[i] > Need[i] for any process i, raise an error condition.
    2. If Request[i] > Available for any process i, then that process must wait for resources to become available. Otherwise the process can continue to step 3.
    3. Check to see if the request can be granted safely, by pretending it has been granted and then seeing if the resulting state is safe. If so, grant the request and if not, then the process must wait until its request can be granted safely. The procedure for granting a request is :
        - Available = Available - Request
        - Allocation = Allocation + Request
    4. Need = Need – Request

(c) Example of Determination of State

- Consider the following initial state :

Claim matrix C

	R1	R2	R3
P1	3	2	2
P2	6	1	3
P3	3	1	4
P4	4	2	2

Allocation matrix A

	R1	R2	R3
P1	1	0	0
P2	6	1	2
P3	2	1	1
P4	0	0	2

C – A

	R1	R2	R3
P1	2	2	2
P2	0	0	1
P3	1	0	3
P4	4	2	0

Resource vector R

R1	R2	R3
9	3	6

Available vector V

R1	R2	R3
0	1	1

(a) Initial sate

Claim matrix C

	R1	R2	R3
P1	3	2	2
P2	0	0	0
P3	3	1	4
P4	4	2	2

Allocation matrix A

	R1	R2	R3
P1	1	0	0
P2	0	0	0
P3	2	1	1
P4	0	0	2

C – A

	R1	R2	R3
P1	2	2	2
P2	0	0	0
P3	1	0	3
P4	4	2	0

(b) P2 runs to completion

	R1	R2	R3
	9	3	6

Resource vector R

	R1	R2	R3
	6	2	3

Available vector V

	R1	R2	R3
P1	0	0	0
P2	0	0	0
P3	3	1	4
P4	4	2	2

Claim matrix C

	R1	R2	R3
P1	0	0	0
P2	0	0	0
P3	2	1	1
P4	0	0	2

Allocation matrix A

	R1	R2	R3
P1	0	0	0
P2	0	0	0
P3	1	0	3
P4	4	2	0

C – A

(c) P1 runs to completion

	R1	R2	R3
	9	3	6

Resource vector R

	R1	R2	R3
	7	2	3

Available vector V

	R1	R2	R3
P1	0	0	0
P2	0	0	0
P3	0	0	0
P4	4	2	2

Claim matrix C

	R1	R2	R3
P1	0	0	0
P2	0	0	0
P3	0	0	0
P4	0	0	2

Allocation matrix A

	R1	R2	R3
P1	0	0	0
P2	0	0	0
P3	0	0	0
P4	4	2	0

C – A

	R1	R2	R3
	9	3	6

Resource vector R

	R1	R2	R3
	9	3	4

Available vector V

(d) P3 runs to completion

- What will be the next process?
- **Safe Sequence :** P2 → P1 → P3 → P4.

Note : After satisfying a particular process for its resources need, it is generally recommended that process that has made request earlier shall be considered first and then subsequently other next processes. This is the reason that after satisfying process P2, we picked up process P1 instead of process P3.

Program 3.1 : Bankers Algorithm in C

```c
#include <studio.h> #include<conio.h>
 void main()
 {
   intprocess,resource,i,j,instanc,k=0,count1=0,count2=0;//count,k variables are taken for counting purpose
   printf("\n\t Enter No. of Process:-\n");
   printf("\t\t");
   scanf("%d",&process);                //Entering No. of Processes
   printf("\n\tEnter No. of Resources:-\n");
   printf("\t\t");
   scanf("%d",&resource);               //No. of Resources
   intavail[resource],max[process][resource],allot[process][resource],need[process][resource],completed[process];
   for(i=0;i<process;i++)
   completed[i]=0;                      //Setting Flag for uncompleted Process
   printf("\n\tEnter No. of Available Instances\n");
   for(i=0;i<resource;i++)
   {
    printf("\t\t");
    scanf("%d",&instanc);
    avail[i]=instanc;                   // Storing Available instances
   }
   printf("\n\tEnter Maximum No. of instances of resources that a Process need:\n");
   for(i=0;i<process;i++)
   {
     printf("\n\t For P[%d]",i);
     for(j=0;j<resource;j++)
     {
       printf("\t");
       scanf("%d",&instanc);
       max[i][j]=instanc;
     }
   }
   printf("\n\t Enter no. of instances already allocated to process of a resource:\n");
   for(i=0;i<process;i++)
   {
```

```c
        printf("\n\t For P[%d]\t",i);
        for(j=0;j<resource;j++)
         {
           printf("\t\t");
           scanf("%d",&instanc);
           allot[i][j]=instanc;
           need[i][j]=max[i][j]-allot[i][j];     //calculating Need of each process
         }
    }
    printf("\n\t Safe Sequence is:- \t");
    while(count1!=process)
    {
     count2=count1;
    for(i=0;i<process;i++)
     {
       for(j=0;j<resource;j++)
        {
           if(need[i][j]<=avail[j])
             {
                k++;
             }
        }
        if(k==resource && completed[i]==0 )
         {
           printf("P[%d]\t",i);
           completed[i]=1;
           for(j=0;j<resource;j++)
             {
               avail[j]=avail[j]+allot[i][j];
             }
             count1++;
         }
         k=0;
      }
        if(count1==count2)
         {
```

```
        printf("\t\t Stop ..After this.....Deadlock \n");
        break;
    }
}
    getch();
}
```

3.8 DEADLOCK DETECTION

- If deadlocks are not avoided, then another approach is to detect when they have occurred and recover somehow.
- In addition to the performance hit of constantly checking for deadlocks, a policy or algorithm must be in place for recovering from deadlocks and there is potential for lost work when processes must be aborted or have their resources preempted.

(a) Single Instance of Each Resource Type
- Wait-for-Graph, which is variation of resource allocation graph, can be used if each resource category has a single instance.
- We construct wait-for-graph from resource allocation graph by eliminating the resources and collapsing the associated edges. This is shown in Fig. 3.8.
- An arc from P_i to P_j in a wait-for graph indicates that process P_i is waiting for a resource that process P_j is currently holding.

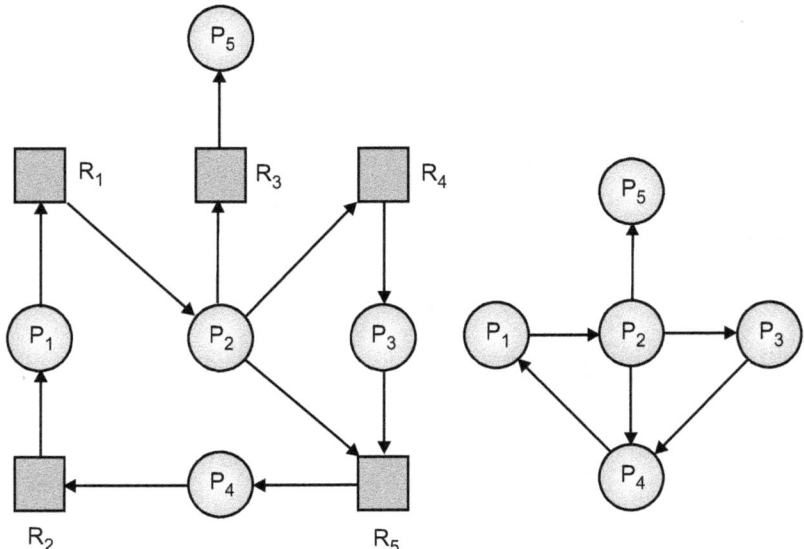

Fig. 3.8 : (a) Resource allocation graph (b) Corresponding wait-for graph

- As before, cycles in the wait-for graph indicate deadlocks.
- This algorithm must maintain the wait-for graph and periodically search it for cycles.

(b) Several Instances of a Resource Type

- The detection algorithm outlined here is essentially the same as the Banker's algorithm, with two subtle differences :
    - In step 1, the Banker's Algorithm sets Finish[i] to false for all i. The algorithm presented here sets Finish[i] to false only if Allocation[i] is not zero. Finish[i] is set to true when currently allocated resources for this process is zero. This is essentially a clear assumption that if all of the other processes can finish then this can also finish. Furthermore, this algorithms looks for processes that are involved in deadlock situation. Process that does not have any resources allocated cannot be involved in a deadlock and so can be removed from any further consideration.
    - Steps 2 and 3 are unchanged.
    - In step 4, the basic Banker's algorithm says that if Finish[i] == true for all i, that there is no deadlock. This algorithm is more specific, by stating that if Finish[i] == false for any process Pi, then that process is specifically involved in the deadlock which has been detected.

Note : An alternative method was presented above, in which Finish held integers instead of Booleans. This vector would be initialized to all zeros and then filled with increasing integers as processes are detected which can finish. If any processes are left at zero when the algorithm completes, then there is a deadlock and if not, then the integers in finish describe a safe sequence. To modify this algorithm to match this section of the text, processes with allocation = zero could be filled in with N, N - 1, N - 2, etc. in step 1 and any processes left with Finish = 0 in step 4 are the deadlocked processes.

Consider, for example, the following state and determine if it is currently deadlocked :

	Allocation A B C	Request A B C	Available A B C
P_0	0 1 0	0 0 0	0 0 0
P_1	2 0 0	2 0 2	
P_2	3 0 3	0 0 0	
P_3	2 1 1	1 0 0	
P_4	0 0 2	0 0 2	

Now suppose that process P_2 makes a request for an additional instance of type C, yielding the state shown below. Is the system now deadlocked?

	Allocation A B C	Request A B C	Available A B C
P_0	0 1 0	0 0 0	0 0 0
P_1	2 0 0	2 0 2	
P_2	3 0 3	0 0 1	
P_3	2 1 1	1 0 0	
P_4	0 0 2	0 0 2	

(c) Detection-Algorithm Usage
- When should the deadlock detection be done? Frequently, or infrequently?
- The answer may depend on how frequently deadlocks are expected to occur, as well as the possible consequences of not catching them immediately.
- If deadlocks are not removed immediately when they occur, then more and more processes can "back up" behind the deadlock, making the eventual task of unblocking the system more difficult and possibly damaging to more processes.
- There are two obvious approaches, each with trade-offs :
  1. Do deadlock detection only when there is some clue that a deadlock may have occurred, such as when CPU utilization reduces to 35% or some other magic number. The advantage is that deadlock detection is done much less frequently, but the down side is that it becomes impossible to detect the processes involved in the original deadlock and so deadlock recovery can be more complicated and damaging to more processes.
  2. It is good to do deadlock detection after every resource allocation which cannot be immediately granted. This has the advantage of detecting the deadlock, while the minimum numbers of processes are involved in the deadlock. One might consider that the process whose request triggered the deadlock condition is the "cause" of the deadlock, but realistically all of the processes in the cycle are equally responsible for the resulting deadlock. The down side of this approach is the extensive overhead and performance hit caused by checking for deadlocks so frequently.
  3. Third alternative is to keep historical log of resource allocations, since the last known time of no deadlock. You can do check for deadlock regularly. Historical log can be used for further use.

3.9 RECOVERY FROM DEADLOCK

- Recovery from deadlock is possible with given three approaches :
  1. Inform the system operator so that he performs manual intervention.
  2. Terminate one or more processes involved in the deadlock.
  3. Preempt resources.

(a) Process Termination
- Two basic approaches, both of which recover resources allocated to terminated processes :
  1. Terminate all processes involved in the deadlock. This definitely solves the deadlock, but at the expense of terminating more processes than would be absolutely necessary.
  2. Terminate processes one by one until the deadlock is broken. This is more conservative, but requires doing deadlock detection after each step.

- In the latter case there are many factors that can go into deciding which processes to terminate next :
  1. Process priorities.
  2. How long the process has been running and how close it is to finishing?
  3. How many and what type of resources is the process holding? Are they easy to preempt and restore?
  4. How many more resources does the process need to complete?
  5. How many processes will need to be terminated?
  6. Whether the process is interactive or batch?
  7. Whether or not the process has made non-restorable changes to any resource?

(b) Resource Preemption

- When preempting resources to relieve deadlock, there are three important issues to be addressed :
  1. **Selecting a Victim :** Deciding which resources to preempt from which processes involves many of the same decision criteria outlined above.
  2. **Rollback :** Ideally one would like to roll back a preempted process to a safe state prior to the point at which that resource was originally allocated to the process. Unfortunately it can be difficult or impossible to determine what such a safe state is and so the only safe rollback is to roll back all the way back to the beginning. (i.e. abort the process and make it start over)
  3. **Starvation :** How do you guarantee that a process will not starve because its resources are constantly being preempted? Priority system can be thought as one option. Job of priority system is to increase priority of process every time its resources get preempted. Subsequently is should get a high enough priority that it won't get preempted any more.

B. MEMORY MANAGEMENT

3.10 INTRODUCTION TO MEMORY MANAGEMENT

Memory Management is the act of managing computer memory. In its simpler forms, this involves providing ways to allocate portions of memory to programs at their request and freeing it for reuse when no longer needed. The management of main memory is critical to the computer system.

Virtual memory systems separate the memory addresses used by a process from actual physical addresses, allowing separation of processes and increasing the effectively available amount of RAM using disk swapping. The quality of the virtual memory manager can have a big impact on overall system performance.

Automated allocation or de allocation of computer memory resources for a program is possible by making use of garbage collector. The applications of this are seen in programming languages, for example Java language. Large group of objects can be simultaneously deallocated by making use of explicit memory management. Other variant of explicit memory management is region based memory management.

We have seen that memory management is one of the most important functionalities of operating system. In this, operating system basically manages and controls primary memory. Memory management keeps track that which memory locations are allocated and which are free. It also calculates amount of memory to be allocated to processes. It decides which process will get memory at what time. It updates the status as and when memory locations are allocated or freed.

Base register and limit register are two resisters that memory management uses to provide protection. The base register holds the smallest legal physical memory address and the limit register specifies the size of the range. For example, if the base register holds 300000 and the limit register is 1209000, then the program can legally access all addresses from 300000 through 411999.

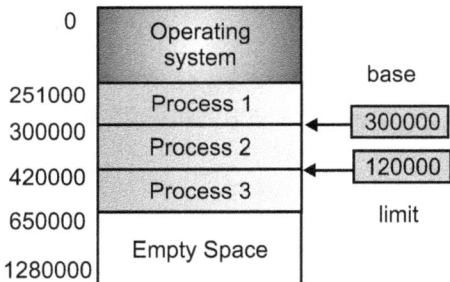

Fig. 3.9 : Memory protection using base register and limit register

Instructions and data to memory addresses can be done in following ways :

- **Compile Time :** When it is known at compile time where the process will reside, compile time binding is used to generate the absolute code.
- **Load Time :** When it is not known at compile time where the process will reside in memory, then the compiler generates re-locatable code.
- **Execution Time :** If the process can be moved during its execution from one memory segment to another, then binding must be delayed to be done at run time.

Dynamic Loading

In dynamic loading, unless routine is called by the program, it is not loaded. All routines are kept on disk in a re-locatable load format. The main program is loaded into memory and is executed. On request, other modules are loaded. Dynamic loading makes better memory space utilization and unused routines are never loaded.

Dynamic Linking

Linking refers to the process of collecting and combining various modules of code and data into one executable file. This file is loaded into memory and then executed. By operating system, system level libraries are linked to program. When libraries are combined at load time, it is called as static linking. When libraries are combined at the time of execution, it os called as dynamic linking.

In static linking code size becomes bigger wherein at dynamic linking, code size remains smaller.

3.10.1 Logical Versus Physical Address Space

Logical address is an address generated by CPU. Physical address is actual available memory unit. Logical address is also known as virtual address.

Logical and physical addresses are the same in compile time and load time address binding schemes wherein they differ in execution time address binding scheme.

Logical address space is a space where the set of all logical addresses generated by program are kept. The set of all physical addresses corresponding to these logical addresses are kept in physical address space.

Memory Management Unit (MMU) is a hardware device which performs runtime mapping from virtual to physical address. Following mechanism is used to convert virtual address to physical address.

- The value in the base register is added to every address generated by a user process which is treated as offset at the time it is sent to memory. For example, if the base register value is 10000, then an attempt by the user to use address location 100 will be dynamically reallocated to location 10100.
- The user program deals with virtual addresses; it never sees the real physical addresses.

3.11 REQUIREMENTS OF MEMORY MANAGEMENT

Memory management systems on multi-tasking operating systems usually deal with the following issues.

Relocation

In systems with virtual memory, programs in memory must be able to reside in different parts of the memory at different times. This is because when the program is swapped back into memory after being swapped out for a while it cannot always be placed in the same location. Memory management in the operating system should therefore be able to relocate programs in memory and handle memory references and addresses in the code of the program so that they always point to the right location in memory.

Protection

Without process permission, other process shall not be able to reference the memory. This is referred as memory protection. Memory protection prevents malicious code in one program from interfering with the other running program.

Sharing

As explained earlier, memory protection is needed. But in few cases we expect memory to be shared among many processes. Sharing memory is one of the fastest techniques of inter-process communication (IPC).

Logical Organization

Programs are often organized in modules. Some of these modules could be shared between different programs, some are read only and some contain data that can be modified. Handling logical organization is the responsibility of memory management. One way to perform logical organization is segmentation.

Important Memory Management Terms

1. **Frame :** Frame is a fixed-length block of main memory.
2. **Page :** Page is a fixed-length block of data in secondary memory (for e.g. disk).
3. **Segment :** Segment is a variable-length block of data that resides in secondary memory.

C. MEMORY PARTITIONING

3.12 FIXED PARTITIONING

- Equal-size partitions
    - Any process whose size is less than or equal to the partition size can be loaded into an available partition.
    - The operating system can swap a process out of a partition, if none are in a ready or running state.
- Fig. 3.10 shows fixed size partition. Size partition considered here is of 8MB in size.

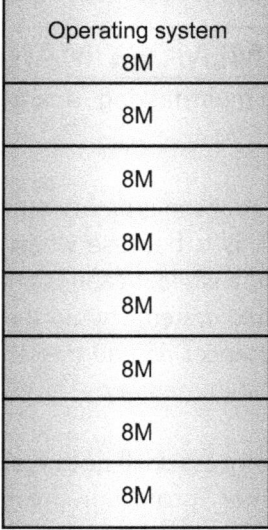

Fig. 3.10 : Fixed size partitions

Fixed Partitioning Problems

- A program may not fit in a partition.
    (i) The programmer must design the program with overlays.

- Main memory use is inefficient.
  - (ii) Any program, no matter how small, occupies an entire partition.
  - (iii) This results in internal fragmentation.

Solution : Unequal Size Partitions

- Above mentioned problems can be solved by this technique. But this does not guarantee to solve them completely.
- In Fig. 3.11
  - (i) Programs up to 16M can be accommodated without overlay.
  - (ii) Smaller programs can be placed in smaller partitions, reducing internal fragmentation.

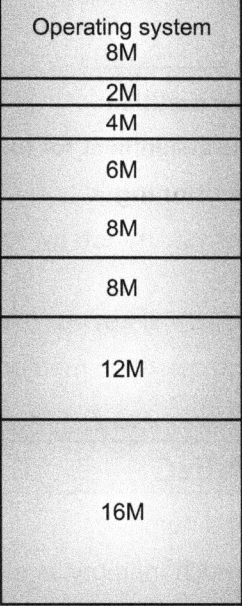

Fig. 3.11 : Equal size partitions

Placement Algorithm

- Equal size :
  - Placement is trivial (no options).
- Unequal size :
  - Can assign each process to the smallest partition within which it will fit.
  - Queue for each partition is needed.
  - Processes are assigned in such a way as to minimize wasted memory within a partition.
- Fig. 3.12 shows queues associated with fixed size partitions. Fig. 3.12 (a) uses separate queue for individual partition where in Fig. 3.12 (b) uses single queue for all partitions.

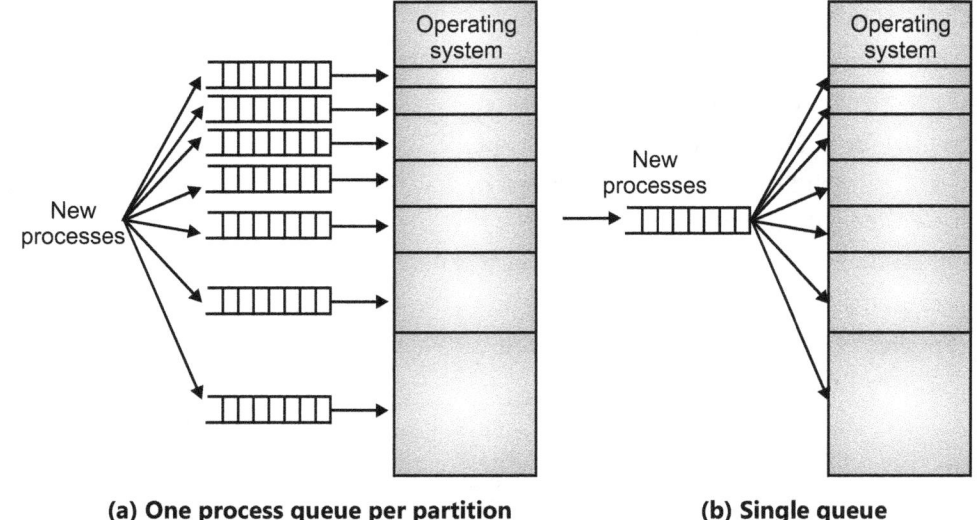

(a) One process queue per partition   (b) Single queue

Fig. 3.12 : Queue assignment for fixed partitioning

Remaining Problems with Fixed Partitioning

- The number of active processes is limited by the system, i.e. limited by the pre-determined number of partitions.
- A large number of very small process will not use the space efficiently :
  1. In either fixed or variable length partition methods

3.13 DYNAMIC PARTITIONING

- Partitions are of variable length and number.
- Process is allocated in exactly as much memory as required. .
- Dynamic partitioning leads to external fragmentation.
- Memory external to all processes is fragmented.
- This problem can be resolved using compaction.
  1. In compaction, OS moves processes so that they are contiguous.
  2. But this is time consuming and wastes CPU time.
- Fig. 3.13 shows process allocation using dynamic partitioning. As shown in Fig. 3.13, P2 used 14M, P4 used 8M and P3 used 18M of memory portions. All of this allocation has been done dynamically on basis of process requirements.
- Out of the available free blocks, operating system must decide which free block to allocate to a process. Operating system makes use of one of the following three algorithms for this purpose.

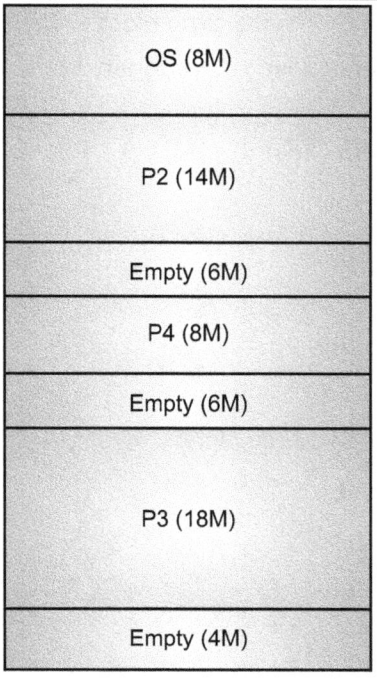

Fig. 3.13 : Process allocation using dynamic partitioning

1. **Best-Fit Algorithm**
   - Chooses the block that is closest in size to the request.
   - Since smallest block is found for process, the smallest amount of fragmentation is left.
   - Memory compaction must be done more often.

2. **First-Fit Algorithm**
   - Scans memory form the beginning and chooses the first available block that is large enough.
   - This is fastest one than other two placement algorithms.

3. **Worst Fit**
   - This uses largest whole to allocate a process.
   - This causes maximum portion of a block to leftover as an unused portion.
   - This is not algorithm that one should use.
   - This causes fragmentation.

4. **Next-Fit**
   - Scans memory from the location of the last placement.
   - More often allocate a block of memory at the end of memory where the largest block is found.
   - The largest block of memory is broken up into smaller blocks.

- Compaction is required to obtain a large block at the end of memory.

Program 3.2 : /* Write a menu driven C program to implement memory management algorithms.
1. FIRST FIT   2. BEST FIT   3. WORST FIT*/

```c
#include<stdio.h>
#include<conio.h>
void accept(int a[],int n)
{
    int i;
    for(i=0;i<n;i++)
    {
        scanf("%d",&a[i]);
    }
}
void display(int a[],int n)
{
    int i;
    printf("\n\n");
    for(i=0;i<n;i++)
    {
        printf("\t%d ",a[i]);
    }
}
void sort(int a[],int n)
{
    int i,j,temp;
    for(i=0;i<n-1;i++)
    {
        for(j=0;j<n-1;j++)
        {
            if(a[j]>a[j+1])
            {
                temp=a[j];
                a[j]=a[j+1];
                a[j+1]=temp;
            }
```

```c
        }
    }
}
void first_fit(int psize[],int np,int msize[],int nm)
{
      int i,j,itot,etot,flag[30]={0};
      itot=etot=0;
    for(i=0;i<np;i++)
    {
        for(j=0;j<nm;j++)
        {
            if(flag[j]==0 && msize[j]>=psize[i])
            {
                flag[j]=1;
                itot=itot+msize[j]-psize[i];
                break;
            }
        }
        if(j==nm)
            printf("\n\nTHERE IS NO SPACE FOR PROCESS %d ",i);
    }
    for(i=0;i<nm;i++)
    {
        if(flag[i]==0)
            etot=etot+msize[i];
    }
    printf("\n\nPROCESSES::");
    display(psize,np);
    printf("\n\nMEMORY HOLES::");
    display(msize,nm);
    printf("\n\nTOTAL SUM OF INTERNAL FRAGMENTATION = %d ",itot);
    printf("\n\nTOTAL SUM OF EXTERNAL FRAGMENTATION = %d ",etot);
}
void best_fit(int psize[],int np,int msize[],int nm)
{
    int i,j,itot,etot,temp[30],flag[30]={0};
```

```c
    itot=etot=0;
    for(i=0;i<nm;i++)
        temp[i]=msize[i];
    sort(temp,nm);
    for(i=0;i<np;i++)
    {
        for(j=0;j<nm;j++)
        {
            if(flag[j]==0 && temp[j]>=psize[i])
            {
                flag[j]=1;
                itot=itot+temp[j]-psize[i];
                break;
            }
        }
        if(j==nm)
            printf("\n\nTHERE IS NO SPACE FOR PROCESS %d ",i);
    }
    for(i=0;i<nm;i++)
    {
        if(flag[i]==0)
            etot=etot+temp[i];
    }
    printf("\n\nPROCESSES::");
    display(psize,np);
    printf("\n\nMEMORY HOLES::");
    display(temp,nm);
    printf("\n\nTOTAL SUM OF INTERNAL FRAGMENTATION = %d ",itot);
    printf("\n\nTOTAL SUM OF EXTERNAL FRAGMENTATION = %d ",etot);
}
void worst_fit(int psize[],int np,int msize[],int nm)
{
    int i,j,itot,etot,temp[30],flag[30]={0};
    itot=etot=0;
    for(i=0;i<nm;i++)
        temp[i]=msize[i];
```

```
    sort(temp,nm);
    for(i=0;i<np;i++)
    {
        for(j=nm-1;j>=0;j--)
        {
            if(flag[j]==0 && temp[j]>=psize[i])
            {
                flag[j]=1;
                itot=itot+temp[j]-psize[i];
                break;
            }
        }
        if(j==nm)
            printf("\n\nTHERE IS NO SPACE FOR PROCESS %d ",i);
    }
    for(i=0;i<nm;i++)
    {
        if(flag[i]==0)
            etot=etot+temp[i];
    }
    printf("\n\nPROCESSES::");
    display(psize,np);
    printf("\n\nMEMORY HOLES::");
    display(temp,nm);
    printf("\n\nTOTAL SUM OF INTERNAL FRAGMENTATION = %d ",itot);
    printf("\n\nTOTAL SUM OF EXTERNAL FRAGMENTATION = %d ",etot);
}
/**********************************************************************/
void main()
{
    int ch,np,nm,psize[30],msize[30];
    clrscr();
    printf("\nENTER NO OF PROCESSES::");
    scanf("%d",&np);
    printf("\n\nENTER SIZES OF PROCESSES::");
    accept(psize,np);
```

```c
printf("\nENTER NO MEMORY HOLES::");
scanf("%d",&nm);
printf("\n\nENTER SIZES OF MEMORY HOLES::");
accept(msize,nm);
while(1)
{
    printf("\n\n\t\t**MAIN MENU**");
    printf("\n\n\tMEMORY MANAGEMENT");
    printf("\n\n\t1.FIRST FIT");
    printf("\n\n\t2.BEST FIT");
    printf("\n\n\t3.WORST FIT");
    printf("\n\n\t4.QUIT");
    printf("\n\nENTER YOUR CHOICE::");
    scanf("%d",&ch);
    switch(ch)
    {
        case 1 :
            printf("\n\nFIRST FIT::\n");
            first_fit(psize,np,msize,nm);
            break;
        case 2 :
            printf("\n\n\tBEST FIT::\n");
            best_fit(psize,np,msize,nm);
            break;
        case 3 :
            printf("\n\n\tWORST FIT::\n");
            worst_fit(psize,np,msize,nm);
            break;
        case 4 :
            exit(0);
        default:
            printf("\n\nPLEASE ENTER CORRECT CHOICE!!");
    }
    getch();
}
}
```

OUTPUT

```
/*OUTPUT
ENTER NO OF PROCESSES::5
ENTER SIZES OF PROCESSES::10 20 15 30 45
ENTER NO MEMORY HOLES::7
ENTER SIZES OF MEMORY HOLES::5 15 10 35 25 20 25
**MAIN MENU**
    MEMORY MANAGEMENT
    1.FIRST FIT
    2.BEST FIT
    3.WORST FIT
    4.QUIT
ENTER YOUR CHOICE::1
FIRST FIT::
THERE IS NO SPACE FOR PROCESS 3
THERE IS NO SPACE FOR PROCESS 4
PROCESSES::
    10   20   15   30   45
MEMORY HOLES::
    5   15   10   35   25   20   25
TOTAL SUM OF INTERNAL FRAGMENTATION = 30
TOTAL SUM OF EXTERNAL FRAGMENTATION = 60
ENTER YOUR CHOICE::2
    BEST FIT::
THERE IS NO SPACE FOR PROCESS 4
PROCESSES::
    10   20   15   30   45
MEMORY HOLES::
    5   10   15   20   25   25   35
TOTAL SUM OF INTERNAL FRAGMENTATION = 5
TOTAL SUM OF EXTERNAL FRAGMENTATION = 55
ENTER YOUR CHOICE::3
    WORST FIT::
```

```
PROCESSES::
    10   20   15   30   45
MEMORY HOLES::
    5   10   15   20   25   25   35
TOTAL SUM OF INTERNAL FRAGMENTATION = 40
TOTAL SUM OF EXTERNAL FRAGMENTATION = 50
ENTER YOUR CHOICE::4
```

D. MEMORY ALLOCATION

3.14 ALLOCATION STRATEGY

We just saw four memory allocation algorithms that operating system uses to allocate a process. They are namely best fit, first fit, next fit and worst fit. Fig. illustrates allocation of process using all these four techniques. As shown in Fig., it is recommended that operating system uses best fit strategy. By using best fit at-least there would be less unused space left after allocation. Fig. 3.14. shows example of memory configuration before and after allocation of 16KB block using all four memory allocation algorithms.

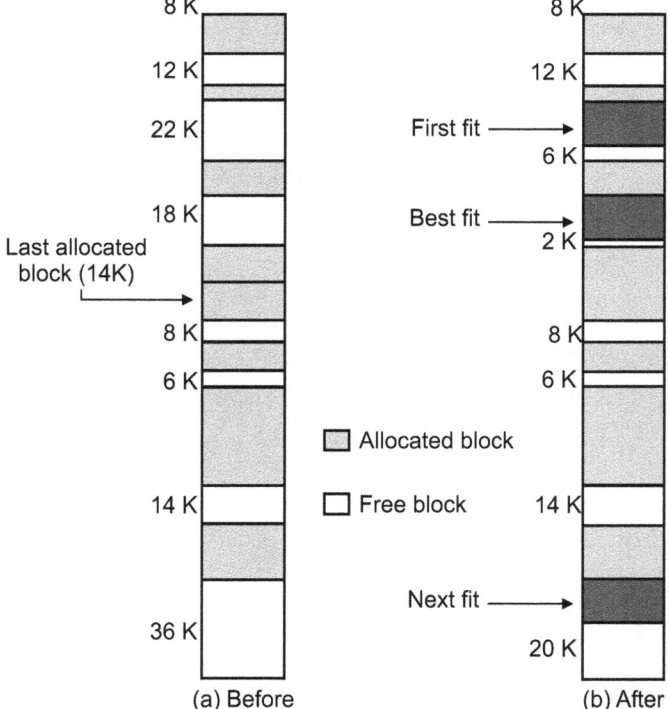

Fig. 3.14 : Example memory configuration before and after allocation of 16KB block

3.15 SWAPPING

Swapping is a mechanism in which a process can be swapped temporarily out of main memory to a backing store and then brought back into memory for continued execution.

Backing store is a usually a hard disk drive or any other secondary storage which is fast in access and large enough to accommodate copies of all memory images for all users. It must be capable of providing direct access to these memory images. Major time consuming part of swapping is transfer time. Total transfer time is directly proportional to the amount of memory swapped. Let us assume that the user process is of size 100KB and the backing store is a standard hard disk with transfer rate of 1 MB per second. The actual transfer of the 100K process to or from memory will take 100KB /1000KB per second = 1/10 second = 100 milliseconds.

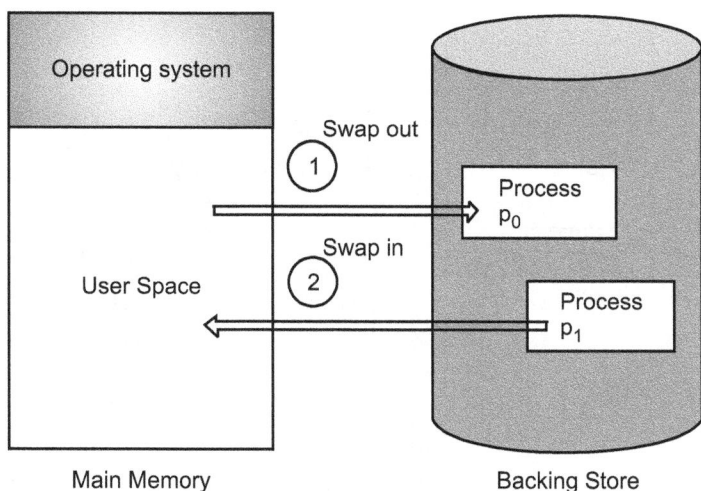

Fig. 3.15 : Swapping mechanism

Fig. 3.15 focus on swapping mechanism used in operating system. Swap out is done from main memory to backing store and swap in is done between backing store to main memory.

When the physical memory in the system runs out and a process needs to bring a page into memory then the operating system must decide what to do. It must fairly share the physical pages in the system between the processes running in the system, therefore it may need to remove one or more pages from the system to make room for the new page to be brought into memory. How virtual pages are selected for removal from physical memory affects the efficiency of the system. Linux uses a page aging technique to fairly choose pages which might be removed from the system. This scheme involves every page in the system having an age which changes as the page is accessed. The more that a page is accessed, the younger it is; the less that it is accessed the older it becomes. Old pages are good candidates for swapping.

If the page to be removed came from an image or data file and has not been written to then the page does not need to be saved. Instead it can be discarded and if the process needs that page again it can be brought back into memory from the image or data file again. However, if the page has been written to then the operating system must preserve the contents of that page so that it can be accessed at a later time.

This type of page is known as a *dirty* page and it is saved in a special sort of file called the swap file. These unwanted *dirty* virtual pages are stored on hard disk in the swap file. Accesses to the disk are very long relative to the speed of the CPU and the operating system must juggle the need to write pages to disk with the need to retain them in memory to be used again. The operating system must use an algorithm which fairly swaps out the less used pages of the processes competing for resources. If the swapping algorithm is not efficient then a condition known as *thrashing* occurs. In this case, pages are constantly being written to disk and then being read back and the operating system is too busy to allow much real work to be performed

Memory Allocation

Main memory usually has two partitions :

1. **Low Memory** - Operating system resides in this memory.
2. **High Memory** - User processes then held in high memory.

Operating system uses the following memory allocation mechanism.

S.N.	Memory Allocation	Description
1	Single-partition allocation	In this type of allocation, relocation-register scheme is used to protect user processes from each other and from changing operating-system code and data. Smallest physical address is stored in relocation register and logical address is kept in limit register. Each logical address must be less than the limit register.
2	Multiple-partition allocation	In this type of allocation, main memory is divided into a number of fixed-sized partitions where each partition should contain only one process. When a partition is free, a process is selected from the input queue and is loaded into the free partition. When the process terminates, the partition becomes available for another process.

3.16 FRAGMENTATION

As processes are loaded and removed from memory, the free memory space is broken into little pieces. It happens after sometimes that processes cannot be allocated to memory blocks considering their small size and memory blocks remains unused. This problem is known as fragmentation.

Fragmentation is of two types :

S.N.	Fragmentation	Description
1	External fragmentation	Total memory space is enough to satisfy a request or to reside a process in it, but it is not contiguous so it cannot be used.
2	Internal fragmentation	Memory block assigned to process is bigger. Some portion of memory is left unused as it cannot be used by another process.

External fragmentation can be reduced by compaction or shuffle memory contents to place all free memory together in one large block. To make compaction feasible, relocation should be dynamic.

Internal Fragmentation

Internal fragmentation occurs when the memory allocator leaves extra space empty inside of a block of memory that has been allocated for a client. This usually happens because the processor's design stipulates that memory must be cut into blocks of certain sizes for example, blocks may be required to be evenly be divided by four, eight or 16 bytes. When this occurs, a client that needs 57 bytes of memory, for example, may be allocated a block that contains 60 bytes, or even 64. The extra bytes that the client doesn't need go to waste and over time these tiny chunks of unused memory can build up and create large quantities of memory that can't be put to use by the allocator. Because all of these useless bytes are inside larger memory blocks, the fragmentation is considered internal.

External Fragmentation

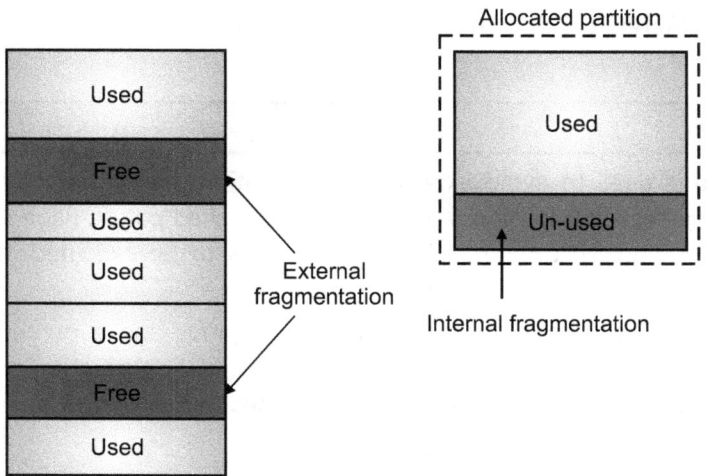

Fig. 3.16 : External and Internal Fragmentation

External fragmentation happens when the memory allocator leaves sections of unused memory blocks between portions of allocated memory. For example, if several memory blocks are allocated in a continuous line but one of the middle blocks in the line is freed (perhaps because the process that was using that block of memory stopped running), the free block is fragmented. The block is still available for use by the allocator later if there's a need for memory that fits in that block, but the block is now unusable for larger memory needs. It cannot be lumped back in with the total free memory available to the system, as total memory must be contiguous for it to be useable for larger tasks. In this way, entire sections of free memory can end up isolated from the whole that are often too small for significant use, which creates an overall reduction of free memory that over time can lead to a lack of available memory for key tasks.

Showing diagrammatically external and internal fragmentation in Fig. 3.16.

Fragmentation can Mean Big Problems for Systems

Fragmentation can become an issue because it builds up over time, creating small and useless blocks of memory and limiting the amount of a computer's available free memory. As it progresses, fragmentation can cause system performance to become slow and sluggish in the short term; in the long term, fragmentation can shorten the life of a computer or server by 30 percent on average. Of the two types of fragmentation, internal is more predictable than external because the amount of wasted space is determined by the memory allocator's parameters (how big the allocated blocks must be), which is a constant. In addition, the amount of overall memory lost to internal fragmentation is usually less than what's lost to external fragmentation, although it can gradually accumulate. External fragmentation, on the other hand, is harder to predict because in most cases several processes are regularly starting and stopping in the system and blocks of memory that are used for varying lengths of time are freed up in a different order than they were filled, leaving gaps in the available memory.

3.17 PAGING

Paging technique is used to avoid external fragmentation. Paging is a technique in which physical memory is broken into blocks of the same size called pages. Page size is power of 2, between 512 bytes and 8192 bytes. When a process is to be executed, its corresponding pages are loaded into any available memory frames.

Logical address space of a process can be non-contiguous and a process is allocated to physical memory whenever the free memory frame is available. Operating system keeps track of all free frames. Operating system needs 'n' free frames to run a program of size 'n' pages.

Address generated by CPU is divided into

- **Page Number (p):** page number is used as an index into a page table which contains base address of each page in physical memory.
- **Page Offset (d):** page offset is combined with base address to define the physical memory address.

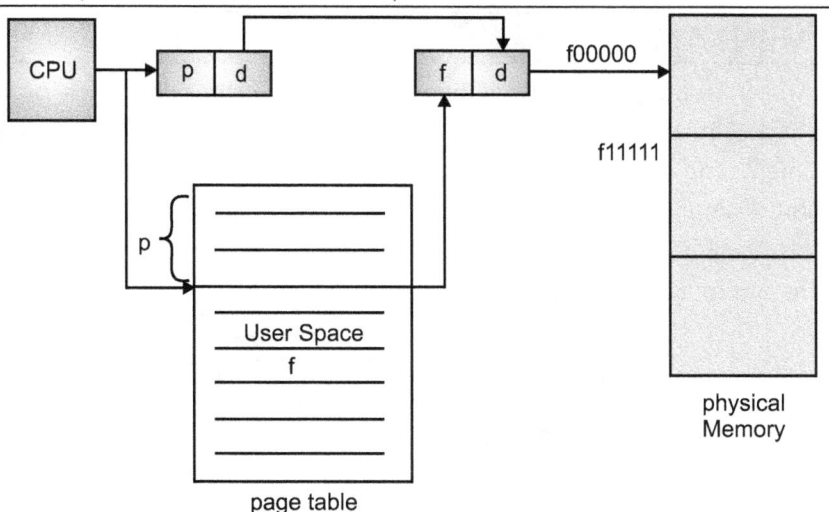

Fig. 3.17 : Address translation using paging mechanism

Fig. 3.17 shows paging mechanism. Page number fetches respective page table entry. This entry and earlier offset given by CPU, when combined together, generates physical address which is an actual entry in physical memory.

Fig. 3.18 shows the paging table architecture. Logical memory holds page numbers. Page number works as an index in page table. Values at these indexes serves as an index of physical memory.

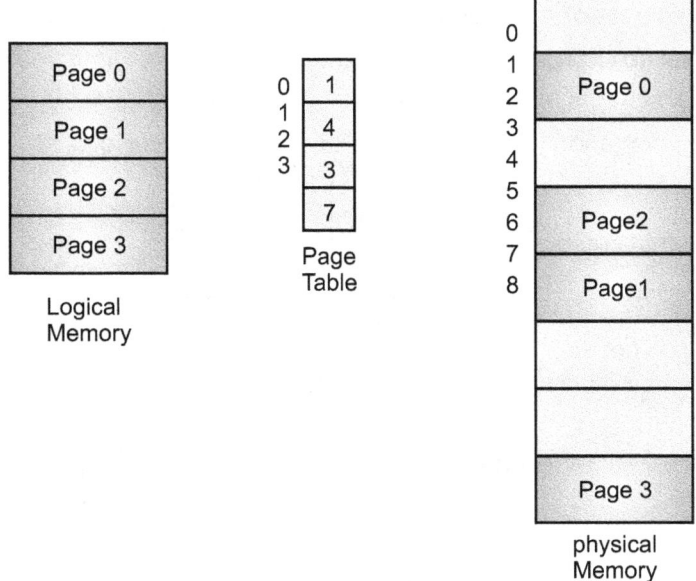

Fig. 3.18 : Paging table architecture

3.18 SEGMENTATION

Segmentation is a technique to break memory into logical pieces. Each of these pieces represents group of related information. Examples of such logical pieces are data segments or code segment for each process, data segment for operating system and so on. Implementation of segmentation is possible with or without paging.

Unlike paging, segments are varying in size. Due to this, it eliminates internal fragmentation. External fragmentation still exists but to lesser extent.

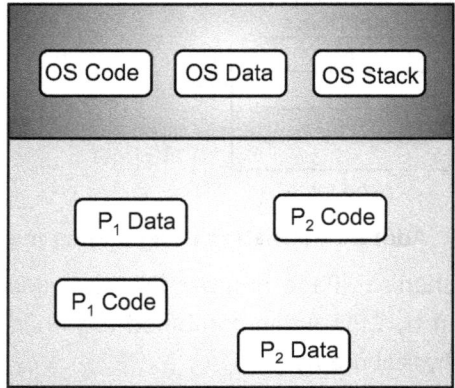

Fig. 3.19 : Logical address space

In this technique, address generated by CPU is divided into

- **Segment Number (s) :** segment number is used as an index into a segment table which contains base address of each segment in physical memory and a limit of segment.
- **Segment Offset (o) :** segment offset is first checked against limit and then is combined with base address to define the physical memory address.
- Working of segmentation for address translation is shown in Fig. 3.20

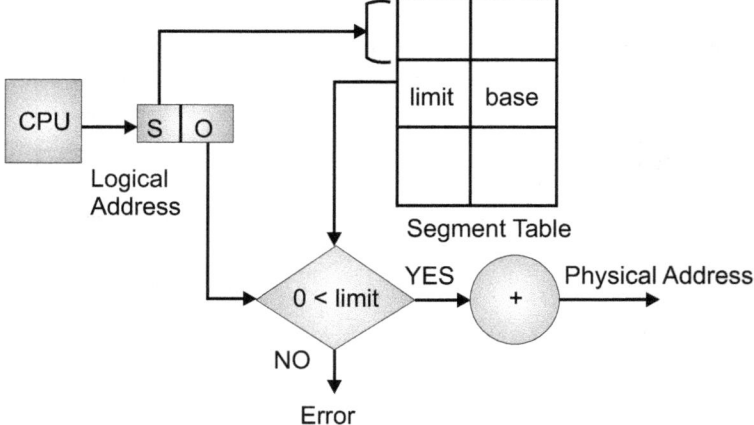

Fig. 3.20 : Address translation using segmentation mechanism

E. VIRTUAL MEMORY MANAGEMENT

3.19 INTRODUCTION TO VIRTUAL MEMORY MANAGEMENT

Processes which are not available completely in memory, for them also virtual memory has made possible execution. The main benefit of using virtual memory is that even though programs are larger than main memory, with the help of virtual memory, they can be executed well. It is said that virtual memory is a separation of user's logical memory from main memory. So when only smaller main memory is available, this separation allows extremely large virtual memory to be provided. Few considerations about virtual memory :

- User written error handling routines are used only when an error occurs in the data or computation.
- User rarely uses certain options and features of program.
- Many tables are assigned a fixed amount of address space even though only a small amount of the table is actually used.
- There are many benefits of having an ability to execute a program that resides only partially in memory.
- To swap or load each user program, less number of I/O would be needed.
- A program would no longer be constrained by the amount of physical memory that is available.
- Each user program could take less physical memory. More programs could be run the same time, with a corresponding increase in CPU utilization and throughput.
- Fig. 3.21 shows mapping of virtual memory to physical memory. In this, virtual memory uses memory map to make mapping to physical memory. It mean pages that are available in virtual memory, with the help of memory map, will be loaded into physical memory as and when needed. Physical memory does take benefit from backing store.

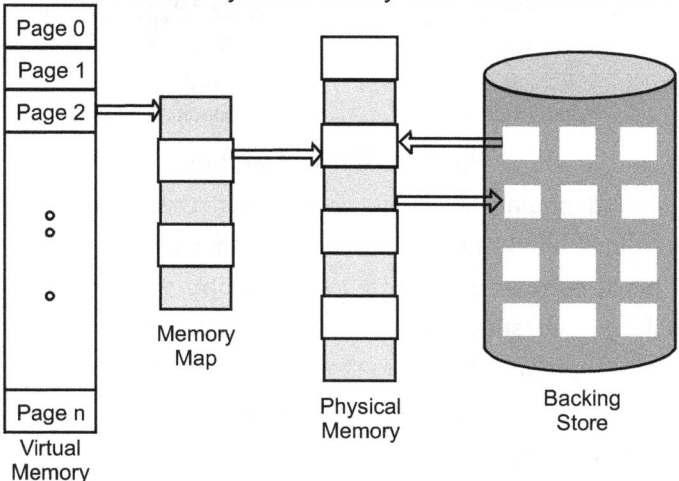

Fig. 3.21 : Mapping of virtual memory to physical memory

Demand paging is commonly used to implement virtual memory. Segmentation can also be used for this purpose. Demand segmentation is also another alternative.

3.19.1 Demand Paging

A demand paging system is quite similar to a paging system with swapping. Process is swapped into memory when it needed to be executed. A lazy swapper called pager is used rather than swapping an entire process.

When a process to be swapped in, a pager guess which page will be used before process is swapped out again. The job of pager would be to swap only essential part of process into main memory instead of entire process. This helps to decrease the swap time as well as amount of physical memory needed.

Hardware support is required that makes use of valid-invalid bit scheme to distinguish between pages that are in memory and pages that are on the disk. Valid and invalid pages can be checked by checking the bit. If process never attempts to access the page then marking a page does not any effect. Execution proceeds normally when process executes and accesses pages that are memory resident.

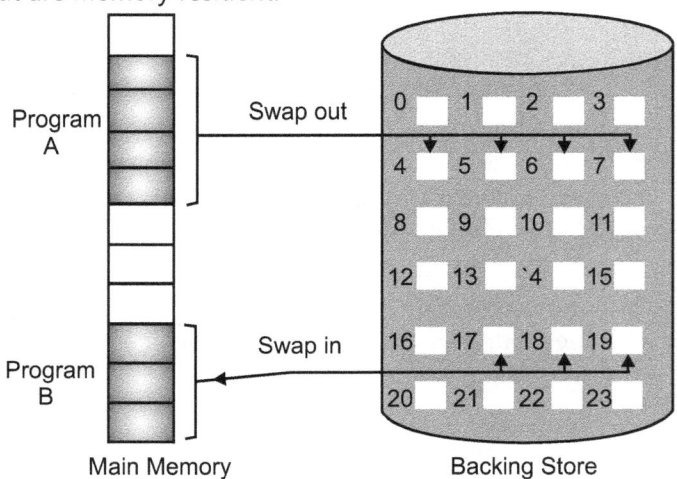

Fig. 3.22 : Demand paging

Fig. 3.22 shows demand paging. As name suggest, in this scheme only pages that are demanded are taken into main memory. For e.g. as shown in Fig. 3.22, program B needs pages available at block number 17,18 and 19 in backing store which are swapped in the main memory. Similarly program A pages are not needed in main memory, so they are swapped out from main memory to backing store and kept at block numbers 4,5,6 and 7.

Access to a page marked invalid causes a page-fault trap. This trap is the result of the operating system's failure to bring the desired page into memory. It is desirable to reduce page faults to the minimum count. Page fault can be handled as following :

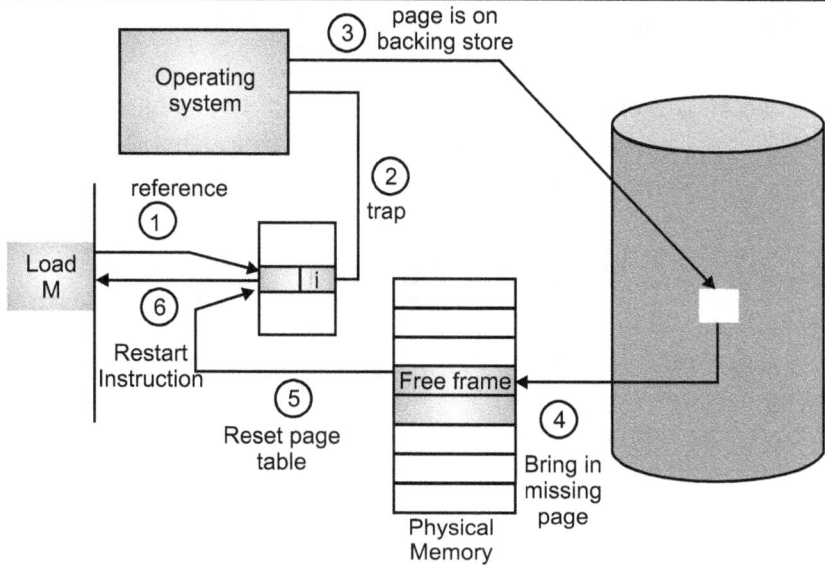

Fig. 3.23 : Handling page faults

Step	Description
Step 1	Determine whether the reference to process was a valid or invalid memory access. Check internal table for this purpose.
Step 2	Terminate the process if the reference was invalid. If it was valid, next stage is to bring it.
Step 3	Find a free frame.
Step 4	Schedule a disk operation to read the desired page into the newly allocated frame.
Step 5	When the disk read is complete, modify the internal table kept with the process and the page table to indicate that the page is now in memory.
Step 6	Restart the instruction that was interrupted by the illegal address trap. The process can now access the page as though it had always been in memory. Therefore, the operating system reads the desired page into memory and restarts the process as though the page had always been in memory.

Advantages of Demand Paging

Following are the advantages of demand paging

- Provides large virtual memory.
- Enables more efficient use of memory.
- Deals with unconstrained multiprogramming. There is no limit on degree of multiprogramming.

Disadvantages of Demand Paging

Following are the disadvantages of demand paging
- Number of tables and amount of processor overhead for handling page interrupts are greater than in the case of the simple paged management techniques.
- Due to the lack of explicit constraints on jobs, address space size is more.

3.20 PAGE REPLACEMENT ALGORITHM

Page replacement algorithms are the techniques using which operating system decides which memory pages to swap out, write to disk when a page of memory needs to be allocated. Paging happens whenever a page fault occurs and a free page cannot be used for allocation purpose accounting to reason that pages are not available or the number of free pages is lower than required pages.

When the page that was selected for replacement and was paged out is referenced again then it has to read in from disk and this requires for I/O completion. This process determines the quality of the page replacement algorithm : the lesser the time waiting for page-ins, the better is the algorithm. A page replacement algorithm looks at the limited information about accessing the pages provided by hardware and tries to select which pages should be replaced to minimize the total number of page misses, while balancing it with the costs of primary storage and processor time of the algorithm itself. There are many different page replacement algorithms. We evaluate an algorithm by running it on a particular string of memory reference and computing the number of page faults.

Reference String

Reference string is term which is used to refer string of memory references.

The string of memory references is called reference string. Reference strings are generated artificially. It can also be generated by tracing a given system and recording the address of each memory reference. The latter choice produces a large number of data, where we note two things.
- We do not consider the entire address, we just consider page number for a given page size.
- If we have a reference to a page p, then any immediately following references to page p will never cause a page fault. Page p will be in memory after the first reference; the immediately following references will not have fault.
- For example, consider the given sequence of addresses - 123,215,600,1234,76,96
- If page size is 100 then the reference string is 1,2,6,12,0,0

1. **First in First Out (FIFO) Algorithm**
- In this, the page which is the oldest one will be selected for replacement.
- This algorithm is easy to implement.
- It maintains a list and replaces pages from the tail and adds new pages at the head.

Reference string : 0, 2, 1, 6, 4, 0, 1, 0, 3, 1, 2, 1

Misses   : x x x x x x   x x x

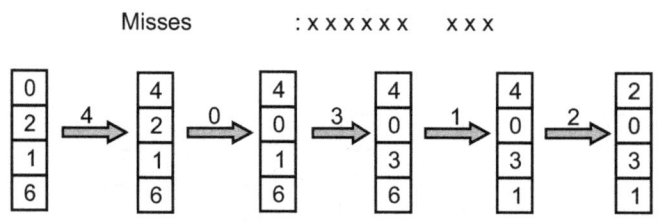

Fault rate = 9/12 = 0.75

Fig. 3.24 : Example of FIFO

As shown in Fig. 3.24, lets consider reference string 0,2,1,6,4,0,1,0,3,1,2,1 with frame size 4. First four pages, means 0,2,1,6 are not available in memory. So initial page miss or page faults are four. Now next page to be brought into memory in '4' and there is no free frame. So decision need to be taken on which page to be replaced to put new page. As we need to use FIFO strategy, page '0' was the oldest one and this has to get replace. So we replace page '0' by page '4' and this cause one more page fault. Subsequently other pages are brought into memory and replacement is needed. Total page fault occurred are : 9.

2. **Optimal Page Replacement Algorithm**
- An optimal page replacement algorithm has the lowest page-fault rate of all algorithms.
- The page which is not used for longest time will be replaced first. It means future reference of page is checked before replacement.

Reference string : 0, 2, 1, 6, 4, 0, 1, 0, 3, 1, 2, 1

Misses   : x x x x x   x

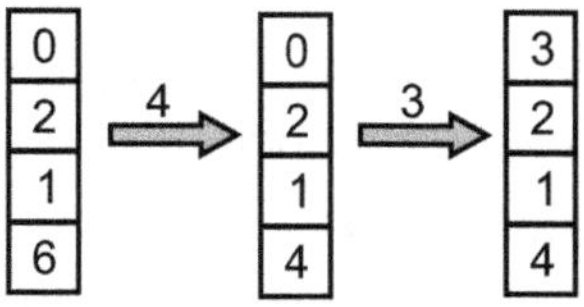

Fault rate = 6/12 = 0.50

Fig. 3.25 : Page replacement example

As shown in Fig. 3.25, consider the reference string 0,2,1,6,4,0,1,0,3,1,2,1. Initial page faults are 4. Next page to be brought in memory is '4'. As you can see, page '6' is not needed in near future, so this is the best one to be replaced by page '4'. At this position one more page fault occurs. When page '3' is needed to be brought in memory, it is replaced by page '0'. Total page faults accured are : 6.

3. **Least Recently Used (LRU) Algorithm**
- Page which has not been used for the longest time in main memory is the one which will be selected for replacement.
- This algorithm is easy to implement.

- It keeps a list and replaces pages by looking back into time.

Reference string : 0, 2, 1, 6, 4, 0, 1, 0, 3, 1, 2, 1

Misses : x x x x x x   x x

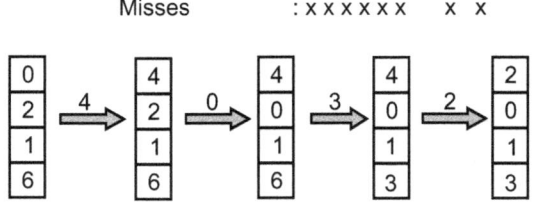

Fault rate = 8/12 = 0.67

Fig. 3.26 : LRU example

As shown in Fig. 3.26, consider reference string 0,2,1,6,4,0,1,0,3,1,2,1. Initial page faults are 4. Next page to be brought in memory is '4'. As you can see, page '0' is not used since longest, so this is replaced by page '4'. At this position one more page fault occurs. Next page '0' is needed to be brought in memory, it is replaced by page '2' as it has not been used since longest. Subsequently other new pages are replaced. Total page faults accured are : 8.

4. **Page Buffering Algorithm**
- Keep a pool of free frames to start process quickly.
- On page fault, select a page to be replaced.
- Write new page in the frame of free pool, mark the page table and restart the process.
- Dirty page is needed to be written out of disk. Place the frame holding replaced page in free pool.

5. **Least Frequently Used (LFU) Algorithm**
- Page with the smallest count is the one which will be selected for replacement.
- This algorithm suffers from the situation in which a page is used heavily during the initial phase of a process, but then is never used again.

6. **Most Frequently Used (MFU) Algorithm**
- This algorithm is based on the argument that the page with the smallest count was probably just brought in and has yet to be used.

Program 3.3 : Write a program for page replacement algorithm.

```
#include<stdio.h>
int n,pg[30],fr[10];
void fifo();
void optimal();
void lru();
void main()
{
    int i,ch;
```

```c
    printf("\nEnter total number of pages:");
    scanf("%d",&n);
    printf("\nEnter sequence:");
    for(i=0;i<n;i++)    //accepting sequence
        scanf("%d",&pg[i]);
    do
    {
        printf("\n\tMENU\n");
        printf("\n1)FIFO");
        printf("\n2)OPTIMAL");
        printf("\n3)LRU");
        printf("\n4)Exit");
        printf("\nEnter your choice:");
        scanf("%d",&ch);
        switch(ch)
        {
            case 1 : fifo();
                break;
            case 2 : optimal();
                break;
            case 3 : lru();
                break;
        }
    }while(ch!=4);
    getchar();
}
void fifo()
{
    int i,f,r,s,count,flag,num,psize;
    f=0;
    r=0;
    s=0;
    flag=0;
    count=0;
```

```c
printf("\nEnter size of page frame:");
scanf("%d",&psize);
for(i=0;i<psize;i++)
{
    fr[i]=-1;
}
while(s<n)
{
    flag=0;
    num=pg[s];
    for(i=0;i<psize;i++)
    {
        if(num==fr[i])
        {
            s++;
            flag=1;
            break;
        }
    }
    if(flag==0)
    {
        if(r<psize)
        {
            fr[r]=pg[s];
            r++;
            s++;
            count++;
        }
        else
        {
            if(f<psize)
            {
                fr[f]=pg[s];
                s++;
```

```c
                    f++;
                    count++;
                }
                else
                    f=0;
            }
        }
        printf("\n");
        for(i=0;i<psize;i++)
        {
            printf("%d\t",fr[i]);
        }
    }
printf("\nPage Faults=%d",count);
getchar();
}
void optimal()
{
    int count[10],i,j,k,fault,f,flag,temp,current,c,dist,max,m,cnt,p,x;
    fault=0;
    dist=0;
    k=0;
    printf("\nEnter frame size:");
    scanf("%d",&f);
    //initilizing distance and frame array
    for(i=0;i<f;i++)
    {
        count[i]=0;
        fr[i]=-1;
    }
    for(i=0;i<n;i++)
    {
        flag=0;
        temp=pg[i];
```

```
        for(j=0;j<f;j++)
        {
            if(temp==fr[j])
            {
                flag=1;
                break;
            }
        }
        if((flag==0)&&(k<f))
        {
            fault++;
            fr[k]=temp;
            k++;
        }
        else if((flag==0)&&(k==f))
        {
            fault++;
            for(cnt=0;cnt<f;cnt++)
            {
                current=fr[cnt];
                for(c=i;c<n;c++)
                {
                    if(current!=pg[c])
                        count[cnt]++;
                    else
                        break;
                }
            }
            max=0;
            for(m=0;m<f;m++)
            {
                if(count[m]>max)
                {
                    max=count[m];
```

```c
                p=m;
            }
        }
        fr[p]=temp;
    }
    printf("\n");
    for(x=0;x<f;x++)
    {
        printf("%d\t",fr[x]);
    }
  }
  printf("\nTotal number of faults=%d",fault);
  getchar();
}
void lru()
{
    int count[10],i,j,k,fault,f,flag,temp,current,c,dist,max,m,cnt,p,x;
    fault=0;
    dist=0;
    k=0;
    printf("\nEnter frame size:");
    scanf("%d",&f);
    //initilizing distance and frame array
    for(i=0;i<f;i++)
    {
        count[i]=0;
        fr[i]=-1;
    }
    for(i=0;i<n;i++)
    {
        flag=0;
        temp=pg[i];
        for(j=0;j<f;j++)
        {
```

```
            if(temp==fr[j])
            {
                flag=1;
                break;
            }
        }
        if((flag==0)&&(k<f))
        {
            fault++;
            fr[k]=temp;
            k++;
        }
        else if((flag==0)&&(k==f))
        {
            fault++;
            for(cnt=0;cnt<f;cnt++)
            {
                current=fr[cnt];
                for(c=i;c>0;c--)
                {
                    if(current!=pg[c])
                        count[cnt]++;
                    else
                        break;
                }
            }
            max=0;
            for(m=0;m<f;m++)
            {
                if(count[m]>max)
                {
                    max=count[m];
                    p=m;
                }
```

```c
            }
            fr[p]=temp;
        }
        printf("\n");
        for(x=0;x<f;x++)
        {
            printf("%d\t",fr[x]);
        }
    }
    printf("\nTotal number of faults=%d",fault);
    getchar();
}
```

OUTPUT

----------Output for PAGE REPLACEMENT ALGORITHM----------
Enter total number of pages:16
Enter sequence:0 1 2 3 0 1 2 3 0 1 2 3 4 5 6 7
    MENU
1)FIFO
2)OPTIMAL
3)LRU
4)Exit
Enter your choice:1
Enter size of page frame:3

0	-1	-1
0	1	-1
0	1	2
3	1	2
3	0	2
3	0	1
3	0	1
2	0	1
2	3	1
2	3	0
2	3	0

```
1   3   0
1   2   0
1   2   3
1   2   3
4   2   3
4   5   3
4   5   6
4   5   6
7   5   6
```
Page Faults=16

```
    MENU
1)FIFO
2)OPTIMAL
3)LRU
4)Exit
```
Enter your choice:2
Enter frame size:3

```
0   -1  -1
0   1   -1
0   1   2
0   1   3
0   1   3
0   1   3
0   2   3
0   2   3
0   2   3
1   2   3
1   2   3
1   2   3
4   2   3
5   2   3
6   2   3
7   2   3
```
Total number of faults=10

```
      MENU
1)FIFO
2)OPTIMAL
3)LRU
4)Exit
Enter your choice:3
Enter frame size:3
0    -1    -1
0     1    -1
0     1     2
3     1     2
3     0     2
1     0     2
1     0     2
1     3     2
0     3     2
1     3     2
1     3     2
1     3     2
4     3     2
4     3     5
6     3     5
6     7     5
Total number of faults=13
```

3.21 THRASHING

In operating systems that implement a virtual memory space, the programs allocate memory from an address space that may be much larger than the actual amount of RAM the system possesses. The operating system is responsible for deciding which programs need to be in actual RAM.

While programs are "out", it needs a place to keep things. This is called swap space as operating system is swapping the processes in and out as and when needed. Swapping is a time consuming task. Thrashing is a situation in which maximum time of CPU is just wasted in doing swap in and swap out.

Thrashing can be avoided by running fewer programs, writing programs that use memory more efficiently, adding RAM to system and some time may be even increasing swap size.

In another terms, thrashing is a state in which CPU performs "productive" work less and "swapping" more. CPU is busy in swapping the pages so much that it cannot respond to user program as quick as it should.

3.21.1 Reason behind Thrashing to Occur

In computer system thrashing occurs when there are too many pages in memory and each page refers to another page. The real memory shortens in capacity to have all the pages in it, so it uses "virtual memory". When each page in execution demands that page that is not currently in real memory (RAM), it keeps some pages on virtual memory and then makes an adjustment of the required page on RAM. If CPU is so much busy in doing this task, thrashing occurs.

Thrashing occurs when a system spends more time processing page faults than executing transactions. While processing page faults is necessary to in order to appreciate the benefits of virtual memory, thrashing has a negative affect on the system.

As the page fault rate increases, more transactions need processing from the paging device. The queue at the paging device increases, resulting in increased service time for a page fault. While the transactions in the system are waiting for the paging device, CPU utilization, system throughput and system response time decrease, resulting in below optimal performance of a system.

Thrashing becomes a greater threat as the degree of multiprogramming of the system increases.

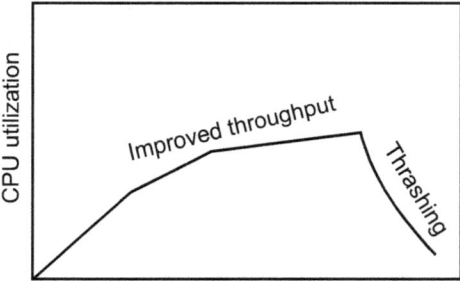

Fig. 3.27 : Degree of Multiprogramming

This graph shows that there is a degree of multiprogramming that is optimal for system performance CPU utilization reaches a maximum before a swift decline as the degree of multiprogramming increases and thrashing occurs in the over-extended system. This indicates that controlling the load on the system is important to avoiding thrashing. In the system represented by the graph, it is important to maintain the multiprogramming degree that corresponds to the peak of the graph.

The selection of a replacement policy to implement virtual memory plays an imporant part in the elimination of the potential for thrashing. A policy based on the local mode will tend to limit the effect of thrashing. In local mode, a transaction will replace pages from its assigned partition. Its need to access memory will not affect transactions using other partitions. If other transactions have enough page frames in the partitions they occupy, they will continue to be processed efficiently.

A replacement policy based on the global mode is more likely to cause thrashing. Since all pages of memory are available to all transactions, a memory-intensive transaction may occupy a large portion of memory, making other transactions susceptible to page faults and resulting in a system that thrashes.

Other ways of preventing thrashing include using the working set strategy, preparing a transactions partition and increasing page size.

QUESTIONS

1. What is deadlock? Explain with an example.
2. What are the necessary conditions for deadlock to exist?
3. What is resource allocation graph? How it can be used to show deadlock presence.
4. Explain with example deadlock avoidance and deadlock detection.
5. Define safe state and unsafe state.
6. What is banker's algorithm? Use given initial state to explain more about it.

	R1	R2	R3
P1	3	2	2
P2	6	1	3
P3	3	1	4
P4	4	2	2

Claim matrix C

	R1	R2	R3
P1	1	0	0
P2	6	1	2
P3	2	1	1
P4	0	0	2

Allocation matrix A

	R1	R2	R3
P1	2	2	2
P2	0	0	1
P3	1	0	3
P4	4	2	0

C – A

R1	R2	R3
9	3	6

Resource vector R

R1	R2	R3
0	1	1

Available vector V

(a) Initial state

7. Explain at-least two strategies to be applied for deadlock recovery.
8. Why memory management is important? Explain base register and limit register used in memory protection.
9. Define following terms in concern with memory management
   a. Logical address
   b. Physical address
   c. Static linking

d. Dynamic linking
   e. Frame
   f. Segment
10. Why memory partitioning is needed? Explain any two memory partitioning techniques.
11. Explain with examples following memory allocations algorithms
    a. First fit
    b. Best fit
    c. Worst fit
12. Differentiate between internal fragmentation and external fragmentation.
13. Explain address translation using paging mechanism with neat diagram.
14. Explain address translation using segmentation mechanism with neat diagram.
15. What is page fault? How it can be handled?
16. Use FIFO, Optimal and LRU page replacement algorithm and calculate number of page faults. Given reference string is {0,2,1,6,4,0,1,0,2,1,3,1} with frame size 4.
17. What is thrashing? Why it needs to be avoided?

Unit - IV

STORAGE MANAGEMENT

4.0 INTRODUCTION

This unit focus on overall storage management required in operating system. Here we start with get to know more about basics concepts of file, file organization like sequential organization, line sequential organization, indexed sequential organization etc. We see in detail different file access methods and directory structures like single level, two level, tree structured and acyclic graph structure etc. Besides this, we discuss disk space allocation methods in terms of contiguous and non-contiguous (which includes chained and indexed allocation) At the last in this unit we present disk scheduling algorithms like FCFS, SSTF, SCAN, C-SCAN, LOOK etc. With their examples and discuss their advantages and disadvantages.

4.1 GENERAL CONCEPTS OF FILE

File system can be thought as a data structure. It helps to organize files and directories on storage disk. It simplifies retrieval of files as and when needed. On a disk partition, only one file system resides.

File is referred as collection of records. Inode is a structure which stores all file related information into it.

Directory is a container which stores files and other directories inside it. Directory is seen as another type of file.

So simply speaking, files and directories, when combined together, makes up file system. File is usually a sequence of bytes with two views :

- Logical (programmer) view, as the users see it (how they are used and what properties they have).
- Physical (OS) view, as it actually resides on secondary storage.

File creator defines what information a file shall have in it. At generalized level we say that file represents programs and data.

- Data files may be binary, numeric, alphabetic or alphanumeric.
- Files may be free form, such as text files, or may be formatted rigidly.

In general, a file is a sequence of bits, bytes, lines, or records, the meaning of which is defined by the file's creator and user.

Depending on file type, it has a certain defined structure.

4.1.1 File Structure

Operating system keeps file structure in such format which it can understand.

- As mentioned earlier, depending on file type a particular structure is associated with each file.
- A text file is a collection of characters organized into lines.
- A source file is a sequence of procedures and functions.
- An object file is understandable by the machine. It is basically sequence of bytes organized into blocks.
- When operating system defines different file structures, it also contains the code to support these file structure. UNIX, MS-DOS support minimum number of file structure.

File Type

File type helps to distinguish one file from other. The regular file types are text file, source file, binary files, etc. Operating system like MS-DOS and UNIX have the following types of files :

1. **Ordinary Files**
- Ordinary file contains user information.
- Ordinary file holds text, databases and executable program.
- Add, delete, modify are the usual operations which user performs on file.

2. **Directory Files**

As name suggests, these are the files that holds list of file names and related information of such files.

3. **Special Files**
- Device file is alternative term to special file.
- They are called device files as they represent device like printers, tape drives, networks, disks, etc.
- There are two categories of these files as mentioned below.
- **Character Special Files :** It means data is handled character by character.

   For e.g. terminal and printer.
- **Block Special Files :** It means data is handled in blocks. For example disks and tapes.

Program 4.1 : Source Code to Perform File I/O Operations

```
#include<stdio.h>
#include<string.h>
#define SIZE 1
#define NUMELEM 5
int main(void)
```

```c
{
   FILE* fd = NULL;
   char buff[100];
   memset(buff,0,sizeof(buff));
   fd = fopen("test.txt","rw+");
   if(NULL == fd)
   {
      printf("\n fopen() Error!!!\n");
      return 1;
   }
   printf("\n File opened successfully through fopen()\n");
   if(SIZE*NUMELEM != fread(buff,SIZE,NUMELEM,fd))
   {
      printf("\n fread() failed\n");
      return 1;
   }
   printf("\n Some bytes successfully read through fread()\n");
   printf("\n The bytes read are [%s]\n",buff);
   if(0 != fseek(fd,11,SEEK_CUR))
   {
      printf("\n fseek() failed\n");
      return 1;
   }
   printf("\n fseek() successful\n");
   if(SIZE*NUMELEM != fwrite(buff,SIZE,strlen(buff),fd))
   {
      printf("\n fwrite() failed\n");
      return 1;
   }
   printf("\n fwrite() successful, data written to text file\n");
   fclose(fd);
   printf("\n File stream closed through fclose()\n");
   return 0;
}
```

Output

```
File opened successfully through fopen()
Some bytes successfully read through fread()
The bytes read are [hello]
fseek() successful
fwrite() successful, data written to text file
File stream closed through fclose()
```

4.2 FILE ORGANIZATION

File organization enables organizing records or data in a file. More preferably file organization indicates how contents of files are added and accessed instead of how files are organized in folders.

File organization is seen in many ways out of which sequential, relative and indexed are most commonly used. In these organizations, the differences lies between complexity in which records can be organized and the way by which records can be accessed.

In this unit we see five methods of organizing files :

1. Sequential
2. Line sequential
3. Indexed sequential
4. Inverted list
5. Direct or hashed access

4.2.1 Sequential Organization

In sequential file, records are organized in the order they were put. In this organization record order is fixed. Storage and sorting of records are done in physical contiguous blocks. Records are kept in sequence in each block. Records in these files can be read or written sequentially. It is difficult to make record shorter or longer after it has been stored in a file. However record can be updated provided length of record is not changed. New record created will always be kept at the end of file.

Sequential organization is not good option if the order of records in a file is not that important. In this case how many records you have in a file also do not matter. In case of report printing, sequential output is useful. Sequential file organization is illustrated in Fig. 4.1 below. As shown below, records are stored one after the other sequentially. So here beginning and end of file is needed.

Fig. 4.1 : Sequential file organization

4.2.2 Line Sequential Organization

Sequential files and line sequential files are somewhat similar except the difference that in line sequential file, records are made up of characters as data part. Native byte stream files of operating system maintain line sequential files. In the COBOL environment, line-sequential files that are created with WRITE statements with the ADVANCING phrase can be directed to a printer as well as to a disk.

Record delimiter is used to separate one record from the other in line sequential files. A carriage return (x"0D") and a line feed (x"0A") character are used in operating systems like OS/2, Windows and DOS. Line sequential files always contains variable length records as these characters are inserted after a last non space character.

We say report files are line sequential as most PC printers indentifies end of each record by seeing carriage return and / or line feed character.

Most PC editors produce line sequential files and these files can therefore be edited with almost any PC editor.

The main use of line sequential files is for display-only data.

Caution : It is not recommended to use line sequential files for binary or packed data fields.

Line sequential files are also known as text files, or flat ASCII files.

In COBOL, SELECT clause is used to declare a file as line sequential file.

Example :

Creating a line sequential file :

```
file-control.
    select lineseq
        assign to "line.dat"
        organization is line sequential.
file section.
fd lineseq
    record contains 80 characters.
01 lineseq-fd-record       pic x(80).
```

4.2.3 Indexed Sequential Organization

In an indexed sequential file, the file contains data records and pointers to the records. In indexed sequential file, data records and record pointers are arranged in buckets. They consist of an integral number of physically contiguous 512-byte disk blocks. In order to locate individual record within a file, specification of keys, that means indexes are associated with the records. Primary key is needed in indexed sequential file. Primary key is a field within the records which uniquely distinguishes one record from other record in a file. There can be 254 alternate keys in indexed sequential file which need not to have unique values.

According to primary key, RMS (Record Management System) writes records to indexed file in collating sequence. These records are put in buckets that are chained together. So sequential access to a file is possible with any key.

Fig. 4.2 below illustrates an indexed sequential file with a single key.

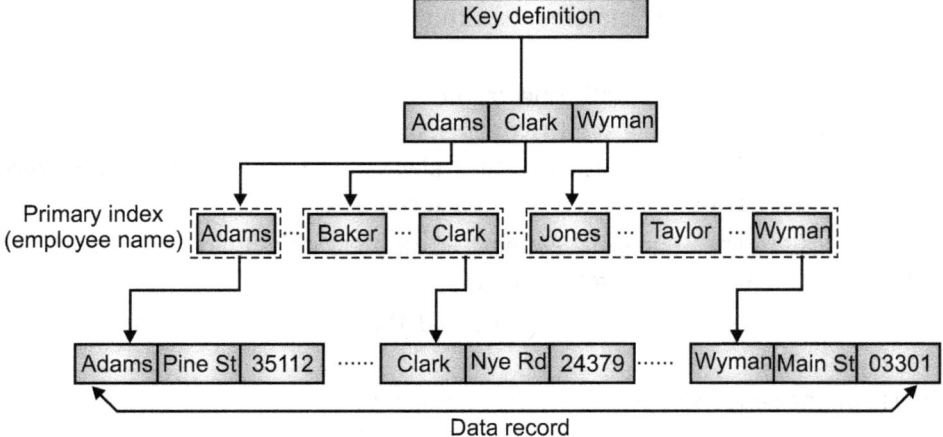

Fig. 4.2 : An indexed sequential file

The records in the file illustrated in Fig. 4.2 above consist of address data that might have been defined in a PL/I structure as follows :

```
DECLARE 1
ADDRESS_FILE,
      2 EMPLOYEE_NAME CHARACTER(30),
      2 ADDRESS,
        3 STREET CHARACTER(20),
        3 ZIP_CODE CHARACTER(5);
```

In this file, the key is the employee name.

RMS helps to build and maintains a tree like structure of key values and location pointers, when it writes records to an indexed sequential file. RMS uses the tree to locate the individual records when records are accessed by key. Thus, when a PL/I program accesses the record whose key value is JONES, RMS traverses the indexes to locate the record.

Some time it happens that when new records are added to an indexed sequential file, a data bucket may not have enough room to accommodate a new record. In this case bucket splitting is performed by RMS. In this it inserts a new bucket in the chain of data buckets. To preserve primary key sequence, it moves enough records from the previous bucket. In PL/I program, the bucket splitting is transparent. The program just knows that it has added a record to file.

4.2.3.1 Defining and Creating an Indexed Sequential File

As shown in Fig. 4.3 below, an indexed sequential file must first be defined then created. Open File Definition Language (FDL) is used to define characteristics of your indexed sequential file. Later on to create the indexed sequential file for use by your program, you use the definition that is resulting FDL file.

Several methods like an Open VMS editor, a PI/I program, or the FDL facility can be used to create FDL definition file. The following steps are keyed to the callout numbers in Fig. 4.3 below :

1. Use an editor to describe the data file.
2. An FDL language source file defines the data file.
3. You can use a program to create an FDL language source file and call FDL$CREATE to create a data file.
4. You can use FDL to create a data file.
5. The data file is created.

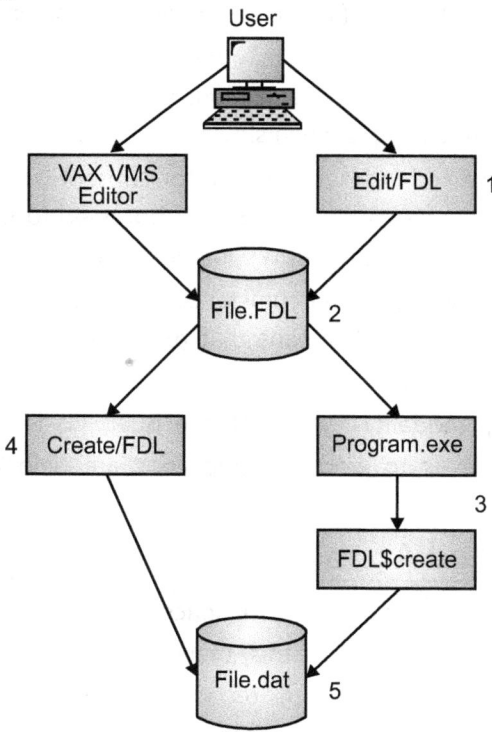

Fig. 4.3 : Creating a data file

Key searches are improved by this system too. The single-level indexing structure is the simplest one where a file, whose records are pairs, contains a key pointer. This pointer is the position in the data file of the record with the given key. A subset of the records, which are evenly spaced along the data file, is indexed, in order to mark intervals of data records.

This is How a Key Search is Performed : the search key is compared with the index keys to find the highest index key coming in front of the search key, while a linear search is performed from the record that the index key points to, until the search key is matched or until the record pointed to by the next index entry is reached. Regardless of double file access (index + data) required by this sort of search, the access time reduction is significant compared with sequential file searches.

4.2.4 Inverted List

In file organization, this is a file that is indexed on many of the attributes of the data itself. This is a method in which for each key type, there is a single index. It is not necessary to keep store records in a sequence. Records are placed into data storage area. And subsequently indexes are updated for record keys and location.

Let's consider an example. In a company file, an index could be maintained for all products and the other one might be maintained for product types. Thus, rather than searching records, it is faster to search an index. Such types of files are known as Inverted Indexes.

There in one drawback in such files. They take more media space, so storage devices may quickly get full with this type of file organization. Benefit of such file organization is that searching is faster wherein updating is much slower.

Practical applications of inverted indexes are seen for content based queries in text retrieval systems. In such systems, data items are stored in compressed form that slow down the data retrieval process, but selecting proper compression algorithm may solve the issue.

When querying a file, there are certain circumstances that need to be considered. When the query is designed to be Modal which means that rules are set which require that different information to be held on index.

Here's an example of this modality : when phrase querying is undertaken, the particular algorithm requires that offsets to word classifications are held in addition to document numbers.

4.2.5 Direct or Hashed Access

With Direct or Hashed Access a portion of disk space is reserved and a "hashing" algorithm computes the record address. Because of this, there is an additional space required for this kind of file in the store. In this approach, record placement in a file is done randomly. Address specifies disk location that is used to access record.

This approach takes benefit of disk storage instead of tape. Even though there is an excellent search retrieval performance, one must need to take care of indexes while maintaining them. It is desirable that back up of this kind of files shall be taken on regular basis because problem may occur when indexes become corrupt. This protects valuable data.

4.3 ACCESS METHODS

Information in the file can be accessed by several means. There are some systems that provide just a single access method to their files. However, there are other systems too that provide multiple access methods to access their files. The big design issue would be which one to pick up as applications requirements are different.

4.3.1 Sequential Access

As name suggest, this type of access method ensures file processing sequentially. It means records are processed one after the other. This is one of the most common access methods. For example computer editors usually access files by this approach.

A read operation reads the next portion of the file and automatically advances the file pointer. Similarly, a write appends to the end of the file and advances to the end of the newly written material (the new end of file). It is possible to reset such file to the beginning and on some system a program may be able to skip forward or backward n records, for some integer n. Sequential access is based on tape model of a file. Fig. 4.4 below demonstrates sequential access and random access to a file.

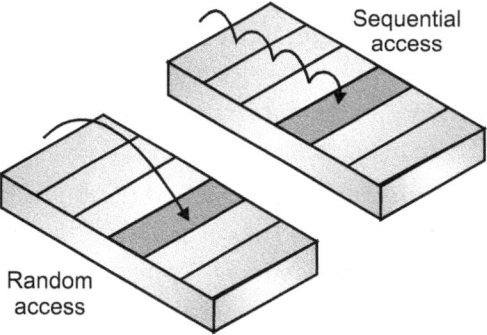

Fig. 4.4 : Demonstrating sequential access and random access

4.3.2 Direct Access

Direct access is based on a disk model of a file. For direct access, the file is viewed as a numbered sequence of block or records. Direct access is a term which is also known as machine access or random access.

A direct-access file allows arbitrary blocks to be read or written. Thus, after block 20 has been read, block 55 could be next and then block 4. As far as writing and reading of direct access file is concerned, there are no restrictions on ordering. If intermediate access to large amount of information is expected, direct access files are of great use.

There are no restrictions on the order of reading and writing for a direct access file. Direct access files are of great use for intermediate access to large amounts of information.

The file operations must be modified to include the block number as a parameter. Thus, we have "read n", where n is the block number, rather than "read next" and "write n", rather than "write next". An alternative approach is to retain "read next" and "write next" and to add an operation; "position file to n" where n is the block number. Then, to effect a "read n", we would issue the commands "position to n" and then "read next".

Not all OS support both sequential and direct access for files. Some systems allow only sequential file access; others allow only direct access. Some systems require that a file be defined as sequential or direct when it is created; such a file can be accessed only in a manner consistent with its declaration.

4.3.3 Indexed Sequential Access

- This approach is built upon sequential access.
- In this, index is created which serves as a pointer for various blocks.
- Index is searched sequentially and its pointer is used to access the file directly.

4.3.4 Other Access Methods

Other access methods can be built on top of a direct-access method. These additional methods include construction of an index for a file. As said earlier, index contains pointer to different blocks. So whenever entry in the file needs to be searched, first index is searched and then pointer is used to access file directly.

For large files, index also becomes large and then it becomes difficult to keep indexes in memory. So solution is to create an index for index file itself. It means there would be primary index file and secondary index file. Primary index file holds pointer to secondary index file which in turn points to actual data items.

For example, IBM's Indexed Sequential Access Method (ISAM) uses a small master index that points to disk blocks of a secondary index. The secondary index blocks point to the actual file blocks. The file is kept sorted on a defined key. To find a particular item, we first make a binary search of the master index, which provides the block number of the secondary index. This block is read in and again a binary search is used to find the block containing the desired record. Finally, this block is searched sequentially. In this way, any record can be located from its key by at most direct access reads.

4.4 DIRECTORY STRUCTURE

File system tend to differ for two main areas. 1. The structure of the directories. 2. The relationship among them. This has the most significant effect on the user interface provided by the file system. Following are the most common directory structures used by multi-user systems are :

1. Single-level directory
2. Two-level directory
3. Tree-structured directory
4. Acyclic directory

4.4.1 Single-Level Directory

As name suggest, all file are placed in one directory. On single user OS this is found commonly.

There is a significant limitation of this kind of directory structure. That is whenever the number of files increases or when there is more than user associated to single directory, complexity also increases. File name need to be given uniquely as all files are in same directory. If there are two users who call their data file "test", then the unique-name rule is violated. Although file names are generally selected to reflect the content of the file, they are often quite limited in length.

Even with a single-user, as the number of files increases, it becomes difficult to remember the names of all the files in order to create only files with unique names.

Fig. 4.5 below illustrates single level directory structure. As shown in Fig. 4.5, directory "cat" contains one file, directory data contains one file and similarly other directories contains one-one file each.

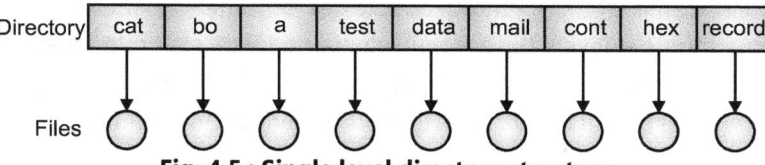

Fig. 4.5 : Single level directory structure

4.2.2 Two-Level Directory

In this directory scheme master block is maintained by system. This block contains one entry for each user. It contains the addresses of the directory of the users.

Two level directory structure has few problems. This is the structure which isolates one user form other effectively. This could be advantageous when users are completely different from each other. But on the other side, there is disadvantage when users want to cooperate on some task and access files of other users. There are some systems (for example UNIX, Linux) that do not allow local files to be shared by other users.

Fig. 4.6 below illustrates two-level directory structure. As shown in Fig. 4.6, we see four users user 1, user 2, user 3 and user 4. Each of them is having their own set of directories, which in terns holds file with them. For example, user 1 is owner of directories cat, bo and test. Each one of these directories has one file under them.

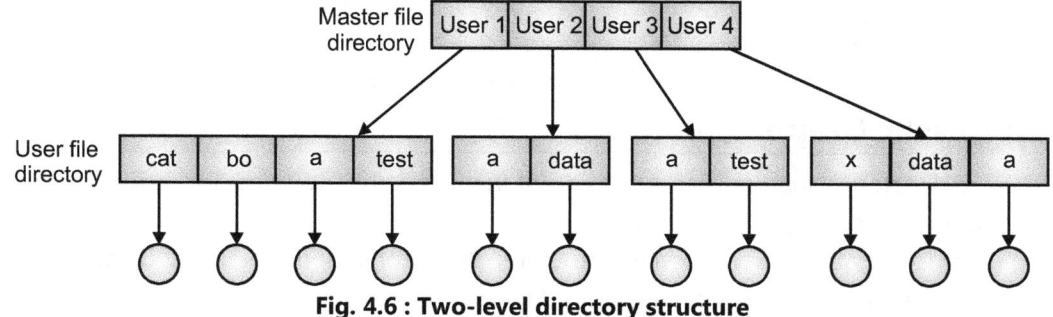

Fig. 4.6 : Two-level directory structure

4.3.3 Tree-Structured Directories

In the tree-structured directory, the directory themselves are files. This leads to the possibility of having sub-directories that can contain files and sub-subdirectories.

Important policy decision need to be made when there is a need to delete directory. Empty directory deletion is simple. While deleting empty directory, just entry in containing directory can simply be deleted. However, suppose the directory to be deleted is not empty, but contains several files, or possibly sub-directories, some systems will not delete a directory unless it is empty. Simply speaking, to delete a directory, firstly it is expected to delete files in that directory. If these are any sub-directories, this procedure must be applied recursively to them, so that they can be deleted also. This approach may result in an insubstantial amount of work. An alternative approach is just to assume that, when a request is made to delete a directory, all of that directory's files and sub-directories are also to be deleted.

Fig. 4.7 below illustrates tree-structured directories scheme. As shown in Fig. 4.7, in this directory scheme, multiple levels have been maintained. For example, directory "pgm" have three sub-directories, namely "p", "e", "mail"; where in "e" sub-directory have two sub-directories, namely "last" and "first" and these sub-directories holding one-one file under them.

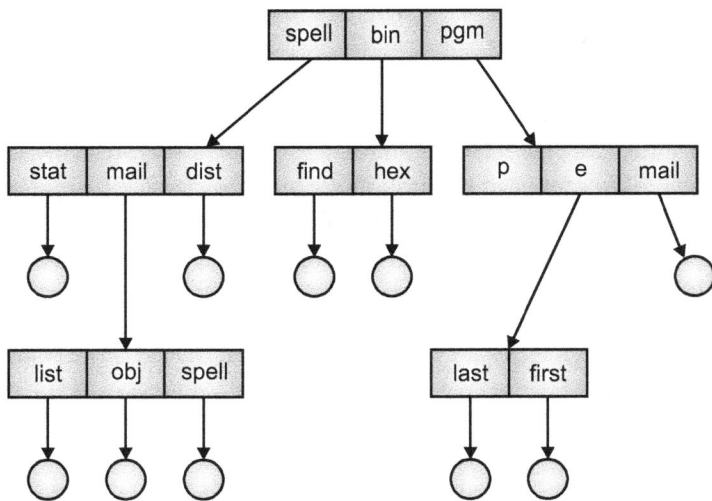

Fig. 4.7 : Tree-structured directories

4.4.4 Acyclic Graph Directories

The acyclic directory structure is an extension of the tree-structured directory structure. In the tree-structured directory, files and directories starting from some fixed directory are owned by one particular user. In the acyclic structure, this prohibition is taken out and thus a directory or file under directory can be owned by several users.

Fig. 4.8 below illustrates acyclic directory structure.

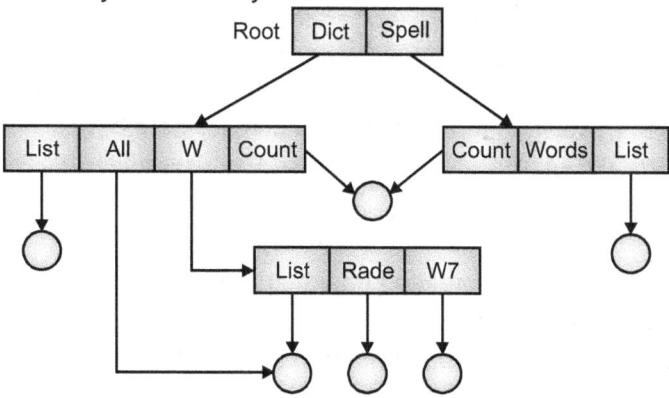

Fig. 4.8 : Acyclic directory structure

B. ALLOCATION OF DISK SPACE

4.5 ALLOCATION OF DISK SPACE

Utilizing disk space effectively is a big concern in file management. This management must include efficient space allocation for files. Two major methods that are used for disk space allocation are :
1. Contiguous
2. Non-contiguous
    a. Linked
    b. Indexed

Each one of these has their advantages and disadvantages. Depending on systems requirement, these methods are used. Preferably system will use method to be used for all files. Let's discuss these methods one by one.

4.5.1 Contiguous Allocation

As name suggests, this method allocates set of contiguous address space on disk to each file. Disk addresses define a linear ordering on the disk. As linear ordering is used, accessing block b+1 after block b usually requires no head movement. Even though, whenever head movement is needed (say from the last sector of one cylinder to the first sector of the next cylinder), it would be just one track. This means number of disk seeks required for accessing contiguous allocated files is minimal. Disk address and length of first block defines contiguous allocation of file. If the file is n blocks long and starts at location b, then it occupies blocks b, b+1, b+2,.., b+n-1. Directory entry contains address of starting block and length of the area allocated for a particular file.

Finding required space for a new file in contiguous allocation method is little difficult. For example, if new file created is n blocks long in length then operating system must have to search for free n contiguous blocks first. As discussed in unit 3, first fit, best fit and worst fit strategies are the most common strategies used to select a free hole from the set of available holes. Simulations have shown that both first-fit and best-fit are better than worst-fit in terms of both time and storage utilization. Neither first-fit nor best-fit is clearly best in terms of storage utilization, but first-fit is generally faster.

These algorithms do suffer from external fragmentation. This is because as files are allocated and deleted, the free disk space is broken into little pieces. External fragmentation means, to satisfy a request, there is a sufficient disk space exists but the space is not contiguous. This means storage is fragmented into large number of small holes.

Another problem with contiguous allocation is to determine how much disk space is needed for a file? When new file is created, it is expected that space requirements of file shall be known and shall be allocated. But do not you feel that being a creator of file, it is actually difficult for you to know in advance the size of file. In some cases, this determination may be fairly simple (for example copying an existing file), but in general the size of an output file may be difficult to estimate.

The Fig. 4.9 depicts a contiguous allocation method.

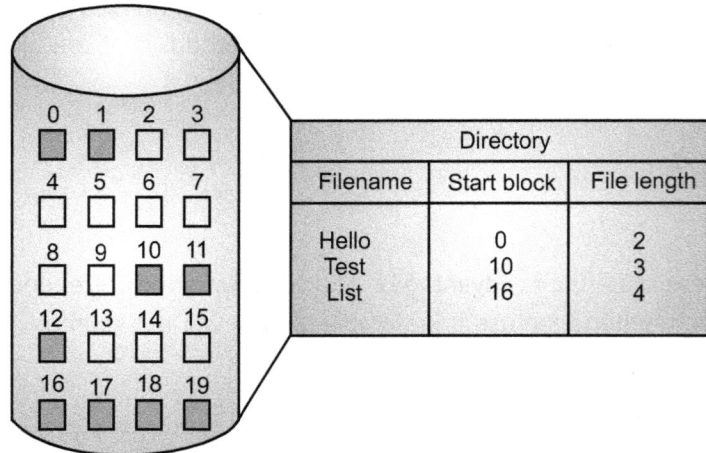

Fig. 4.9 : Contiguous allocation method

As shown in the Fig. 4.9, 'Hello' file is stored on disk and the starting block from where the file begins is block number 0 (zero) and the length of the file is 2 blocks long. So, block number 0 and 1 are allocated for the file 'Hello'. Same way allocation for 'Test' and 'List' file will be done. As you can see, this Fig. exhibits similar fragmentation problems as in variable memory partitioning. This is because the allocation and disk location could result in regions of free disk space broken into chunks (pieces) within active space, which is called external fragmentation.

User specifies in advance the size of the area needed to hold a file to be created. File cannot be created if desired amount of contiguous space is not available. This method supports both direct accessing and sequential accessing. For sequential access, almost no seeks are required. Even direct access to seek and read is fast. Also, calculation of blocks holding data is quick and easy as we need just offset from the start of the file.

Program 4.2 : Source Code for Contiguous File Allocation Using Compaction Algorithm

```c
#include<stdio.h>
#include<conio.h>
void create(int,int);
void del(int);
void compaction();
void display();
int fname[10],fsize[10],fstart[10],freest[10],freesize[10],m=0,n=0,start;
int main()
 {
   int name,size,ch,i;
   int *ptr;
   // clrscr();
   ptr=(int *)malloc(sizeof(int)*100);
   start=freest[0]=(int)ptr;
   freesize[0]=500;
   printf("\n\n");
   printf(" Free start address  Free Size \n\n");
   for(i=0;i<=m;i++)
     printf("    %d %d\n",freest[i],freesize[i]);
     printf("\n\n");
    while(1)
  {
    printf("1.Create.\n");
    printf("2.Delete.\n");
    printf("3.Compaction.\n");
    printf("4.Exit.\n");
    printf("Enter your choice: ");
      scanf("%d",&ch);
    switch(ch)
```

```
    {
      case 1 :
        printf("\nEnter the name of file: ");
         scanf("%d",&name);
        printf("\nEnter the size of the file: ");
         scanf("%d",&size);
        create(name,size);
        break;
      case 2 :
        printf("\nEnter the file name which u want to delete: ");
         scanf("%d",&name);
        del(name);
        break;
      case 3 :
         compaction();
         printf("\nAfter compaction the tables will be:\n");
         display();
         break;
      case 4 :
         exit(1);
      default:
         printf("\nYou have entered a wrong choice.\n");
    }
  }
}
void create(int name,int size)
 {
   int i,flag=1,j,a;
    for(i=0;i<=m;i++)
   if( freesize[i] >= size)
     a=i,flag=0;
    if(!flag)
    {
   for(j=0;j<n;j++);
```

```
      n++;
   fname[j]=name;
   fsize[j]=size;
   fstart[j]=freest[a];
   freest[a]=freest[a]+size;
         freesize[a]=freesize[a]-size;
         printf("\n The memory map will now be: \n\n");
   display();
    }
   else
    {
    printf("\nNo enough space is available.System compaction......");
     flag=1;
     compaction();
     display();
    for(i=0;i<=m;i++)
       if( freesize[i] >= size)
     a=i,flag=0;
   if(!flag)
    {
    for(j=0;j<n;j++);
       n++;
    fname[j]=name;
    fsize[j]=size;
    fstart[j]=freest[a];
    freest[a]+=size;
    freesize[a]-=size;
    printf("\n The memory map will now be: \n\n");
    display();
    }
    else
    printf("\nNo enough space.\n");
    }
 }
void del(int name)
 {
```

```c
  int i,j,k,flag=1;
   for(i=0;i<n;i++)
     if(fname[i]==name)
        break;
   if(i==n)
    {
 flag=0;
 printf("\nNo such process exists......\n");
    }
    else
    {
    m++;
    freest[m]=fstart[i];
    freesize[m]=fsize[i];
   for(k=i;k<n;k++)
          {
      fname[k]=fname[k+1];
           fsize[k]=fsize[k+1];
           fstart[k]=fstart[k+1];
          }
          n--;
    }
    if(flag)
    {
   printf("\n\n After deletion of this process the memory map will be : \n\n");
   display();
    }
  }
void compaction()
 {
   int i,j,size1=0,f_size=0;
    if(fstart[0]!=start)
    {
   fstart[0]=start;
   for(i=1;i<n;i++)
    fstart[i]=fstart[i-1]+fsize[i-1];
```

```
    }
    else
    {
    for(i=1;i<n;i++)
     fstart[i]=fstart[i-1]+fsize[i-1];
    }
    f_size=freesize[0];
    for(j=0;j<=m;j++)
     size1+=freesize[j];
    freest[0]=freest[0]-(size1-f_size);
    freesize[0]=size1;
    m=0;
}
void display()
  {
    int i;
    printf("\n ***  MEMORY MAP TABLE ***     \n");
    printf("\n\nNAME    SIZE    STARTING ADDRESS    \n\n");
    for(i=0;i<n;i++)
     printf(" %d%10d%10d\n",fname[i],fsize[i],fstart[i]);
    printf("\n\n");
    printf("\n\n*** FREE SPACE TABLE ***\n\n");
    printf("FREE START ADDRESS      FREE SIZE    \n\n");
    for(i=0;i<=m;i++)
     printf("     %d              %d\n",freest[i],freesize[i]);
  }
```

Output

The memory map will be now be :

*** MEMORY MAP TABLE ***

NAME	SIZE	STARTING ADDRESS
12	200	2688

*** FREE SPACE TABLE ***

FREE START ADDRESS	FREE SIZE
2888	300

Free start address	Free Size
2888	300

1. Create.

2. Delete.
3. Compaction.
4. Exit.
Enter your choice : 1
Enter the name of file : 12
Enter the size of the file : 200

4.5.2 Non-Contiguous Allocation

This scheme is basically replacement for previous one. This method is popular. The reason is that files either grow or shrink over the time. So users rarely know how large their files will be in contiguous. Storage allocation systems are being replaced by more dynamic non-contiguous storage allocation systems. In this method, we study two schemes :

4.5.2.1 Linked / Chained Allocation

Linked allocation is essentially a disk-based version of the linked list. Disk blocks are scattered any where on the disk. As far as directory is concerned, it holds pointer to first and last block of the file. Each block also contains pointer to next block, but this information is not available to the user. This is something where one can think to have sequential access but it may generate long seeks between blocks.

Now bottleneck here is that this scheme requires extra storage space for pointers. If there is damage or loss to any pointer may raise the reliability question on this scheme. Fig. 4.10 depicts linked /chained allocation.

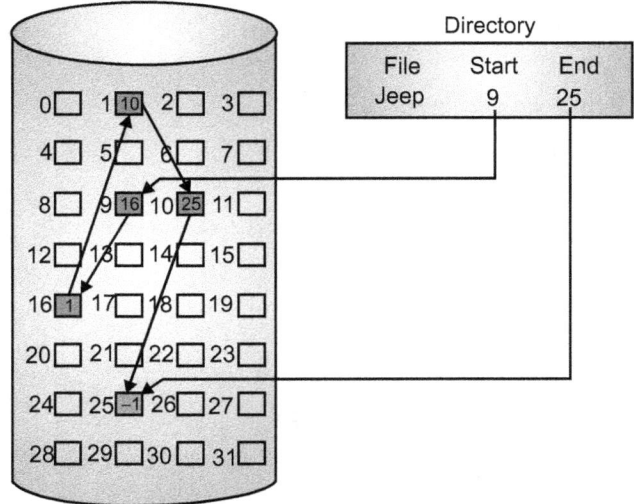

Fig. 4.10 : Linked / chained allocation

As shown in Fig. 4.10, file "jeep" has got disk space from block no 9 and from block no 9 to 25, chain is maintained to depict which is the next block is liked with the previous one. In this, current block holds pointer to next block in chain.

FAT (File Allocation Table), which is another variation to linked list is used by MS-DOS and OS/2. In this beginning of each partition contains a table. This table has one entry for each block and is indexed by the block number. The directory entry contains the block number of the first block of the file. The table entry indexed by block number contains the block number of the next block in the file. The Table pointer of the last block in the file has an EOF pointer value. Until EOF table entry in encountered, this chain continues. Even though we do not have to go to disk for each of them, we still have to traverse linearly next pointers. 0 (Zero) table value indicates an unused block. So, allocation of free blocks with FAT scheme is straightforward, just search for the first block with a 0 table pointer. The OS/2 and MS-DOS use this scheme. The Fig. 4.11 shows File Allocation Table (FAT).

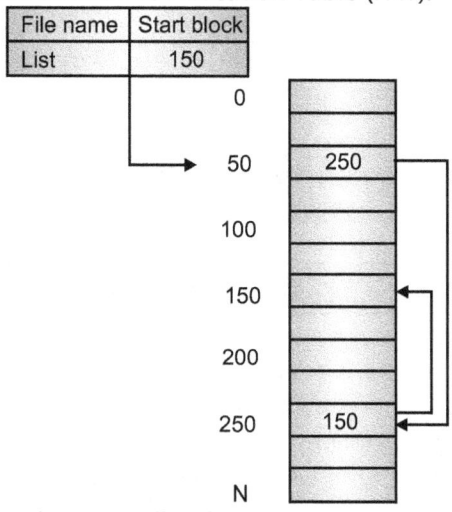

Fig. 4.11 : File allocation table (FAT)

4.5.2.2 Indexed Allocation

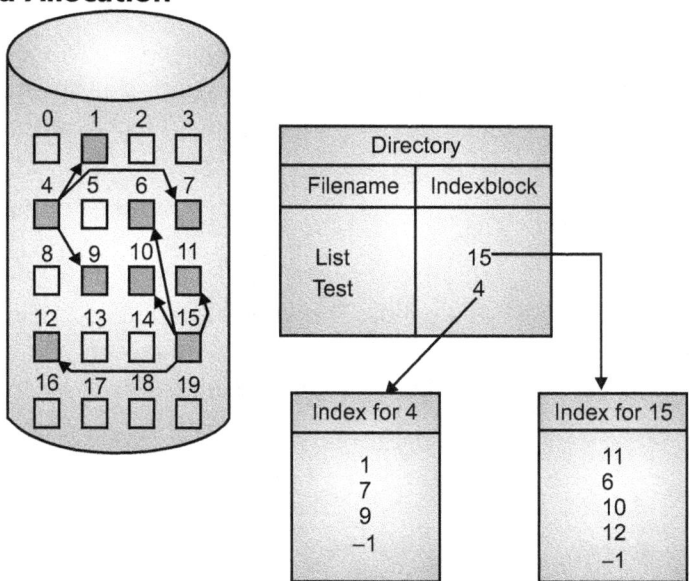

Fig. 4.12 : Indexed allocation scheme

Problems of contiguous and chained allocation have been addressed by indexed allocation. This scheme contains separate one level index for each file in file allocation table. An has one entry for each portion allocated to a file. Typically, the file indexes are not physically stored as part of the file allocation table. Rather separate block is used to keep index for a file and entry for the file in the allocation table points to that block. The basis for allocation might be variable size portions or fixed size blocks. The indexed allocation scheme is diagrammatically shown in above Fig. 4.12.

This scheme supports both, sequential and random access. This turns to be advantageous of this scheme. The searching may take place in index blocks themselves. To maximize the seek time; an index block can be kept close together in secondary storage. In this scheme space is wasted on index which is not very large. There is no external fragmentation involved in this scheme.

C. DISK SCHEDULING

4.6 CONCEPT OF DISK SCHEDULING

We expect that on single computer we shall be able to run many operations at a time. To achieve this, effective management is needed to do so. With the help or advent of the Multi-programming we can execute many programs at a Time. So concept of disk scheduling is used by operating system for controlling and providing memory to all the process.

Disk scheduling decides at what time which process shall get executed by the CPU. In this, time of CPU is divided among the various processes and care is taken for all processes proper working. Scheduling means to execute all the processes those are given to a CPU at a Time.

Scheduling is used for divide the total time of the CPU between the Number of Processes, so that the processes can execute concurrently at a single time. For sharing the time or for dividing total number of time of the CPU, various scheduling techniques are used. They are explained with example in next section.

4.7 FIRST COME FIRST SERVE (FCFS)

In this jobs or processes are executed in the manner in which they are entered into the system. For this reason, CPU creates a queue. This queue is helpful to maintain the sequence order in which processes need to be executed and the sequence in which CPU will execute them. The job which has been requested first for an execution will be the job that will be executed first by the CPU.

4.8 SHORTEST SEEK TIME FIRST (SSTF)

In this scheme, operating system search for the job that needs short time to run out of the other jobs. It mean a job that will take less time of CPU for running will be chosen and will be executed. For simplicity, operating system arranges all jobs in a sequence or some time they are arranged as per their priority order. Here the priority of the process will be the total time which a process will use for execution.

4.9 C-SCAN SCHEDULING

In this scheme, circular list is used to arrange all processes. In circular list, there is no start and end point of the list. It means, we can say that end of the list is the starting of the list. In this scheme, CPU searches for the process in the list.

Many times it happens that when a CPU is executing the processes then user may want to enter some data. In this case, CPU will again execute the process after the input operation is completed. This means by making use of this scheme, executing the same process again and again is possible.

4.10 LOOK SCHEDULING

In the Look scheduling, CPU scans the list from starting to end of the disk in which the various processes are running.

Above explained algorithms are not hard to understand, but they can confuse someone because they are so similar. What we are striving for by using these algorithms is keeping head movements (# tracks) to the least amount as possible. The less the head has to move, the faster the seek time will be. In following section we see why C-LOOK is the best algorithm to use in trying to establish less seek time.

Given the following queue : 95, 180, 34, 119, 11, 123, 62, 64 with the read-write head initially at the track 50 and the tail track being at 199, let us now discuss the different algorithms.

1. **FCFS**

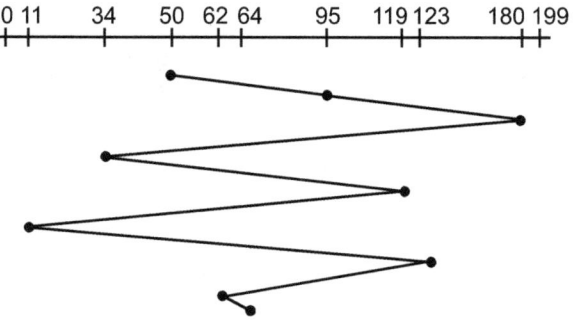

Fig. 4.13 : FCFS simulation

In this scheme as said earlier, all incoming requests are placed at the end of the queue. The one that will be next in queue will be served next. To determine the number of head movements you would simply find the number of tracks it took to move from one request to the next.

For this case it went from 50 to 95 to 180 and so on. From 50 to 95 it moved 45 tracks. If you tally up the total number of tracks you will find how many tracks it had to go through before finishing the entire request. In this example, it had a total head movement of 640 tracks.

The disadvantage of this algorithm is noted by the oscillation from track 50 to track 180 and then back to track 11 to 123 then to 64. As you will soon see, this is the worse algorithm that one can use.

2. SSTF

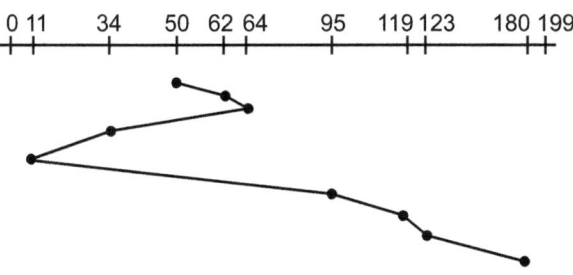

Fig. 4.14 : SSTF simulation

In this scheme, request is serviced according to next shortest distance. Starting at 50, the next shortest distance would be 62 instead of 34 since it is only 12 tracks away from 62 and 16 tracks away from 34. This continues till all processes are considered. For example the next case would be to move from 62 to 64 instead of 34 since there are only 2 tracks between them and not 18 if it were to go the other way.

Although this seems to be a better service as it moved total of 236 tracks, this is not an optimal one. In this scheme, we cannot deny the probability of starvation. The reason is, if there were a lot of requests close to each other, the other requests will never be handled since the distance will always be greater.

3. Elevator (SCAN)

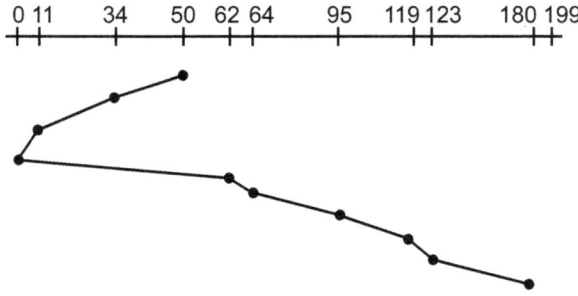

Fig. 4.15 : SCAN simulation

This approach works like an elevator does. It scans down towards the nearest end and then when it hits the bottom it scans up servicing the requests that it didn't get going down. If a request comes in after it has been scanned, it will not be serviced until the process comes back down or moves back up. This process moved a total of 230 tracks. Once again this is more optimal than the previous algorithm, but it is not the best.

4. C-SCAN

Circular scanning works just like the elevator to some extent. It begins its scan toward the nearest end and works all the way to the end of the system. Once it hits the bottom or top, it jumps to the other end and moves in the same direction.

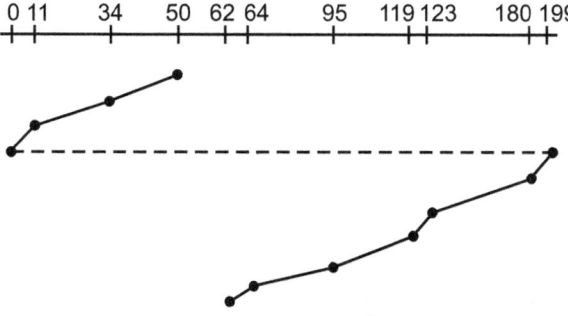

Fig. 4.16 : C-SCAN simulation

Keep in mind that the huge jump doesn't count as a head movement. The total head movement for this algorithm is only 187 tracks, but still this isn't the most sufficient.

5. C-LOOK

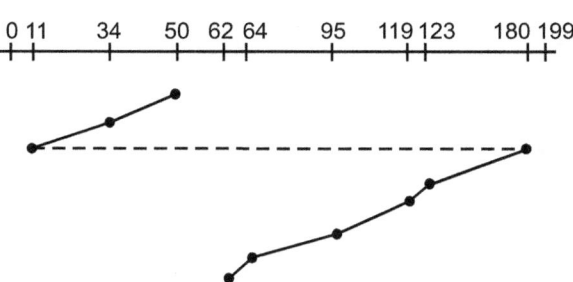

Fig. 4.17 : C-LOOK simulation

C-LOOK is an enhanced version of C-SCAN. In this scheme, the scanning doesn't go past to the last request in the direction that it is moving. It too jumps to the other end but not all the way to the end. Just to the furthest request. C-SCAN had a total movement of 187 but this scan (C-LOOK) reduced it down to 157 tracks.

From this you were able to see a scan change from 644 total head movements to just 157. You should now have an understanding as to why your operating system truly relies on the type of algorithm it needs when it is dealing with multiple processes.

Note : It is important that you draw out the sequence when handling algorithms like this one. One would have a hard time trying to determine which algorithm is best by just reading the definition. There is a good chance that without the drawings there could be miscalculations.

Program 4.3 : Source code for scheduling techniques.

```
#include<stdio.h>
#include<math.h>
```

```c
void fcfs(int noq, int qu[10], int st)
{
 int i,s=0;
 for(i=0;i<noq;i++)
 {
  s=s+abs(st-qu[i]);
  st=qu[i];
 }
 printf("\n Total seek time :%d",s);
}
void sstf(int noq, int qu[10], int st, int visit[10])
{
 int min,s=0,p,i;
 while(1)
 {
  min=999;
  for(i=0;i<noq;i++)
   if (visit[i] == 0)
   {
     if(min > abs(st - qu[i]))
      {
       min = abs(st-qu[i]);
       p = i;
      }
   }
 if(min == 999)
  break;
 visit[p]=1;
 s=s + min;
 st = qu[p];
 }
 printf("\n Total seek time is: %d",s);
}
void scan(int noq, int qu[10], int st, int ch)
{
```

```c
int i,j,s=0;
for(i=0;i<noq;i++)
{
 if(st < qu[i])
 {
  for(j=i-1; j>= 0;j--)
  {
   s=s+abs(st - qu[j]);
   st = qu[j];
  }
  if(ch == 3)
  {
   s = s + abs(st - 0);
   st = 0;
  }
  for(j = 1;j < noq;j++)
  {
   s= s + abs(st - qu[j]);
   st = qu[j];
  }
  break;
 }
}
printf("\n Total seek time : %d",s);
}
int main()
{
 int n,qu[20],st,i,j,t,noq,ch,visit[20];
 printf("\n Enter the maximum number of cylinders : ");
 scanf("%d",&n);
 printf("enter number of queue elements");
 scanf("%d",&noq);
 printf("\n Enter the work queue");
 for(i=0;i<noq;i++)
 {
  scanf("%d",&qu[i]);
```

```c
  visit[i] = 0;
 }
printf("\n Enter the disk head starting posision: \n");
scanf("%d",&st);
while(1)
{
 printf("\n\n\t\t MENU \n");
 printf("\n\n\t\t 1. FCFS \n");
 printf("\n\n\t\t 2. SSTF \n");
 printf("\n\n\t\t 3. SCAN \n");
 printf("\n\n\t\t 4. EXIT \n");
 printf("\nEnter your choice: ");
scanf("%d",&ch);
if(ch > 2)
 {
 for(i=0;i<noq;i++)
 for(j=i+1;j<noq;j++)
 if(qu[i]>qu[j])
 {
  t=qu[i];
  qu[i] = qu[j];
  qu[j] = t;
 }
 }
 switch(ch)
  {
  case 1 : printf("\n FCFS \n");
       printf("\n*****\n");
       fcfs(noq,qu,st);
       break;
  case 2 : printf("\n SSTF \n");
       printf("\n*****\n");
       sstf(noq,qu,st,visit);
       break;
  case 3 : printf("\n SCAN \n");
       printf("\n*****\n");
       scan(noq,qu,st,ch);
       break;
```

```
    case 4 : exit(0);
}
}
}
```

OUTPUT :

"disksche.c" 122L, 2076C written

[anandh@localhost ~]$ cc disksche.c

[anandh@localhost ~]$ ./a.out

 Enter the maximum number of cylinders : 200

enter number of queue elements 5

Enter the work queue23

89

132

42

187

Enter the disk head starting posision:

100

        MENU
        1. FCFS
        2. SSTF
        3. SCAN
        4. EXIT

Enter your choice: 1

 FCFS

*****

 Total seek time : 421

        MENU
        1. FCFS
        2. SSTF
        3. SCAN
        4. EXIT

Enter your choice: 2

SSTF

*****

 Total seek time is: 273

        MENU

```
                1. FCFS
                2. SSTF
                3. SCAN
                4. EXIT
Enter your choice : 3
SCAN
*****
 Total seek time : 287
            MENU
                1. FCFS
                2. SSTF
                3. SCAN
                4. EXIT
Enter your choice: 4
```

QUESTIONS

1. Define file. What are the different types of file?
2. What do you mean by organizing a file? State the benefits of file organization.
3. Out of the five file organization methods which one will you use? Why?
4. Differentiate sequential, line sequential and indexed sequential file organization methods.
5. Write short note on inverted list and direct/hashed access methods.
6. Explain different file access methods with example.
7. Why directory structure is important? Explain with example.
8. Compare single level directory structure with two level directory structure.
9. How tree structured directories are different from acyclic graph directories? Explain with example.
10. What strategies will you apply while allocating disk space?
11. Which allocation strategy is better, contiguous or non contiguous? Why?
12. Explain in detail linked/chained allocation and indexed allocation with example.
13. Explain the disk scheduling and its importance.
14. Explain with example FCFS and SSTF disk scheduling schemes.
15. Explain with example SCAN disk scheduling and LOOK disk scheduling schemes.

✠ ✠ ✠

Unit - V

SECONDARY STORAGE STRUCTURE, PROTECTION AND SECURITY, INTRODUCTION TO UNIX

5.0 INTRODUCTION

This unit focus on disk management which includes disk formatting, disk partitioning, details about boot block and bad block. Swap space in any operating system plays an important role. Here, we discuss in detail, what is swap space? How to use it? This part includes overall swap space management of UNIX like system. Now days, every system owner wants good protection to his / her system. Keeping this fact in mind, we present goals of protection, domain of protection, threats and standard security attacks. Later on in this unit, we focus on UNIX operating system history and its architecture. More to this, here we study in details internal representation of files by looking into the details few important things like inode, structure of regular file, super block and pipe as an inter-process communication mechanism. At last in this unit, we cover process creation, process system calls (fork() and exec()) and process state transition.

A. DISK MANAGEMENT

Disk management includes management of disk based hardware. Provision of disk management is different for different operating systems. This includes management of flash drives, optical disk drives, external or internal hard disk drives, etc. It is also used to format a drive, to partition a drive, to assign letter to drive so that they can be distinguished from others and so on.

5.1 DISK FORMATTING

Disk Formatting is the process of preparing a data storage device such as a hard disk drive, solid-state drive, floppy disk or USB flash drive for initial use. Sometimes, one or more new files are created due to formatting operation. There are two types of formatting can be given : low level formatting and high level formatting. Low Level formatting is one in which we perform basic medium preparation. High Level formatting mostly includes generating a new file system all together. As a general rule, formatting a disk leaves most if not all existing data on the disk medium. In case of data loss, it can be recovered using special tools.

Formatting a hard drive allows you to use it on your computer to store files and install programs on. The format you choose for the drive determines the drive's compatibility.

Formatting a drive will erase all of the data currently on the drive, so ensure you have everything you need backed up. You can format a second (or third, or fourth...) drive from within your operating system, or you can format your boot drive by using your OS installation disc. If you need to erase data securely, there are free tools that will allow you to completely erase your drive so that nothing can be recovered.

5.1.1 Formatting a Secondary Hard Drive (Windows)

1. **Back up Any Data on the Drive you Want to Save :** Formatting a drive will erase all of the data on a drive, so make sure that everything you need to save is backed up to a safe location. You can then restore this data to your new drive.
   - You cannot back up installed programs. These will need to be reinstalled on your new drive. You can, however, usually back up settings and preference files.
2. **Install the Hard Drive :** If you are formatting a new drive, it will need to be installed in your system.
3. Open the Computer/My Computer/This PC window. This can be accessed from the Start menu, or by pressing ⊞ Win+E. This window displays all of the drives connected to your computer.
4. **Right-Click on the Drive you Want to Format :** Select *Format...* This will open the Windows disk formatting tool.
   - Make sure you select the right drive. Everything will be deleted when the drive is formatted.
5. **Select the File System :** The file system is the way that the hard drive stores and catalogs files. The file system will determine what the drive is compatible with. If the drive is internal and you are only using it with your Windows computer, select NTFS. If the drive is external, select FAT32 or exFAT.
   - FAT32 and exFAT can be written to and read by all newer operating systems. FAT32 is an older system and doesn't support files larger than 4 GB, but can be read by virtually any operating system. exFAT has no restrictions, but won't work with older operating systems like Windows 95.
   - In general, exFAT will be the best option for an external drive. It is compatible with the most systems and can store the largest files.
6. **Give the Drive a Name :** If you are primarily using the drive for one use, giving it a name will help you identify what's on it. For example, if you are using a second drive to store your music, movies and pictures, naming it "Media" will quickly let you know what it contains.
7. **Choose Whether or Not to Quick Format :** A Quick Format will perform the format much quicker than a standard format and is fine for most users. Only perform a regular format if you suspect that the drive may have errors. A regular format may be able to correct some of these errors.

- The Quick Format option does not affect how securely the data is erased. If you need to securely wipe the drive, see the last section of this article.
8. **Start the Format :** Click Start to begin the format. Click OK to confirm that you understand everything will be erased. If you selected Quick Format, the process should only take a few seconds.

5.1.2 Formatting you Boot Drive (Windows)

1. **Back up Any Data on the Drive you Want to Save :** Formatting your boot drive will erase your operating system and all the files stored on it, so be prepared to reinstall the operating system on the drive. Having a back up of your important files will make transitioning much easier.
2. **Insert your Windows Installation Disc :** You can also use a boot disk or LiveCD. This will allow you to boot to this disk instead of the hard drive, which will allow you to format it.
3. **Set your Computer to Boot from the Disc :** You will need to set your boot order in the BIOS in order to boot from the disc. See this guide for details on setting your boot order.
   - To open your BIOS, reboot your computer and press the setup key. This is usually F2, F10, or ⊠ Del.
4. **Navigate through the Installation Screens :** You will need to start the installer and navigate past the first few pages until you reach the screen with a list of your installed drives. You will be initiating a Custom Installation of Windows.
5. **Select the Drive you Want to Format :** You will see a list of all your drives and the partitions they contain. Select the drive you want to format and then click the "Format" button at the bottom of the list. The drive will be formatted as NTFS.
   - You can only format your boot drive as NTFS.
6. **Reinstall Windows :** Now that the drive has been formatted, you can reinstall Windows, or install Linux on it. You will need an operating system on your computer in order to use it.
   - Reinstall Windows 7
   - Reinstall Windows 8
   - Install Linux.

5.2 BOOT BLOCK

(a) Introduction to Book Block

A boot sector is a region of floppy disk, optical disk, hard disk or other data storage device that contains machine code to be loaded into RAM by a computer system's built-in firmware. Boot sector is also referred as boot block. Boot sector allows boot process to load a program stored on same storage device. The design of computer platform decides the size of boot sector.

On an IBM PC compatible machine, the BIOS selects a boot device, then copies the first sector from the device (which may be a MBR, VBR or any executable code), into physical memory at memory address 0x7C00. On other systems, the process may be quite different.

(b) Kinds of Boot Sector

On IBM PC compatible floppy disk, hard disk and similar storage device, different types of boot sector can be encountered.

- A Master boot record (MBR) is the first sector of data storage device that have been partitioned. MBR contains code to locate active partition and invoke volume boot record.
- The first sector of data storage devices, that has not been partitioned are called volume boot record (VBR).

(c) Operation

The firmware simply loads and runs the first sector of the storage device. A VBR is used when device is a USB flash drive or floppy disk. There will be MBR if device is hard disk. It is the code in the MBR which generally understands disk partitioning and in turn, is responsible for loading and running the VBR of whichever primary partition is set to boot (the *active* partition).

Furthermore, whatever is stored in the first sector of a floppy diskette, USB device, hard disk or any other *bootable* storage device, is not required to immediately load any bootstrap code for an OS, if ever. The BIOS merely passes control to whatever exists there, as long as the sector meets the very simple qualification of having the boot record signature of 0x55, 0xAA in its last two bytes. This is why it's easy to replace the usual bootstrap code found in an MBR with more complex loaders, even large multi-functional boot managers (programs stored elsewhere on the device which can run without an operating system), allowing users a number of choices in what occurs next. Abuse often occurs in the form of boot sector viruses with this kind of freedom.

(d) Writing Boot Block

A PC Master Boot Sector is just 512 bytes of machine code that the BIOS loads at bootup. It's basically unchanged since 1981 with the original IBM PC, although there is a new different standard called as EFI that is just now catching on with the original interface.

The boot sector is a fixed 512 bytes long. If you need more data, the boot sector code needs to read it in manually.

It's 16-bit x86 code, so it starts with "BITS 16". Because we're in 16 bit mode, "eax" isn't available, but "ax" is!

It's in raw binary machine code format, so you compile with "-f bin".

The sector MUST end with the two bytes "dw 0xAA55", or the BIOS won't boot it. It's also got some partition information in the 64 bytes before this.

It's totally full raw access to the machine, so "cli" (clear interrupts) is a good way to avoid problems at startup.

Here's an example :
BITS 16 ; everything here is 16 bit code
; Code gets loaded by the PC BIOS into address 0x7C00 and executed.
    mov al,'H'
    mov ah,0x0e ; print command
    int 0x10 ; talk to video card
    mov al,'i'
    mov ah,0x0e ; print command
    int 0x10 ; talk to video card
hang :
    jmp hang
; Pad data out to magic boot sector identifier
times 512-2-($-$$) db 0
    db 0x55
    db 0xaa

You compile your little boot block with :

    nasm -f bin -o boot.bin yourcode.S

This should make a 512 byte file full of machine code. If you point a virtual machine emulator at this as a tiny hard drive image, it should boot and run! On a Linux machine, you can copy this onto a flash drive or floppy using "dd":

    sudo dd if=boot.bin of=/dev/sdX

This will actually boot any machine using pre-EFI BIOS.

5.3 BAD BLOCK

A Bad block is damaged area of magnetic storage media. As it is damaged, it is not reliable either to store or retrieve data from bad block.

In magnetic storage media, bad blocks can happen when a location on a hard disk is defective or when the cyclic redundancy checks (CRC) for a particular storage block does not match the data read by the disk. To write over the original file is the one of the best ways to fix a file that has been caused by bad block. This is how data or CRC can be fixed.

As flash is not magnetic medium, still it can experience bad blocks. Managing bad blocks is an important part of improving the reliability and endurance of NAND flash drives. Blocks can become worn from use, making them unusable after a certain number of write and erase cycles. To ensure that no block has excessive use compared with other blocks, wear-leveling algorithm can be implemented. This management is done by writing software to do this all which in turns extends the life of solid state device. To avoid bad blocks, software checks device's Bad Block Table (BBT). This is done before reading from or writing to a NAND device. There are two types of BBT's :

1. **NAND-Resident BBT's :** These are preserved across system boots.
2. **RAM-Resident BBT's :** These must be created each time system is booted.

Bad blocks, also called bad sectors, are sections of magnetic storage media (i.e., hard disks and floppy disks) that cannot be reliably used for storing and retrieving data.

A block is a uniform unit of the storage media whose size is determined at the time of high-level formatting (i.e., creation of a filesystem). If the mke2fs command (which is used to create the standard Linux ext2 and ext3 filesystems) is used, valid block size values are 1024, 2048 or 4096 bytes. The default block size on a typical Red Hat 9 Linux installation is 4096 bytes.

New disks are given a low level formatting at the factory, which consists of writing the track and sector markers on the blank magnetic media. If one of these new sectors cannot be read or write correctly, then it is marked as bad or invalid and a spare sector is used to replace it. Similarly, if, in use, a block does not record correctly after several attempts, it is marked bad and is remapped to a spare defect-free block.

The list of bad blocks is provided to the filesystem, which stores it in a special file and remembers not to use those blocks. This relieves the operating system of the task of keeping track of bad blocks and ensures that the computer only sees a well-behaved, defect-free device. The e2fsck command, which is used to check ext2 and ext3 filesystems, automates the process of giving the list to the filesystem and thus is highly reliable.

The badblocks program is used for checking for bad blocks is on Unix-like operating systems. This program should only be used directly when checking a blank partition or a filesystem other than ext2 or ext3. When checking an ext2 or ext3 filesystem partition, e2fsck should be used, which runs badblocks in the background. Some Microsoft Windows operating systems as well as MS-DOS contain a program called ScanDisk to check for bad blocks.

5.3.1 Bad Block Management

Bad block management (BBM) is a critical component of NAND flash drivers to improve the reliability and endurance of the flash. NAND is shipped from the factory with "mostly good" cells, meaning there are some cells that are non-functional even when the flash is new. Blocks can also go bad over time, causing loss of data stored in the flash memory or even a bricked device. To prevent flash memory corruption, the Datalight line of FlashFX products employs patented bad block management technology to map bad sectors and avoid storing data in those areas. Using Datalight FlashFX flash memory drivers makes bad block management worry-free, making NAND flash reliable and reducing warranty returns.

5.4 MOST POPULAR LINUX / UNIX DISK MANAGEMENT COMMANDS

1. **$ fdisk -l :** To outlook the entire accessible partitions of the disk.
2. **$ fdisk -l / dev / sda :** To see all the hard disk partitions for the specific hard disk.
3. **$ fdisk -d :** To delete the partition of the hard disk.
4. **$ fdisk -n :** To create the new partition of the hard disk.
5. **$ fdisk -s :** To see the size of the existing disk partitions.
6. **$ fdisk -f :** To fix the disk partition which you delete, create or modify.

B. SWAP SPACE MANAGEMENT

5.5 OVERVIEW OF SWAP SPACE MANAGEMENT

We know that all computer uses virtual memory to boost up RAM. I mean, virtual memory allows programs to run on your system as if it had more RAM than is actually available. But there are some compromises that you need to do when you use virtual memory, like

- Whatever memory is allocated to your program use, it must be backed up by same amount of swap space. We refer to it as paging space. Swap space is a specially formatted area of your disk that the operating system can use while it is managing the real memory of your computer.

  It means in principle, all or part of virtual memory used by your program can be moved to swap space area at any time by operating system. So whenever there may be shortage of swap space, operating system may cancel the job due to insufficient room to your job to run.

- Performance may suffer when virtual memory used by your program exceeds the available real memory. Performance will be harmed the most when operating system makes rapid transfers between real memory and swap space area. It means, program is repeatedly accessing more virtual memory than the available RAM in system.

  Performance is acceptable only when transfers between real memory and the swap space area are infrequent, that is, when the virtual memory area used by the program is smaller than the available RAM in system.

5.6 SWAP SPACE

5.6.1 Introduction to Swap Space

In Linux, when main memory is full, swap space is used as an alternative. Inactive pages are moved to swap space when system needs more memory resources and RAM. We cannot think swap space as complete replacement for more RAM. Virtual memory helps machine with small RAM. Swap space has slower access time than RAM as it is located on hard drives.

Swap space may have dedicated swap partition, a swap files or both.

Swap should equal 2x physical RAM for up to 2 GB of physical RAM and then an additional 1x physical RAM for any amount above 2 GB, but never less than 32 MB.

So, if :

M = Amount of RAM in GB and S = Amount of swap in GB, then

```
If M < 2
    S = M *2
Else
    S = M + 2
```

Using this formula, a system with 2 GB of physical RAM would have 4 GB of swap, while one with 3 GB of physical RAM would have 5 GB of swap. Creating a large swap space partition can be especially helpful if you plan to upgrade your RAM at a later time.

For systems with really large amounts of RAM (more than 32 GB) you can likely get away with a smaller swap partition (around 1x, or less, of physical RAM).

Important

File systems and LVM2 volumes assigned as swap space cannot be in use when being modified. For example, no system processes can be assigned the swap space, as well as no amount of swap should be allocated and used by the kernel. Use the free and cat /proc/swaps commands to verify how much and where swap is in use.

5.6.2 Adding Swap Space

Sometimes it is necessary that even after installations you have to add more swap space. For e.g. it might be possible to upgrade RAM from 128 MB to 256 MB, but swap space available could be just 256 MB. It is better if you increase swap space to 512 MB when you need to run memory intense operations that require large amount of memory.

Generally there are three options :

1. Create a new partition
2. Create a new swap file
3. Extend swap on existing LVM2 logical volume.

Out of these options, you pick up the third option. It means you extend an existing volume.

5.6.3 Swap Space Management

Swap space is a generic term for disk storage used to increase the amount of apparent memory available on the system. Under Linux, swap space is used to implement *paging*, a process whereby memory pages (a page is 4096 bytes on Intel systems; this value can differ on other architectures) are written out to disk when physical memory is low and read back into physical memory when needed. The process by which paging works is rather involved, but it is optimized for certain cases. The virtual memory subsystem under Linux allows memory pages to be shared between running programs. For example, if you have multiple copies of Emacs running simultaneously, there is only one copy of the Emacs code actually in memory. Also, text pages (those pages containing program code, not data) are usually read-only and therefore not written to disk when swapped out. Those pages are instead freed directly from main memory and read from the original executable file when they are accessed again.

Of course, swap space cannot completely make up for a lack of physical RAM. Disk access is much slower than RAM access, by several orders of magnitude. Therefore, swap is useful primarily as a means to run a number of programs simultaneously that would not otherwise fit into physical RAM; if you are switching between these programs rapidly you'll notice a lag as pages are swapped to and from disk.

At any rate, Linux supports swap space in two forms : as a separate disk partition or a file somewhere on your existing Linux filesystems. You can have up to 16 swap areas, with each swap area being a disk file or partition up to 128 MB in size (again, these values can differ on non-Intel systems). You math whizzes out there will realize that this allows up to 2 GB of swap space. (If anyone has actually attempted to use this much swap, the authors would love to hear about it, whether you're a math whiz or not.)

Note that using a swap partition can yield better performance, because the disk blocks are guaranteed to be continuous. In the case of a swap file, however, the disk blocks may be scattered around the filesystem, which can be a serious performance hit in some cases. Many people use a swap file when they must add additional swap space temporarily for example, if the system is thrashing because of lack of physical RAM and swap. Swap files are a good way to add swap on demand.

5.7 SWAP SPACE USE

An initialized swap space is taken into use with swapon command. This command intimates the kernel that the swap space can be used. The path to the swap space is given as the argument, so to start swapping on a temporary swap file one might use the following command.

```
$ swapon /extra-swap
$
```

Swap spaces can be used automatically by listing them in the /etc/fstab file.

```
/dev/hda8    none    swap    sw    0  0
/swapfile    none    swap    sw    0  0
```

The startup scripts will run the command swapon -a, which will start swapping on all the swap spaces listed in /etc/fstab. Therefore, whenever extra swap is required, swapon command is usually used.

Free command is used to monitor the use of swap spaces. It indicates total amount of swap space used.

```
$ free
             total    used    free    shared   buffers
Mem :        15152   14896     256    12404     2528
-/+ buffers :                12368     2784
Swap : 32452          6684   25768
$
```

The first line of output (Mem :) shows the physical memory. The total column does not show the physical memory used by the kernel, which is usually about a megabyte. The used column shows the amount of memory used (the second line does not count buffers). The free column shows completely unused memory. The shared column shows the amount of memory shared by several processes. The buffers column shows the current size of the disk buffer cache.

That last line (Swap :) shows similar information for the swap spaces. If this line is all zeroes, your swap space is not activated.

The same information is available via top, or using the proc filesystem in file /proc/meminfo. It is currently difficult to get information on the use of a specific swap space.

Swapoff command is used to remove swap space. Except for temporary swap spaces, it is usually not necessary to do it. Any pages in use in the swap space are swapped in first; if there is not sufficient physical memory to hold them, they will then be swapped out (to some other swap space). Linux will start to thrash if there is not enough virtual memory to hold all of the pages. After a long while it should recover, but meanwhile the system unusable. Before removing a swap space, it is important to check whether there is enough free memory available.

All the swap spaces that are used automatically with swapon -a can be removed from use with swapoff -a; it looks at the file /etc/fstab to find what to remove. Any manually used swap spaces will remain in use.

Even though there is a lot of free physical memory available, sometimes there is a lot of swap space can be used. This can happen for instance if at one point there is need to swap, but later a big process that occupied much of the physical memory terminates and frees the memory. Until it is needed, swapped-out data is not automatically swapped in, so physical memory may remain free for a long time.

C. SYSTEM PROTECTION

5.8 OVERVIEW OF SYSTEM PROTECTION

System protection refers to providing protection to computer system resources. Resources include CPU, memory, disk, software programs and most importantly data stored in computer system. Unauthorized users may cause severe damage to computer or data stored in it. Security must be ensured from malicious access to system, viruses, worms and unauthorized access to system.

5.8.1 Goals of Protection

- To prevent misuse of system by unauthorized users or programs.
- To ensure that system policies are strictly followed whenever shared resource is used. System policies need to be set by either system administrators or system designers.
- System administrator and users must implement these mechanisms effectively.
- To ensure that errant programs cause the minimal amount of damage possible.

5.8.2 Principles of Protection

- The principle of least privilege dictates that programs, users and systems be given just enough privileges to perform their tasks.
- This ensures that failures do the least amount of harm and allow the least of harm to be done.
- For example, if a program needs special privileges to perform a task, it is better to make it a SGID program with group ownership of "network" or "backup" or some other pseudo group, rather than SUID with root ownership. This limits the amount of damage that can occur if something goes wrong.
- Usually each user is given with their own account privileges which will be used to modify their own files.
- It is not recommended to use root account for doing day to day activities. Root account shall be used for those tasks that needs root privileges. For other tasks, administrator shall have an ordinary account.

5.9 DOMAIN OF PROTECTION

- We view computer as a collection of hardware and software. Some user views computer as collection of processes and objects.
- The need to know principle states that a process should only have access to those objects it needs to accomplish its task and furthermore only in the modes for which it needs access and only during the time frame when it needs access.
- Depending on object types, modes available gets varied.

5.9.1 Domain Structure

- Resource accessibility to the process is specified by protection domain.
- A set of objects and types of operations that needs to be invoked on each object is defined by each domain.
- An access right is the ability to execute an operation on an object.
- A domain is defined as a set of < object, {access right set} > pairs, as shown below in Fig. 5.1. Note that some domains may be disjoint while others overlap.

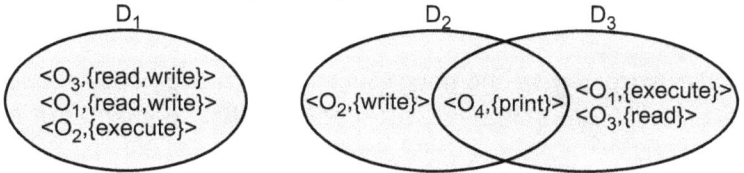

Fig. 5.1 : System with three protection domains

- There can be a static or dynamic association between process and domain :
  1. If the association is static, then the need-to-know principle requires a way of changing the contents of the domain dynamically.
  2. If the association is dynamic, then there needs to be a mechanism for domain switching.
- Domains can be realized in different ways : as users, as process or as procedures. For example if each user corresponds to a domain, then that domain defines the access of that user and changing domains involves changing user ID.

5.9.2 An Example : UNIX

- In UNIX, each user is associated with domains.
- Certain programs operate with the SUID bit set, which effectively changes the user ID. This therefore allows access to domain while program is running. Sometime this lead to some potential for abuse.
- Some systems use an alternative for this. I mean they place privileged programs in special directories which in turn attain the identity of directory owner when they run. Because of this, it is difficult for crackers to place SUID programs in random directories around the system.
- Another alternative is that do not at all allow changing of ID. Instead of this, at boot time, launch special privileged daemons. So whenever user needs special tasks to be performed, they send messages to these daemons.

5.9.3 An Example : MULTICS

- The MULTICS system uses a complex system of rings. In this each ring corresponds to different protection domain. It is shown in Fig. 5.2.

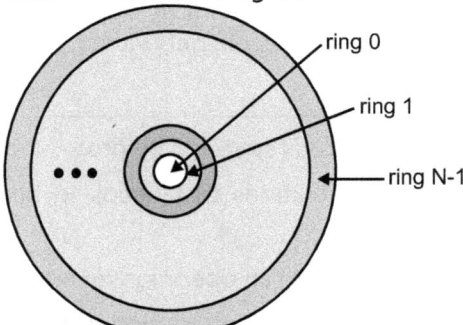

Fig. 5.2 : MULTICS using ring structure

- Rings are numbered from 0 to 7, with outer rings having a subset of the privileges of the inner rings.
- In this, each file is treated as memory segment. Each segment includes some specific details. Details are like ring number associated with that segment, privileges in terms of read, write and execute.
- Each process runs in a ring. According to the *current-ring-number*, a counter is associated with each process.

- A process operating in one ring can only access segments associated with higher (farther out) rings and then only according to the access bits. Segments associated with lower rings are not accessible to processes.
- Domain switching is achieved by a process in one ring calling upon a process operating in a lower ring. This is controlled by several factors stored with each segment descriptor :
  1. An *access bracket*, defined by integers b1 <= b2.
  2. A *limit* b3 > b2
  3. A *list of gates,* identifying the entry points at which the segments may be called.
- If a process operating in ring i calls a segment whose bracket is such that b1 <= i <= b2, then the call succeeds and the process remains in ring i.
- Otherwise a trap to the operating system occurs and is handled as follows :
  1. If i < b1, then the call is allowed, because we are transferring to a procedure with fewer privileges. However if any of the parameters being passed are of segments below b1, then they must be copied to an area accessible by the called procedure.
  2. If i > b2, then the call is allowed only if i <= b3 and the call is directed to one of the entries on the list of gates.
- Overall we say that this approach is less efficient and more complex than other schemes.

5.10 THREATS AND ATTACKS

5.10.1 Security Problems

Here we dealwith protecting systems from deliberate attacks, either internal or external, from individuals intentionally attempting to steal information, damage information, or otherwise deliberately wreak havoc in some manner.

Some of the most common types of violations include :

- **Theft of Service :** This includes unauthorized use of resources. For e.g. theft of CPU cycles, tapping into target's telephone or network services, installation of daemons running unauthorized file server.
- **Breach of Confidentiality :** This includes stealing private or confidential information. For e.g. theft of credit card numbers, patent, secret formulas, trade secrets, medical information, manufacturing procedures, financial information, etc.
- **Breach of Availability :** This includes unauthorized destruction of data, often just for the "fun" of causing havoc. Vandalism of web sites is a common form of this violation.
- **Denial of Service, DOS :** This includes preventing legitimate users to use system. This is done often by overwhelming or overloading system with an excess request for services.
- **Breach of Integrity :** This includes unauthorized modification of data. This may have serious indirect consequences. For e.g. a popular game or other program's source code could be modified to open up security holes on users systems before being released to the public.

5.10.2 Security Attacks

Masquerading is one of the most common attacks on computer system found. In this, the attacker pretends to be a trusted third party. Man-in-the-middle attack is variation of masquerading. In this the attacker masquerades as both ends of the conversation to two targets.

A replay attack involves repeating a valid transmission. Sometimes this can be the entire attack, (such as repeating a request for a money transfer), or other times the content of the original message is replaced with malicious content. Fig. 5.3 illustrates these standard attacks.

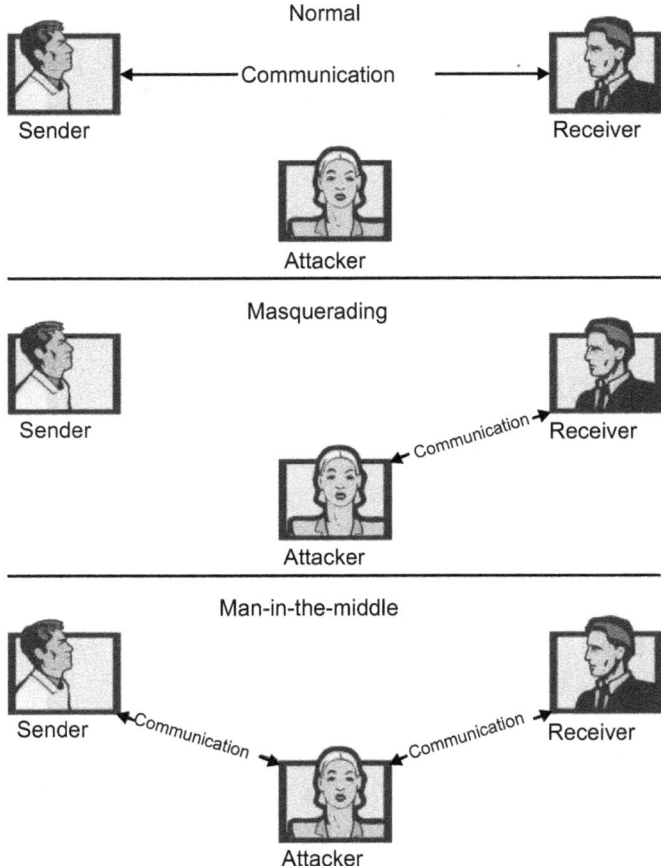

Fig. 5.3 : Standard security attacks

There are four levels at which a system must be protected :
1. **Physical :** The easiest way to steal data is to pocket the backup tapes. If attacker gets an access to root console, by making use of special privileges, attacker may provide harm to the system. This may include rebooting the system as root from removable device/media. Sometimes even general access to terminal in a computer room do provides attacker an opportunity to damage the system. Actually today's high end network services do provide attacker with remote access to the system.

2. **Human :** There is some concern that the humans who are allowed access to a system be trustworthy and that they cannot be coerced into breaching security. However more and more attacks today are made via social engineering, which basically means fooling trustworthy people into accidentally breaching security.
   - **Phishing :** This involves revealing confidential information of people. This is usually done by sending an innocent looking email or by designing a website. For e.g. spam emails.
   - **Dumpster Diving :** This involves searching the trash or other locations for passwords that are written down. (Note : Passwords that are too hard to remember, or which must be changed frequently are more likely to be written down somewhere close to the user's station.)
   - **Password Cracking :** This involves divining user's passwords, either by watching them type in their passwords, knowing something about them like their pet's names, or simply trying all words in common dictionaries. While setting up passwords try to make use of better combination of alphanumeric and special characters. It is recommended that you change the passwords frequently.
3. **Operating System :** It is expected that operating system protects itself form security breaches. Security breaches include denial of service, stack overflow violations, memory access violations and many others.
4. **Network :** In modern computing environment, network communication has become more important and pervasive. It has become mandatory to protect this area. This protection includes protecting local machine that are part of network and network itself from internal and external attacks. This has become challenging issues.

5.10.3 Program Threats

There are many common threats to modern systems. Only few are discussed here :

1. **Trojan Horse**
   - A *Trojan Horse* is a program that secretly performs some maliciousness in addition to its visible actions.
   - Some Trojan Horses are deliberately written as such and others are the result of legitimate programs that have become infected with *viruses*.
   - One dangerous opening for Trojan Horses is long search paths and in particular paths which include the current directory (".") as part of the path. If a dangerous program having the same name as a legitimate program (or a common misspelling, such as "sl" instead of "ls") is placed anywhere on the path, then an unsuspecting user may be fooled into running the wrong program by mistake.
   - Another classic Trojan Horse is a login emulator. It records a user's account name and password, issues a "password incorrect" message and then logs off the system. The user then tries again (with a proper login prompt), logs in successfully and doesn't realize that their information has been stolen.

- Two solutions can be thought for Trojan Horse :
  1. On logouts, present system usage statistics.
  2. On log in, use non trappable key sequence. For example ALT+CTRL+Delete.

  This is how many new systems have started using these solutions.
- **Spyware** is another version of Trojan Horse. It is often included in free software that you download from Internet. Spyware program generate pop-up browser windows and may also accumulate information about the user and deliver it to some central site. Another job that spyware does is sending spam email message. Example of spyware is covert channels in which surreptitious communications occurs.

2. Trap Door

- A *Trap door* is when a designer or a programmer (or hacker) deliberately inserts a security hole that they can use later to access the system.
- If system becomes untrustworthy because of trap door, then that system can be never trustworthy again. Even the backup tapes may contain a copy of some cleverly hidden back door.
- Existence of trap door can be found in many applications. For e.g. if attacker put it into compiler then whatever programs will be compiled through that compiler, will have security holes. This is actually dangerous as code inspection of program being compiled would not reveal any problems.

3. Logic Bomb

- A Logic Bomb is code that is not designed to cause problems all the time. But they will be used when certain set of circumstance or some other noticeable events occurs.
- A classic example is the Dead-Man Switch, which is designed to check whether a certain person (e.g. the author) is logging in every day and if they don't log in for a long time (presumably because they've been fired), then the logic bomb goes off and either opens up security holes or causes other problems.

4. Stack and Buffer Overflow

- This is a classic method of attack. It exploits bugs in system code which then allows buffers to overflow. Consider what happens in the following code, for example, if argv[1] exceeds 256 characters :
  - The strcpy command will overflow the buffer, overwriting adjacent areas of memory.
  - The problem could be avoided using str*n*cpy, with a limit of 255 characters copied plus room for the null byte.

C Program with Buffer Overflow Condition :

```
#include
#define BUFFER_SIZE 256
int main( int argc, char * argv[ ] )
{
 char buffer[ BUFFER_SIZE ];
if( argc < 2 )
```

```
        return -1;
    else {
        strcpy( buffer, argv[ 1 ] );
        return 0;
    }
}
```

5. **Viruses**
- A virus is a fragment of code embedded in an otherwise legitimate program. It is designed to replicate itself. While doing this it infects other programs and eventually wreaks havoc.
- Viruses are more likely to infect computer systems. But this is not applicable to all systems. For example UNIX like system do not allow virus to enter into it.
- Viruses are delivered to systems in a virus dropper, usually some form of a Trojan Horse and usually via e-mail or unsafe downloads.
- Viruses take many forms shown in Fig. 5.4. shows typical operation of a boot sector virus

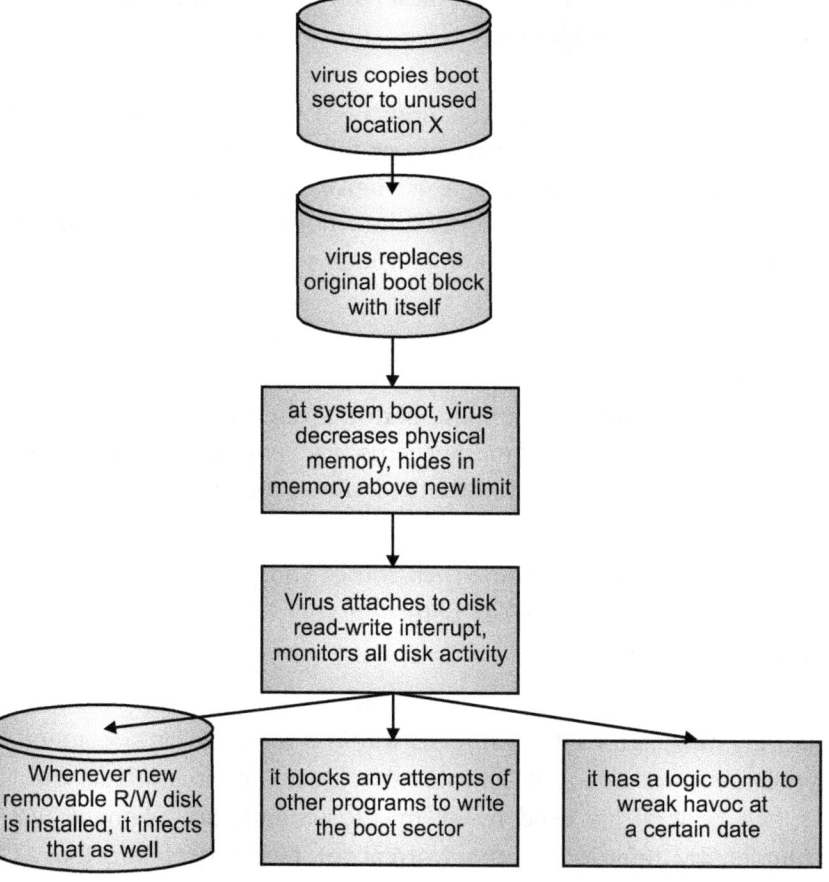

Fig. 5.4 : A boot-sector computer virus

5.10.4 Common Types of Computer Viruses

1. Boot Viruses

Since nobody uses floppy disks anymore, these types of computer virus are left to infect only the master boot records of the hard disk. The boot record program loads the operating system in the memory at startup. These viruses replace the boot record and move it to a different part of the hard disk, or simply overwrite it. As you can imagine, once you start your operating system, it loads into memory, along with the virus. Once the virus is in the memory, it is free to do whatever it was programmed to do. To avoid loading the boot record viruses into memory, you must boot your operating system from another source (another hard drive or a bootable CD/DVD).

2. Program Viruses

These types of computer virus will infect only executable files (with extensions like .BIN, .COM, .EXE, .OVL, .DRV and .SYS). Once executed, these programs load into memory, along with the virus contained within them. Once in the memory, the scenario repeats the virus is free to act and infect other files or simply deliver its payload. These viruses are friendlier than boot viruses and can be removed a lot easier.

3. Multipartite Viruses

These computer viruses are hybrids, derived from boot viruses and program viruses. They infect executable files, just like the program viruses but, once the executable is executed, it infects the master boot records. The scenario is similar to the boot virus's one : once you boot your operating system, the virus is loaded into the memory, from where it is free to infect other programs and replicate itself, ultimately delivering the payload.

4. Stealth Viruses

These viruses are specialized in avoiding detection and will use a number of techniques to do so. Most of them simply redirect the hard disk head, forcing it to read another memory sector instead of their own. Some of them also alter the reading of the file size shown when listing the directory. These types of computer virus are very hard to find by humans, but antivirus software is specially designed to track them down and erase them.

5. Polymorphic Viruses

The polymorphic viruses will always change their source code from one infection to another. Each infection is different and this makes detection very hard. However, detection is still possible, depending on the antivirus.

6. Macro Viruses

This virus is relatively new and it infects macros within a template or document. When you open a word processing document, it activates the virus. The virus infects the Normal.dot template, which is a general file used by all the documents. So, whenever you open an uninfected document, by referring to the Normal.dot file, it gets infected as well. This infection can only spread if infected documents are opened on another machine.

7. Active X Viruses

Most people do not know how to configure ActiveX and Java controls, unconsciously leaving a security hole. Applets are then allowed to run freely on the machine, delivering all ActiveX viruses. By simply turning off some ActiveX and Java controls in the browser, a user can efficiently protect their PC from this type of computer virus.

D. INTRODUCTION TO UNIX

5.11 THE UNIX SYSTEM

The UNIX system is known for multiuser and multitasking system. This means, it allows single or multiprocessor to simultaneously several programs by one or many users. UNIX contains several command interpreters (we refer them as shell) and many utilities. UNIX is highly portable means implementation and use of UNIX system is possible on almost all hardware.

Currently, UNIX systems have a strong foothold in professional and university environments. This has become possible because of its stability, its increased level of security and observance of standards, notably in terms of networks.

5.12 HISTORY OF UNIX

Ken Thompson developed first UNIX system at Bell AT&T laboratory, Murray Hill in New Jersey, USA during 1965. Ken Thompson's aim was to develop a simple interactive operating system called "MULTICS" (Multiplexed Information and Computing System) in order to run a game which he had created (space travel, a simulation of the solar system).

A consortium made up of MIT (Massachusetts Institute of Technology), General Electric Co. and Bell Lab was then formed around MULTICS.

In April 1969, the AT&T laboratories decided to use the GECOS (General Electric Comprehensive Operating System) instead of MULTICS. However, Ken Thompson and Dennis Ritchie who joined the team needed to make the space travel game work on a smaller machine (a DEC PDP-7, Programmed Data Processor which only had 4K of memory to make user programs run), this is why they recreated the system in order to create a limited version of MULTICS called UNICS (UNiplexed Information and Computing Service), quickly shortened to UNIX.

The date of 1st January 1970 is considered as the birth date of the UNIX system, which explains why all system clocks for UNIX operating systems start from this date.

Alongside these activities, D. Ritchie played a large part in the definition of the C language (since he is considered as one of its creators with B. W. Kernighan), so the whole system was entirely rewritten in C in 1973 and called UNIX Time-Sharing System (TSS). When the system passed version 7 in 1979, its development was accompanied by many notable modifications such as :

- The removal of limitations linked to file sizes.
- Better portability of the system (operating on many hardware platforms).
- The addition of many utilities.

A decree dating from 1956 prevented the company ATT, to which Bell Labs belonged, from marketing anything other than telephone or telegraph equipment, this is why the decision was taken in 1973 to distribute UNIX source into universities for educational purposes.

From the end of 1977 researchers from the University of California redeveloped a version of UNIX from source supplied by AT&T in order to run the system on their VAX platforms and called it BSD for Berkeley Software Development.

So two development branches of the source grew :

- The AT&T branch which would become System V from UNIX System Labs (USL).
- BSD (Berkeley Software Development) developed by the University of California.

In 1977 AT&T made the UNIX source available to other companies, although a great number of UNIX-like systems were developed :

- AIX, commercial UNIX based on System V developed in February 1990 by IBM.
- Sun Solaris, commercial UNIX based on System V and BSD developed by SUN Microsystems.
- HP-UX, commercial UNIX based on BSD developed from 1986 by Hewlett Packard.
- Ultrix, commercial UNIX developed by DEC.
- IRIX, commercial UNIX developed by SGI.
- UNIXware, commercial UNIX developed by Novell.
- UNIX SCO, commercial UNIX based on System V developed from 1979 by Santa Cruz Operations and Hewlett Packard.
- Tru64 UNIX, commercial UNIX developed by Compaq.

In 1983 AT&T had the right to market its UNIX, which marked the appearance of UNIX System V, the commercial version of its UNIX system.

In 1985 a Dutch professor called Andrew Tannenbaum developed a minimal operating system called MINIX in order to teach system programming to his students.

In 1991, a student, Linus Torvalds decided to design on the MINIX model, an operating system capable of running on type 386 architectures. He called this operating system "Linux" and posted the following message on the comp.os.minix discussion forum :

1. Hello everybody out there using minix -
2. I'm doing a (free) operating system (just a hobby,
3. won't be big and professional like gnu) for 386(486) AT clones.

5.13 ARCHITECTURE OF UNIX OPERATING SYSTEM

UNIX kernel is hub of the operating system. Its job is to allocate time and memory to programs, to handle file store and communications in response to system calls.

As an illustration of the way that the shell and the kernel work together, suppose a user types on terminal "rm myfile". Here removal of file "myfile" is expected. The shell searches the file store for the file containing the program rm and then requests the kernel, through system calls, to execute the program rm on myfile. When the process "rm myfile" has finished running, the shell then returns the UNIX prompt % to the user, indicating that it is waiting for next commands. Fig. 5.5 shows general architecture of UNIX system.

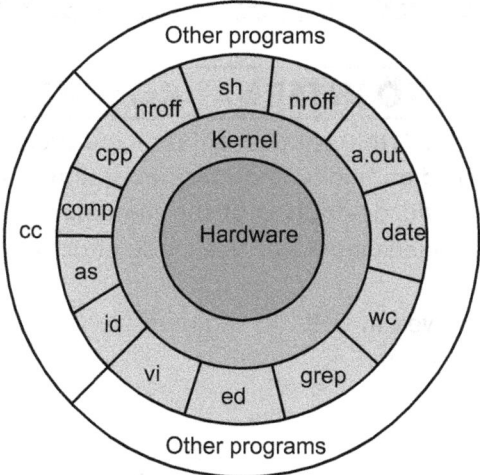

Fig. 5.5 : Architecture of UNIX operating system

Functions performed by the kernel are :
- To manage main memory and to allocate it to each process.
- To schedule work done by CPU.
- To organize file transfer from one machine to another.
- To accept instructions from shell and carry them.
- To enforce access permissions.

The Shell

As said earlier, shell is a command line interpreter (CLI). It acts as an interface between user and the kernel. After successful login, login checks for user details and starts another program called shell. Job of shell is to interpret commands entered by user. After shell terminates as called program (I mean each command does have respective program), it returns user another prompt (usually shown as '%').

Shell customization is possible to user. Users can use different shell on same machine. Shell keeps commands that are executed successfully into buffer, so that if user wants to execute the earlier executed command, he does not need to retype it. Simply by pressing up key on keyboard he can see earlier commands and can select the appropriate one.

You can use any one of these shells if they are available on your system. And you can switch between the different shells once you have found out if they are available.
- Bourne shell (sh).
- C shell (csh).
- TC shell (tcsh).
- Korn shell (ksh).
- Bourne Again SHell (bash).

E. INTERNAL REPRESENTATION OF FILE

5.14 INTRODUCTION TO INTERNAL REPRESENTATION OF FILE

In UNIX based file systems all the entities on disk are treated as a file. The internal representation of a file is called an "inode" (contraction of term - index node) which contains all the required information and description of the file data and its layout on disk. In this section we would build an understanding of this inode structure and also the way the files are organized on the disk.

Reverse tree structure is followed in UNIX to organize file structure. Fig. 5.6 shows a typical organization of files in UNIX system.

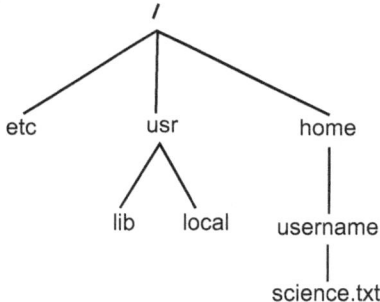

Fig. 5.6 : Typical organization of file in UNIX system

The diagram looks like any upside-down tree. The slash (/) indicates the root directory. Names like etc, usr, local are directories and Science.txt is a file. The regular files in UNIX are the leaves in a tree structure.

In the original Unix file system, Unix divided physical disks into logical disks called *partitions*. Each partition is a standalone file system. We will use the term ``file system'' when referring to a single partition.

Each disk device is given its own *major device number* and each partition has an associated *minor device number* which the device driver uses to access the raw file system.

The major/minor device number combination serves as a handle into the device switch table. That is, the major number acts as an index and the minor number is passed as an argument to the driver routines so that they can recognize the specific instance of a device.

5.14.1 Unix Directory

Internally, Unix stores directories in files. The file type (of the inode) is marked ``directory'' and the file contains pairs of name/inode numbers.

For example, when a user issues *open(`` /etc/passwd'', ...)* the kernel performs the following operations :

1. Because the file name is a full path name, find the inode of the root directory (found in superblock) and search the corresponding file for the entry ``etc''
2. When the entry ``etc'' is found, fetch its corresponding inode and check that it is of type directory
3. Scan the file associated with ``/etc'' looking for ``passwd''
4. Finally, fetch the inode associated with *passwd*'s directory entry, verify that it is a regular file and start accessing the file.

Note : What would the system do when opening ``/dev/tty01''?

Eventually, the system would find the inode corresponding to the device and note that its file type was ``special''. Thus, it would extract the major/minor device number pair from the length field of the inode and use the device number as an index into the device switch table.

Getwd()

How to get string of current directory? Have only the inode of the current directory.

```
get current inode
while (inode != root inode) {
    get inode of parent from ..
    search parent's directory file to match our inode number
```

Where should a file's data blocks be physically located?

To improve performance, we might want to place a file's data blocks in contiguous sectors on disk. However, this leads to inefficiencies in allocating space, or forces the user to specify the size of the file at creation time.

The Unix file system allocates *data blocks* (blocks that contain a file's contents) one at a time from a pool of free blocks. Unix uses 4K blocks. Moreover, a file's blocks are scattered randomly within the physical disk.

5.15 BASIC BUILDING BLOCK IN FILE SYSTEM

1. Inode

Inode is a complex data structure. It holds all the necessary information that specifies a file. Inode detail includes file permissions, access time, memory layout of file on disk, number of different links to file, owner of file, last modification time and so on.

2. Global File Table

As name suggest, it contains information that is global to kernel. For example the byte offset in the file where the user's next read/write will start and the access rights allowed to the opening process.

3. Process File Descriptor Table

It is local to every process and contains information like the identifiers of the files opened by the process. Whenever, a process creates a file, it gets an index from this table primarily known as file descriptor.

4. Disk Blocks

These are sequence of logical blocks of a particular size for example 512, 1024, 2048 bytes etc. This is the amount of data that would be accessed in one single disk read/write.

5. Boot Block

It's the first sector/block in a file system and typically contains the bootstrap code needed to boot the system.

6. Super Block

It specifies the state of a file system like the size of the system, how many files it can store, location of free space on the file system etc.

5.16 BUFFER SYSTEM FOR DISK BLOCK

The simplicity of UNIX file systems lies in the usage of buffer pool for manipulation of disk data. Direct read/write from/to the disk will never be done by kernel. For this purpose, it first allocates in memory buffer and then does the data manipulation. As far as efficiency is concerned, it depends on internal algorithms used for data manipulation and the way buffers are organized.

Allocating space for a sufficiently large number of buffers is done by kernel during system initialization. The data in a buffer is actually a mapping of the data on the disk blocks. Here buffer mean in memory copy of data on the disk. However, the mapping is temporary until the kernel re-maps the buffer to some other data on the disk. Disk block maps only one single buffer otherwise it becomes hard for kernel to figure out which buffer contains the current data.

Buffers are arranged in the form of a hash queues with one header which helps in organizing the buffer list based on the device and block numbers to have a simple and fast search mechanism. Each buffer is associated with state. It can be locked or valid data or free. Kernel makes use of LRU (Least Recently Used) order to maintain free list of buffers. Free list is a circular doubly link list with a dummy head marking the start/end of the list. So when system is booted, every buffer is put on the free list. When kernel needs a particular block in buffer pool, it takes it from the head of the free list. It then removes buffer from free list. When the kernel frees a buffer it attaches it to the tail of the free list. This is diagrammatically represented in Fig. 5.7.

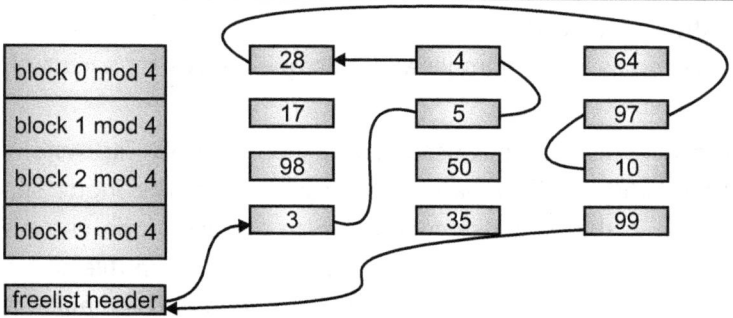

Fig. 5.7 : Buffer list

5.16.1 Buffer Cache

Now we know that the files are stored on the hard drive and the processes can access these files and create new files on the disk. When a process requests for a file the kernel brings the file into the main memory where user process can change, read or access the file.

The kernel read the super block to figure out the details about the hard drive and the inode table to find the meta data information of any file. So the kernel reads the inode into the memory whenever any process want to access the data and write it back onto the hard disk when the process is done using the file.

The kernel could read and write the file directly from the hard disk and put it in memory and vice versa but the response time and throughput will be very low in this case because of disks sow data transfer speed.

To minimize the frequency of disk usage/access the kernel keeps a buffer to store the recently accessed files and/or frequently accessed files. This buffer is called the buffer cache.

When the process want to read a file the kernel attempts to read this file in the buffer cache, if the data is found in the buffer cache the data/file is sent to the process. If the file is not found in the buffer cache then the file is read from the disk and then kept in the buffer cache so that it can be made available to the process.

To minimize the disk access frequency the kernel may also implement the pre-caching or write delay functionalities.

5.17 INODE

5.17.1 Basics

The inode (also known as Index Node) is a very basic concept related to Linux and UNIX filesystem. Each and every object/element in the filesystem is associated with an inode.

You must be aware of the fact that, most of the countries have given a unique identity to their citizens in the form of a unique identification number ('Aadhar Card' in India and 'SSN' in the USA) to identify an individual easily and uniquely. This also leads to make all the paper work corresponding to any citizen easier to be handled.

Just like this identity, UNIX and Linux file system provides unique identity to their every member. This is referred as inode number and it uniquely exists for each and every file on file system.

Only 1% of the available disk space is occupied by inode in UNIX file system. This disk space would be either hard disk itself or partitions present on it. The inode space is helpful to "track" the files saved in the hard disk memory. Size of each inode entry is 128 bytes. The inode entries store metadata about each object of the filesystem (file or directory) that just points to these structures and does not store any kind of data. The metadata, stored by each inode entry, may have the following information about each structure :

- Inode number
- Number of blocks
- File deletion time
- File size
- File type
- Access control list (ACL)
- Status flag
- Group
- Owner
- Extended attribute
- File generation number
- Direct/indirect disk blocks
- File access, change and modification time
- Number of links
- Permissions

Name and inode number, these two entries are given to a file whenever it is created within a directory. Some of you may think that any parent directory contains the entire file and all the information relevant to it. But this might not be always true. So we see that a directory associates a file name with its inode number.

File name is used by user whenever he wants to access the file. But as far internal representation of file is concerned, file name is linked with its inode number. Inode table is maintained by system to get to know about mapping between inode number and respective associated inode.

"You store your information in a file and operating system stores information about a file in inode".

Fig. 5.8 and 5.9 shows inode structure of a file and directory respectively.

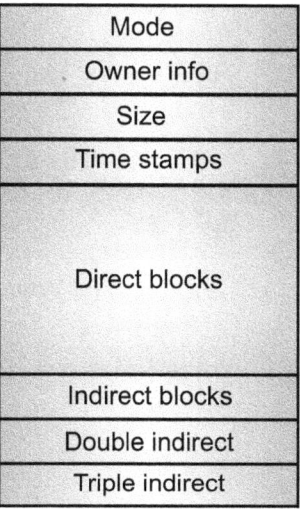

Fig. 5.8 : Inode structure of a file

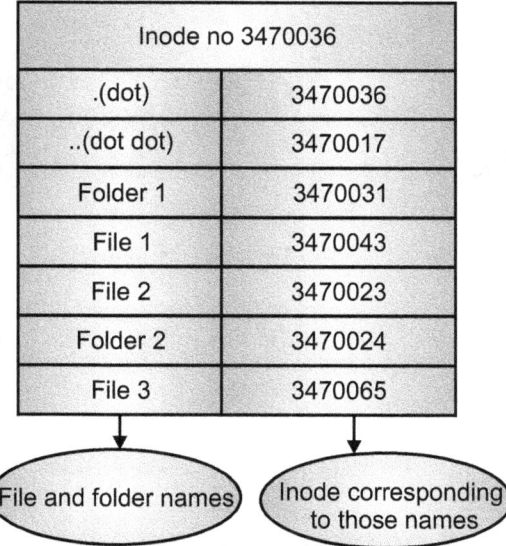

Fig. 5.9 : Inode structure of a directory

5.17.2 Accessing Inode

1. Ls -i command

As we all know, ls is used for listing all the files within a directory. ls command when used with option -i displays the list of files along with their inode numbers.

Syntax

$ ls –i

Example

Fig. 5.10 : Snapshot of ls –i command

2. **Df –i command**

The df command when used with option -i displays inode information.

Syntax

$ df –i

Example

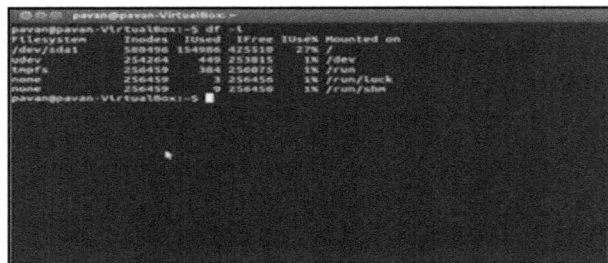

Fig. 5.11 : Snapshot of df –i command

3. **Stat Command**

Stat command is very useful in displaying the file statistics. This command also shows inode number of a file.

Syntax

$ stat [filename]

Example

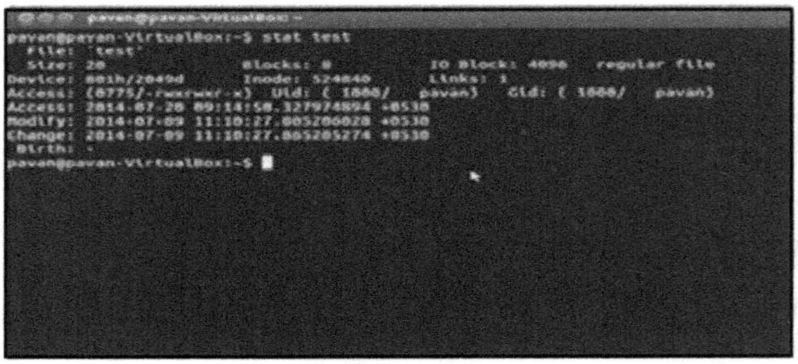

Fig. 5.12 : Snapshot of stat command

5.18 STRUCTURE OF REGULAR FILE

As stated previously inode contains the table of content of the file data on disk. As each disk block can be referenced by a number, the table of content is nothing but a sequence of disk block numbers. The file data may not always be stored in contiguous memory locations; hence we need to keep track of all the block numbers on the disk. The system V UNIX has following 13 entries as the table of contents :

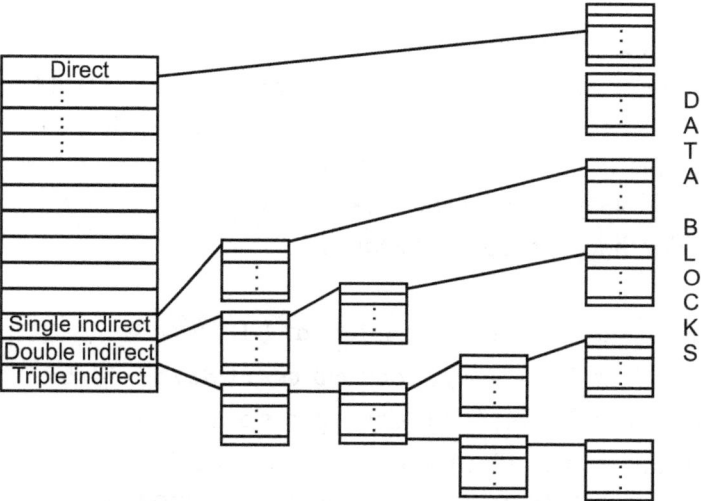

Fig. 5.13 : System V UNIX 13 entries as a table of contents

As shown in Fig. 5.13, the blocks marked "direct" can refer to a single disk block that contains the real data. "Single indirect" block contains the number of a disk block which itself contains a list of block numbers that we can reference and they have the real data. Going on the same line, we have "double indirect" and "triple indirect" blocks. Let's now try to get an estimate of the max limit on the size of a file that UNIX file system can handle.

Assume one block is of 1 Kbytes and a block number is an integer of 4 bytes (32 bits). Thus a block can have 256 block numbers.

> 10 direct blocks => 10 K bytes
> 1 single indirect block with 256 block number entries => 256 K bytes
> 1 double indirect block with 256 single indirect entries => 64 M bytes
> 1 triple indirect block with 256 double indirect entries => 16 G bytes

This is far more than what the 4-byte memory address can handle (2^{32} => 4 G bytes).

So, whenever a process wants to access any particular offset in a file, it will simply use this table of indexes and thus would load the appropriate disk block into memory.

5.19 SUPERBLOCK

A superblock is a record of the characteristics of a *filesystem*, including its size, the *block* size, the empty and the filled blocks and their respective counts, the size and location of the *inode* tables, the disk block map and usage information and the size of the *block groups*.

Each file system is different and they have type like ext2, ext3 etc. Further each file system has size like 5 GB, 10 GB and status such as mount status. In short each file system has a superblock, which contains information about file system such as :

- File system type
- Size
- Status
- Information about other metadata structures

You will be in trouble if this information is lost. For this reason, UNIX maintains multiple redundant copies of the superblock in every file system. This helps in many emergency situations. For example you can use backup copies to restore damaged primary super block. Following command displays primary and backup superblock location on /dev/sda3 :

```
$ dumpe2fs /dev/hda3 | grep -i superblock
```

Output

```
Primary superblock at 0, Group descriptors at 1-1
Backup superblock at 32768, Group descriptors at 32769-32769
Backup superblock at 98304, Group descriptors at 98305-98305
Backup superblock at 163840, Group descriptors at 163841-163841
Backup superblock at 229376, Group descriptors at 229377-229377
Backup superblock at 294912, Group descriptors at 294913-294913
```

The superblock is essentially file system metadata and defines the file system type, size, status and information about other metadata structures (metadata of metadata). The superblock is very critical to the file system and therefore is stored in multiple redundant copies for each file system. The superblock is a very "high level" metadata structure for the file system. For example, if the superblock of a partition, /var, becomes corrupt then the file system in question (/var) cannot be mounted by the operating system. Commonly in this event fsck is run and will automatically select an alternate, backup copy of the superblock and attempt to recover the file system. The backup copies themselves are stored in block groups spread through the file system with the first stored at a 1 block offset from the start of the partition. This is important in the event that a manual recovery is necessary. You may view information about superblock backups with the command dumpe2fs /dev/foo | grep -i superblock which is useful in the event of a manual recovery attempt. Let us suppose that the dumpe2fs command outputs the line Backup superblock at 163840, Group descriptors at 163841-163841. We can use this information and additional knowledge about the file system structure, to attempt to use this superblock backup : /sbin/fsck.ext3 -b 163840 -B 1024 /dev/foo. Please note that I have assumed a block size of 1024 bytes for this example.

5.20 PIPE

UNIX/Linux provides many ways for processes to communicate with each other. One of them is using pipes. This is something which is similar to a pipe that carries water in which water enters from one end and exits from the other. In UNIX pipes data enters from one end and exits from the other.

Pipe() is a system call that is used to create a pipe. Read() and write() system calls are used to read to and write from the pipe respectively. The C library in UNIX provides wrappers around these system calls which make their use much easier.

The function popen() is a wrapper for pipe, which allows us to create a pipe and read or write from it using C functions like fprintf(), fscanf(), etc.

5.20.1 Operation of Pipe

The open() system call creates a pipe and returns two file descriptors.
1. One that can be used to read from the pipe
2. Other that can be used to write into the pipe.

This can be visualized as shown in Fig. 5.14.

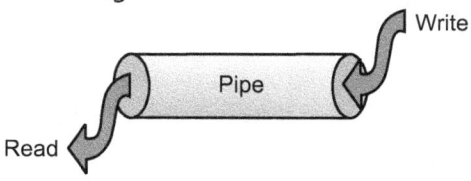

Fig. 5.14 : Visualizing pipe

These two descriptors are given to popen() function which then decides the next step based on what operation is requested by the process, read or write? Second argument to the pipe decides either of (i.e. "r" or "w") the operation. If the second argument was "r" that is the process is going to read from the pipe then the write file descriptor is changed to that of the standard output. Which means when the output of "command", which was passed as the first argument to open, instead of being printed on the standard output will now be sent into the pipe, which can be later read by using fscanf(). Thus the child is able to send data through the pipe to the parent process, achieving the communication between processes. This is visualized in Fig. 5.15 which indicates inter process communication using pipe.

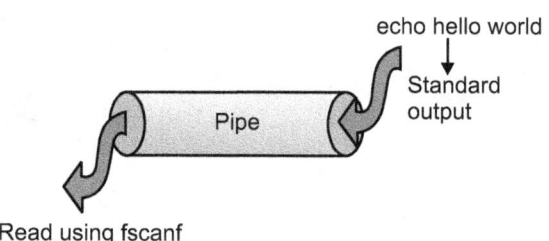

Fig. 5.15 : IPC using pipe

5.20.2 Types of Pipe

1. Anonymous Pipe

Anonymous pipe is also termed as pipe. By making use of pipe, one process stream data to other. As said earlier, pipe has two ends associated with a pair of file descriptors which makes it one to one communication or messaging mechanism. The processes those shares parent-child relationship, only among these processes, anonymous pipe can be setup and used.

2. Named Pipe

Named pipe is a variation to anonymous pipe. It allows communication between processes even though they are not related with each other. In order to communicate using named pipe, process opens special file as FIFO file. It means, one process opens FIFO file for writing while other opens it for reading.

5.20.3 Pipe Example using UNIX Utilities

The "more" command takes the standard input and paginates it on the standard output. This means that if a command displays more information than can be shown on one screen, the "more" program will pause after the first screen full (page) and wait for the user to press SPACE to see the next page or RETURN to see the next line.

Here is an example which will list all the files, with details (-la) in the /dev directory and pipe the output to more. The /dev directory should have dozens of files and hence ensure that more needs to paginate.

```
$ ls -la /dev | more
```

Output

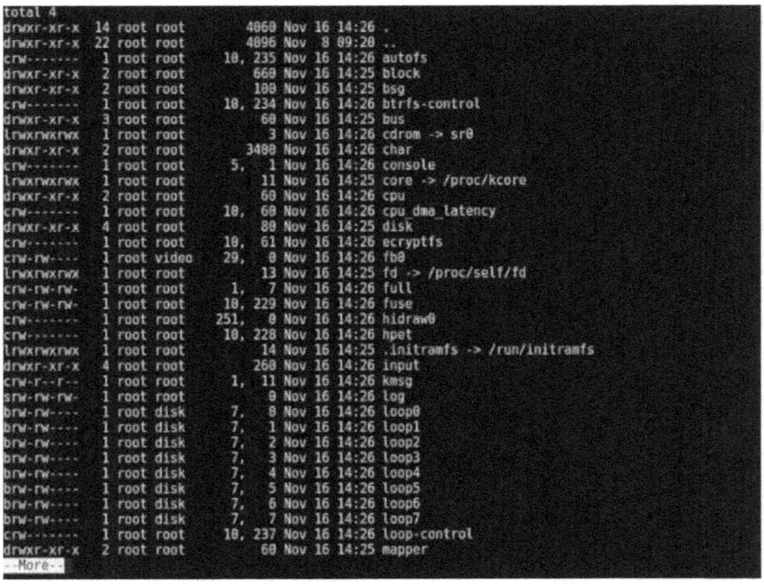

```
total 4
drwxr-xr-x  14 root root        4060 Nov 16 14:26 .
drwxr-xr-x  22 root root        4096 Nov  8 09:20 ..
crw-------   1 root root     10, 235 Nov 16 14:26 autofs
drwxr-xr-x   2 root root         660 Nov 16 14:25 block
drwxr-xr-x   2 root root         100 Nov 16 14:25 bsg
crw-------   1 root root     10, 234 Nov 16 14:26 btrfs-control
drwxr-xr-x   3 root root          60 Nov 16 14:25 bus
lrwxrwxrwx   1 root root           3 Nov 16 14:26 cdrom -> sr0
drwxr-xr-x   2 root root        3400 Nov 16 14:26 char
crw-------   1 root root      5,   1 Nov 16 14:26 console
lrwxrwxrwx   1 root root          11 Nov 16 14:25 core -> /proc/kcore
drwxr-xr-x   2 root root          60 Nov 16 14:26 cpu
crw-------   1 root root     10,  60 Nov 16 14:26 cpu_dma_latency
drwxr-xr-x   4 root root          80 Nov 16 14:25 disk
crw-------   1 root root     10,  61 Nov 16 14:26 ecryptfs
crw-rw----   1 root video    29,   0 Nov 16 14:26 fb0
lrwxrwxrwx   1 root root          13 Nov 16 14:25 fd -> /proc/self/fd
crw-rw-rw-   1 root root      1,   7 Nov 16 14:26 full
crw-rw-rw-   1 root root     10, 229 Nov 16 14:26 fuse
crw-------   1 root root    251,   0 Nov 16 14:26 hidraw0
crw-------   1 root root     10, 228 Nov 16 14:26 hpet
lrwxrwxrwx   1 root root          14 Nov 16 14:25 .initramfs -> /run/initramfs
drwxr-xr-x   4 root root         260 Nov 16 14:26 input
crw-r--r--   1 root root      1,  11 Nov 16 14:26 kmsg
srw-rw-rw-   1 root root           0 Nov 16 14:26 log
brw-rw----   1 root disk      7,   0 Nov 16 14:26 loop0
brw-rw----   1 root disk      7,   1 Nov 16 14:26 loop1
brw-rw----   1 root disk      7,   2 Nov 16 14:26 loop2
brw-rw----   1 root disk      7,   3 Nov 16 14:26 loop3
brw-rw----   1 root disk      7,   4 Nov 16 14:26 loop4
brw-rw----   1 root disk      7,   5 Nov 16 14:26 loop5
brw-rw----   1 root disk      7,   6 Nov 16 14:26 loop6
brw-rw----   1 root disk      7,   7 Nov 16 14:26 loop7
crw-------   1 root root     10, 237 Nov 16 14:26 loop-control
drwxr-xr-x   2 root root          60 Nov 16 14:25 mapper
--More--
```

Fig. 5.16 : Demonstrating pipe using UNIX utilities

Program 5.1 : Program for Pipe using C

```c
#include<unistd.h>
#include<stdlib.h>
#include<stdio.h>
#include<string.h>
int main()
{
int data_processed;
int file_pipes[2];
const char some_data[]= "123";
pid_t fork_result;
if(pipe(file_pipes)==0)
{
fork_result=fork();
if(fork_result==(pid_t)-1)
{
fprintf(stderr,"fork failure");
exit(EXIT_FAILURE);
}
  if(fork_result==(pid_t)0)
{
close(0);
dup(file_pipes[0]);
close(file_pipes[0]);
close(file_pipes[1]);
execlp("od","od","-c",(char *)0);
exit(EXIT_FAILURE);
}
else
{
close(file_pipes[0]);
data_processed=write(file_pipes[1],
some_data,strlen(some_data));
close(file_pipes[1]);
```

```
printf("%d -wrote %d bytes\n",(int)getpid(),data_processed);
}
}
exit(EXIT_SUCCESS);
}
```

The program creates a pipe and then forks. Now both parent and child process will have its own file descriptors for reading and writing. Therefore totally there are four file descriptors.

The child process will close its standard input with *close(0)* and calls duo(*file_pipes[0]*). This will duplicate the file descriptor associated with the read end. Then child closes its original file descriptor. As child will never write, it also closes the write file descriptor, *file_pipes[1]*. Now there is only one file descriptor 0 associated with the pipe that is standard input. Next, child uses the *exec* to invoke any program that reads standard input. The *od* command will wait for the data to be available from the user terminal.

Since the parent never read the pipe, it starts by closing the read end that is file_pipe[0]. When writing process of data has been finished, the write end of the parent is closed and exited. As there are no file descriptor open to write to pipe, the od command will be able to read the three bytes written to pipe, meanwhile the reading process will return 0 bytes indicating the end of the file.

F. PROCESS CONTROL

5.21 DEFINITION OF PROCESS

Let's recall the definition of process.

Process is a program in execution. The execution of a process must progress in a sequential fashion. Definition of process is following.

A process is defined as an entity which represents the basic unit of work to be implemented in the system.

5.21.1 Process Creation

Processes may create other processes through appropriate system calls, such as fork or spawn. The process which does the creating is termed the parent of the other process, wherein newly created process is termed as child.

Each process is uniquely identified because of its process identifier (PID). There is also a parent PID (PPID) for each process.

On typical UNIX systems the process scheduler is termed sched and is given PID 0. The first thing it does at system startup time is to launch init, which gives that process PID 1. Init then launches all system daemons and user logins and becomes the ultimate parent of all other processes. Fig. 5.17 shows a typical process tree for a UNIX like system.

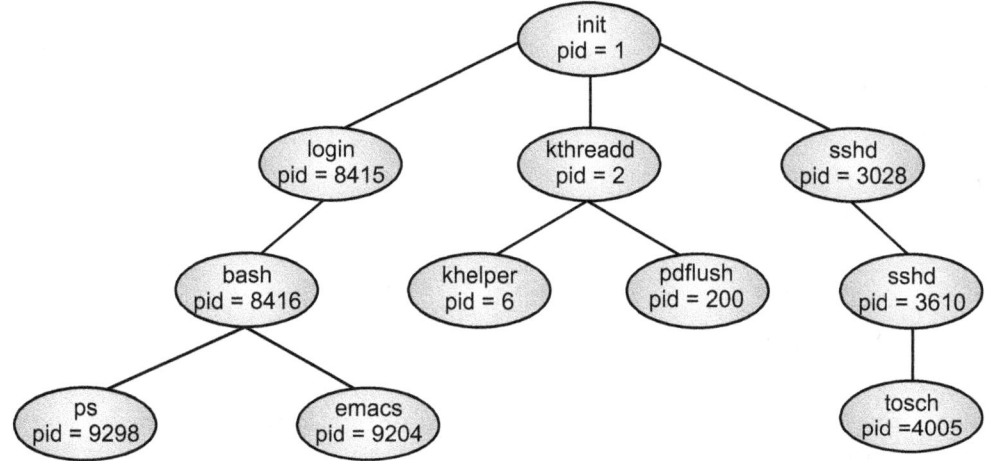

Fig. 5.17 : A tree of processes on typical UNIX like system

Depending on system implementation, a child process may receive some amount of shared resources with its parent. Child processes may or may not be limited to a subset of the resources originally allocated to the parent, preventing runaway children from consuming all of a certain system resource.

There are two options for the parent process after creating the child :

1. Wait for the child process to terminate before proceeding. The parent makes a wait( ) system call, for either a specific child or for any child, which causes the parent process to block until the wait() returns. UNIX shells normally wait for their children to complete before issuing a new prompt.

2. Run concurrently with the child, continuing to process without waiting. This is the operation seen when a UNIX shell runs a process as a background task. It is also possible for the parent to run for a while and then wait for the child later, which might occur in a sort of a parallel processing operation. (E.g. the parent may fork off a number of children without waiting for any of them, then do a little work of its own and then wait for the children.)

Two possibilities for the address space of the child relative to the parent :

1. The child may be an exact duplicate of the parent, sharing the same program and data segments in memory. Each will have their own PCB, including program counter, registers and PID. This is the behaviour of the fork system call in UNIX.

2. The child process may have a new program loaded into its address space, with all new code and data segments. This is the behaviour of the spawn system calls in Windows. UNIX systems implement this as a second step, using the exec system call.

5.22 PROCESS SYSTEM CALLS (FORK() AND EXEC())

1. **Fork()**

   #include <sys/types.h>
   #include <unistd.h>
   pid_t fork(void);

- The fork system call does not take an argument.
- The process that invokes the fork() is known as the parent and the new process is called the child.
- If the fork system call fails, it will return a -1.
- If the fork system call is successful, the process ID of the child process is returned in the parent process and a 0 is returned in the child process.
- When a fork() system call is made, the operating system generates a copy of the parent process which becomes the child process.
- The operating system will pass to the child process most of the parent's process information. However, some information is unique to the child process :
    - The child has its own process ID (PID)
    - The child will have a different PPID than its parent
    - System imposed process limits are reset to zero
        - All recorded locks on files are reset
    - The action to be taken when receiving signals is different

Simple Example of Fork

```
#include <stdio.h>
#include <sys/types.h>
#include <unistd.h>
int main(void)
{
  printf("Hello \n");
  fork();
  printf("bye\n");
  return 0;
}
```

Hello - is printed once by parent process

bye - is printed twice, once by the parent and once by the child

If the fork system call is successful a child process is produced that continues execution at the point where it was called by the parent process.

After the fork system call, both the parent and child processes are running and continue their execution at the next statement in the parent process.

A Summary of Fork() Return Values Follows :

fork_return > 0 : this is the parent

fork_return == 0 : this is the child

fork_return == -1 : fork() failed and there is no child.

2. **Exec()**

```
#include <unistd.h>
extern char **environ;
int execl(const char *path, const char *arg, ...);
int execlp(const char *file, const char *arg, ...);
int execle(const char *path, const char *arg , ..., char * const envp[]);
int execv(const char *path, char *const argv[]);
int execvp(const char *file, char *const argv[]);
```

"The exec family of functions replaces the current process image with a new process image."

Commonly a process generates a child process because it would like to transform the child process by changing the program code the child process is executing.

The text, data and stack segment of the process are replaced and only the u (user) area of the process remains the same.

If successful, the exec system calls do not return to the invoking program as the calling image is lost.

It is possible for a user at the command line to issue an exec system call, but it takes over the current shell and terminates the shell.

exec command [arguments]

The Versions of Exec are :

- execl
- execv
- execle
- execve
- execlp
- execvp

The Naming Convention

- 'l' indicates a list arrangement (a series of null terminated arguments)
- 'v' indicates the array or vector arrangement (like the argv structure).
- 'e' indicates the programmer will construct (in the array/vector format) and pass their own environment variable list.
- 'p' indicates the current PATH string should be used when the system searches for executable files.

5.23 PROCESS STATE TRANSITION

Applications that have strict real-time constraints might need to prevent processes from being swapped or paged out to secondary memory. Here's a simplified overview of UNIX process states and the transitions between states :

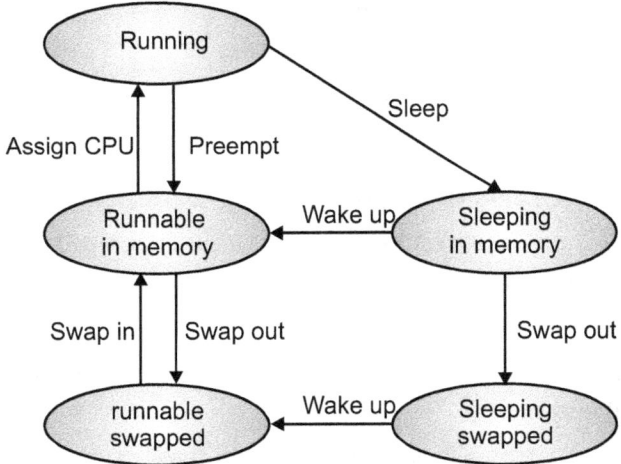

Fig. 5.18 : Process state transition diagram

An active process is normally in one of the five states in the diagram. Arrow direction shows changes in states.

- We say process is running when CPU is assigned to it.
- A process is running if it is assigned to a CPU. Sometime process is preempted which cause change in process state. This is done by scheduler when some other higher priority process needs CPU. A process is also preempted if it consumes its entire time slice and a process of equal priority is runnable.
- A process is runnable in memory if it is in primary memory and ready to run, but is not assigned to a CPU.
- A process is sleeping in memory if it is in primary memory but is waiting for a specific event before it can continue execution. For example, a process is sleeping if it is waiting

for an I/O operation to complete, for a locked resource to be unlocked, or for a timer to expire. When the event occurs, the process is sent a wake up signal; if the reason for its sleep is gone then the process becomes runnable.

- A process is runnable and swapped if it is not waiting for a specific event but has its whole address space written to secondary memory to make room in primary memory for other processes.
- A process is sleeping and swapped if it is both waiting for a specific event and has had its whole address space written to secondary memory to make room in primary memory for other processes.
- There will be a need for swapping some address space to secondary memory when system does not have sufficient main memory to hold all its active processes.
- When the system is short of primary memory, it writes individual pages of some processes to secondary memory but still leaves those processes runnable. When a process runs, if it accesses those pages, it must sleep while the pages are read back into primary memory.
- When the system gets into a more serious shortage of primary memory, it writes all the pages of some processes to secondary memory and marks those processes as swapped. Such processes get back into a state where they can be scheduled only by being chosen by the system scheduler daemon process and then read back into memory.

Both, paging and swapping, cause delay when a process is ready to run again. For processes that have strict timing requirements, this delay can be unacceptable. To avoid swapping delays, real-time processes are never swapped, though parts of them can be paged. A program can prevent paging and swapping by locking its text and data into primary memory. How much memory can be locked is limited by how much memory is configured. Also, locking too much can cause intolerable delays to processes that do not have their text and data locked into memory.

5.24 PROCESS MANAGEMENT

When you execute a program on your UNIX system, the system creates a special environment for that program. This environment contains everything needed for the system to run the program as if no other program were running on the system.

Whenever you issue a command in UNIX, it creates, or starts, a new process. When you tried out the ls command to list directory contents, you started a process. A process, in simple terms, is an instance of a running program.

The operating system tracks processes through a five digit ID number known as the pid or process ID. Each process in the system has a unique pid.

Pids eventually repeat because all the possible numbers are used up and the next pid rolls or starts over. At any one time, no two processes with the same pid exist in the system because it is the pid that UNIX uses to track each process.

- Starting a Process :

When you start a process (run a command), there are two ways you can run it :

- Foreground Processes
- Background Processes

5.24.1 Foreground Processes

By default, every process that you start runs in the foreground. It gets its input from the keyboard and sends its output to the screen.

You can see this happen with the ls command. If I want to list all the files in my current directory, I can use the following command :

$ls ch*.doc

This would display all the files whose name start with ch and ends with .doc :

ch01-1.doc ch010.doc ch02.doc ch03-2.doc
ch04-1.doc ch040.doc ch05.doc ch06-2.doc
ch01-2.doc ch02-1.doc

The process runs in the foreground, the output is directed to my screen and if the ls command wants any input (which it does not), it waits for it from the keyboard.

While a program is running in foreground and taking much time, we cannot run any other commands (start any other processes) because prompt would not be available until program finishes its processing and comes out.

5.24.2 Background Processes

A background process runs without being connected to your keyboard. If the background process requires any keyboard input, it waits.

The advantage of running a process in the background is that you can run other commands; you do not have to wait until it completes to start another!

The simplest way to start a background process is to add an ampersand (&) at the end of the command.

$ls ch*.doc &

This would also display all the files whose name start with ch and ends with .doc :

ch01-1.doc ch010.doc ch02.doc ch03-2.doc
ch04-1.doc ch040.doc ch05.doc ch06-2.doc
ch01-2.doc ch02-1.doc

Here if the ls command wants any input (which it does not), it goes into a stop state until I move it into the foreground and give it the data from the keyboard.

That first line contains information about the background process - the job number and process ID. You need to know the job number to manipulate it between background and foreground.

If you press the Enter key now, you see the following :

```
[1]  +  Done          ls ch*.doc &
$
```

The first line tells you that the ls command background process finishes successfully. The second is a prompt for another command.

5.24.3 Listing Running Processes

It is easy to see your own processes by running the ps (process status) command as follows :

```
$ps
PID        TTY      TIME       CMD
18358      ttyp3    00:00:00   sh
18361      ttyp3    00:01:31   abiword
18789      ttyp3    00:00:00   ps
```

One of the most commonly used flags for ps is the -f (f for full) option, which provides more information as shown in the following example :

```
$ps -f
UID        PID PPID C STIME    TTY TIME  CMD
amrood    6738 3662 0 10:23:03 pts/6 0:00 first_one
amrood    6739 3662 0 10:22:54 pts/6 0:00 second_one
amrood    3662 3657 0 08:10:53 pts/6 0:00 -ksh
amrood    6892 3662 4 10:51:50 pts/6 0:00 ps -f
```

Here is the description of all the fileds displayed by ps -f command :

Column	Description
UID	User ID that this process belongs to (the person running it).
PID	Process ID.
PPID	Parent process ID (the ID of the process that started it).
C	CPU utilization of process.
STIME	Process start time.
TTY	Terminal type associated with the process
TIME	CPU time taken by the process.
CMD	The command that started this process.

There are other options which can be used along with ps command :

Option	Description
-a	Shows information about all users
-x	Shows information about processes without terminals.
-u	Shows additional information like -f option.
-e	Display extended information.

5.24.4 Stopping Processes

Ending a process can be done in several different ways. Often, from a console-based command, sending a CTRL + C keystroke (the default interrupt character) will exit the command. This works when process is running in foreground mode.

If a process is running in background mode then first you would need to get its Job ID using ps command and after that you can use kill command to kill the process as follows :

```
$ps -f
UID      PID PPID C STIME    TTY   TIME CMD
amrood  6738 3662 0 10:23:03 pts/6 0:00 first_one
amrood  6739 3662 0 10:22:54 pts/6 0:00 second_one
amrood  3662 3657 0 08:10:53 pts/6 0:00 -ksh
amrood  6892 3662 4 10:51:50 pts/6 0:00 ps -f
$kill 6738
Terminated
```

Here kill command would terminate first_one process. If a process ignores a regular kill command, you can use kill -9 followed by the process ID as follows :

```
$kill -9 6738
Terminated
```

5.24.5 Zombie and Orphan Processes

Normally, when a child process is killed, the parent process is told via a SIGCHLD signal. Then the parent can do some other task or restart a new child as needed. However, sometimes the parent process is killed before its child is killed. In this case, the "parent of all processes," init process, becomes the new PPID (parent process ID). Sometime these processes are called orphan process.

When a process is killed, a ps listing may still show the process with a Z state. This is a zombie, or defunct, process. The process is dead and not being used. These processes are different from orphan processes. They are the processes that has completed execution but still has an entry in the process table.

5.24.6 Daemon Processes

Daemons are system-related background processes that often run with the permissions of root and services requests from other processes.

A daemon process has no controlling terminal. It cannot open /dev/tty. If you do a "ps -ef" and look at the tty field, all daemons will have a ? for the tty.

More clearly, a daemon is just a process that runs in the background, usually waiting for something to happen that it is capable of working with, like a printer daemon is waiting for print commands.

If you have a program which needs to do long processing then its worth to make it a daemon and run it in background.

5.24.7 The top Command

The top command is a very useful tool for quickly showing processes sorted by various criteria.

It is an interactive diagnostic tool that updates frequently and shows information about physical and virtual memory, CPU usage, load averages and your busy processes.

Here is simple syntax to run top command and to see the statistics of CPU utilization by different processes :

$top

QUESTIONS

1. What is disk management? Why it is important?
2. Write short note on disk formatting.
3. What is MBR? Where it is used?
4. What is swap space? How to manage swap space?
5. What Linux utility you will use to check swap space of system? Explain with example.
6. Write short note on following
   a. Goals of protection
   b. Principles of protection
7. Explain domain of protection with the help of diagram.
8. Define threat to computer system? How will you differentiate threats from attacks?
9. Explain standard security attacks with neat diagram.

10. Write short note on following
    a. Trojan Horse
    b. Trap door
    c. Logic bomb
    d. Stack and buffer overflow
    e. Virus
11. Explain in brief history of UNIX system.
12. With neat diagram explain UNIX system architecture.
13. What is inode? Explain inode structure of a file and inode structure of a directory.
14. What is pipe? Differentiate anonymous pipe and named pipe.
15. What is process? Explain fork() and exec() system calls.
16. Explain process state transition with neat diagram.

✠ ✠ ✠